Schizoanalysis and Schizodrama

Domenico Uhng Hur

Schizoanalysis and Schizodrama

Clinic and Politics

Springer

Domenico Uhng Hur
Graduate Program in Psychology
Universidade Federal de Goiás
Goiânia, Goiás, Brazil

ISBN 978-3-031-94656-1 ISBN 978-3-031-94657-8 (eBook)
https://doi.org/10.1007/978-3-031-94657-8

The original submitted manuscript has been translated into English. The translation was done using artificial intelligence. A subsequent revision was performed by the author(s) to further refine the work and to ensure that the translation is appropriate concerning content and scientific correctness. It may, however, read stylistically different from a conventional translation.
Translation from the Portuguese language edition: "Esquizoanálise e esquizodrama: clínica e política (2a Edição Revisada)" by Domenico Uhng Hur, © Grupo Átomo e Alínea 2023. Published by Alínea Editora. All Rights Reserved.

This Springer imprint is published by the registered company Springer Nature Switzerland AG.
The registered company address is: Gewerbestrasse 11, 6330 Cham, Switzerland

In memory of the masters Gregorio Baremblitt (1936–2021) and Jorge Bichuetti (1960–2022), guerrillas of power and becoming, who departed at twilight, but who always taught us how to dawn.

Contents

About the Author

Domenico Hur is a psychologist, master, and doctor in Social Psychology from the University of São Paulo (USP-Brazil), with a doctoral internship at the Autonomous University of Barcelona (UAB) and post-doctorate at the University of Santiago de Compostela (USC-Spain). He is Professor of Psychology at the Federal University of Goiás (Brazil), with dozens of articles, chapters, and books on Schizoanalysis, Schizodrama, and critical Political Psychology. He runs the blog https://domenicohur.wordpress.com/ with his texts and the channel https://www.youtube.com/@DomenicoHur with his lectures and courses.

List of Figures

List of Tables

Chapter 1
The Problem of the Crossing from Philosophy to Clinic

Schizoanalysis is configured as a *trans* field, of analysis and intervention on hypercomplex, metastable systems, which orchestrates a set of knowledge and practices aimed at intervening directly in reality, with the purpose of enhancing life and the expression of difference, multiplicities, and their dissents. It dispenses with mediations via symbolic, structure, normalizations, and articulates knowledge from various areas, such as Philosophy, Psychoanalysis, Art, Politics, Linguistics, Biology, operating unusual connections and methodological displacements. Schizoanalysis was created in the early 1970s and expresses the insurgency of new social movements, emerging after the mythical May 68 in France.[1] Philosophy of difference, Pragmatics, Micropolitics, Stratoanalysis, Nomadology, Nomadopraxis, Active Utopia, and Pop analysis are some of the terms used to name it.

Although it refers to different fields of knowledge, schizoanalysis is closer to a philosophy. However, it has been adopted as an important foundation in several areas of the humanities and health in Latin America, being studied and performed by numerous professionals in Psychology, Education, Arts, Anthropology, Social Sciences, etc., becoming a fruitful source of concepts and propositions. Brazil is

[1] The French May 68 expressed a *tsunami* of labor and student protests that stopped the country. They were demonstrations that were not limited to traditional political agendas, restricted to parties and unions but to the multitude in general. Slogans such as "Let's be realistic, demand the impossible" were uttered. Instituting mobilization that created a new circuit, which did not wish to take power from the State, but to express a molecular revolution, new and desiring political practices, where the political was widespread in everything and not just in its traditional entities. There, desire was politics, and politics was desiring. From May 68, political movements were reconfigured and new modes of subjectivation were generated, giving rise, for example, to social movements of gender and sexual diversity, as well as Non-Governmental Organizations (NGOs) such as Doctors Without Borders. Not only there, but political and molecular movements occurred worldwide, not restricted to the field of politics. In Brazil, in addition to the libertarian guerrilla struggles, this era was marked by Tropicalism in music, Glauber Rocha's *Cinema Novo* and a different relationship with sexuality, which obviously brought a new relationship with the body, with others, a new conception of sex/gender and the production of a new subjectivation.

D. U. Hur, *Schizoanalysis and Schizodrama*,
https://doi.org/10.1007/978-3-031-94657-8_1

possibly the country with the largest number of schizoanalysts who create new readings and interventions from this theoretical and practical repertoire.

Thus, we arrive at the complex fold of articulation between two different fields: the crossing of concepts from philosophy to the "applied field" of research and intervention. Turning philosophy into a clinic, or a policy, is evidently a complex, tortuous task, perhaps even impossible, but that has already been carried out in different ways by many people, thinkers, clinicians, activists, and artists.

Since we wrote *Psicologia, Política e Esquizoanálise* [*Psychology, Politics and Schizoanalysis*[2]] (Hur, 2018), started in 2006 (with our PhD thesis), there have been quite a few works published on schizoanalysis in Brazil and Latin America. Obviously not as much as psychoanalysis, and not as much as we would like to see. Written not only by famous intellectuals, from a schizoanalytic *mainstream*, but also by "*young*" researchers, among whom I include myself.

In that book, we worked on how some concepts from this theoretical-practical field contribute to an analysis of the political and social. But we missed something; we considered that the work was a little more "sociological" than expected, even though it deals with psychic, affective, and subjective issues. Nevertheless, after a closer partnership with Gregorio Baremblitt (in memoriam—1936–2021), Margarete Amorim, Jorge Bichuetti (in memoriam—1960–2022), Gregorio Kazi, and other companions of the Gregorio Baremblitt Institute (IGB), besides the great learning obtained and joint production (Amorim et al., 2021; Baremblitt et al., 2020), we found that it is important to make schizoanalysis even more accessible and operative for people's daily lives and more "applicable" in the clinical and institutional field, mainly in its schizodramatic aspect. It is in the schizoanalytic interventions that we undertake experiments and the search for clues that allow us to think and create new possibilities of *praxis*, which materialize in this book: *Schizoanalysis and Schizodrama: Clinic and Politics.*[3] The contents developed here arise from a writing process that has as its first station the activities we developed in the *Schizodrama Immersions* of the IGB. Texts whose writing touched upon the readings and concepts worked on in each session and that after experimented with new schizodramatic devices took on new reflective and affective hues. The second station was carried out after the immersions, when the texts were dismembered, reformulated, merged, and developed in the cartography of this book.

This book intends to work on methodological issues of schizoanalysis to provide clues for intervention in the field of clinic, arts, in concrete institutions, and references for a psychopolitical analysis. It seeks to make the transition from philosophy to the "applied" field of intervention, offering reflections for a clinic-politics, with strong inspiration from one of its derivatives: the schizodrama, invented by Baremblitt and which is an expression of an original Latin American schizoanalysis.

[2]Book also published in Spanish, with the title *Esquizoanálisis: política y psicología [Schizoanalysis: politics and psychology*] (Hur, 2022b).

[3]This book was originally published in Portuguese in Brazil (Hur, 2022a).

The working method started from the theoretical study on the entire work of Gilles Deleuze, Félix Guattari, and Gregorio Baremblitt, articulated to clinical and social practice. From a schizodramatic perspective, or *baremblittian*, we did not just reproduce dogmatically certain concepts, in the traditional eurocolonized academic method. Without abandoning the rigor, we produced more associations, new regimes of visibility, affections, and enunciations. We operate a certain smuggling, migration, between borders, in which philosophical concepts inspire the production and polishing of new tools, both in the realm of reflection, as in the production of intervention devices.

We chose fundamental concepts from the field such as desire, forces, becoming, intensities, body without organs, cartography, haptic dimension, consciousness, device, to weave how they can be operationalized and produce more senses about everyday experience. Each chapter functions as a *plateau*, to allude to the definition of Gregory Bateson (1972) of a zone of continuous variation, and seeks to bring conceptual and pragmatic elements to reference interventions and clinical procedures and creation. They do not need to be read linearly, and the reader can start the book by his chapter of interest.

Chapter 2 provides a brief introduction to schizoanalysis and schizodrama, being more directed to the beginning scholar in the theme. *Chapter 3* presents our working apparatus, discussing the device, the cartography, the logic of intensities, and a new sensitivity: the haptic dimension. *Chapters 4 and 5* have a more cartographic character and develop the relationship between desire and forces, our "units of analysis," as well as their actualization in different desiring circuits: the state, the neoliberal, and the neofascist. But they also bring elements for their transmutation, with the *klinics* of difference–repetition and production–reproduction–antiproduction. *Chapters 6 and 7* work with two crucial concepts of schizoanalysis: becoming and body without organs. Both start with a dense philosophical discussion and are articulated with contemporary phenomena (such as psychedelics and possession), possibilities of intervention, and clues for a theory of technique. *Chapters 8 and 9* are more directed to intervention. The *eighth* brings a controversial and very current theme which is the theorization of the management of "altered states of consciousness" as a way to reach the processes of deterritorialization, much worked by Baremblitt. The *ninth* proposes an unprecedented model of group analysis, resulting from schizoanalysis and schizodrama, which is different from traditional psychoanalytic models, and provides subsidies for a new reading on the social and political and minority movements. *Chapter 10* concludes the book with some schizoanalytic movements directed to the production of life in these times of death, such as the power of encounters, the valorization of the infinitely small, affect as passage, *multiplicitation*, and transduction. Movements that can be actualized not only in the clinic, but also in political movements, and even in life itself.

We warn the beginning scholar that understanding schizoanalysis is a slow learning process. With the need for immediacy of information absorption, an expression of neoliberal logic, there are those who want to understand schizoanalysis overnight, watching videos on *YouTube*, taking one course or another, but little studying or reading the work of Deleuze and Guattari. And as they usually can't, they get frustrated and even start to criticize the field of knowledge itself. Hence, this book aims to provide both introductory conceptual issues, as clues for its operationalization, and the migration of contents from philosophy to the clinic and intervention. A task that is not easy, since it presupposes not only the internalization of concepts, but also their experimentation. Because it is the practice that attributes senses, produces becomings, and elevates the events provided by theory. Therefore, we consider that this is a book intended both for the beginning scholar and for the initiated.[4]

Our proposal is to produce knowledge, and life, in several spaces. Not only to sacralize the "altar" of the University but to transit through the territory in its different zones of intensity. Not only reproduce research and studies for the elites but also constitute, in alternative ways, knowledge for a potent collective life. With a schizoanalysis that is not only directed to people who seek psychotherapeutic care, in the traditional *psy technology*, but that is intended for everyday life. Not only in moments of sadness, doubt, and venting but also of joy, confidence, and celebrations. Both in crisis and in smoothness, in depression, exhaustion, as in overflow. Not only from the fear of death, but from the affirmation of life. To articulate such powerful theoretical and technical devices to our context and realities, in a nomadic experimentation in which we will reap their results and ramifications. And obviously, starting from our own territoriality of origin, as well as the margins we traipse and the dissents we provoke.

Possibly this work will not please the "Deleuzian fundamentalism," also present in the Academy, in some Faculties of Philosophy and Psychology, where thinking is assimilated to reproducing, memorizing, and obeying. However, this book may please more the experimenters, the *bricoleurs*, the restless and curious, who never tire of questioning, problematizing, and investigating. Perhaps even more to artists rather than academics. Those who consider life to be an eternal discovery, that is, a perpetual invention. And it is up to us to populate and sow this territory, considered by many as the desert of the real. It is not a desert, but forests, fields, mangroves, springs of life that we must not only cross but above all create, collect, and care for. Huge and endless *machinosphere*, producer of *insurgent subjectivations*, as well as captured subjectivities. So, here, where life never tires of insisting and overflowing, we invite this collective of insurgents, experimenters, restless, and disturbed, to an associative flow of ideas and practices that can lead us to paths for the production of other possible worlds, where the lines of desire and flight are the vectors of forces and creation. We do not pretend to exhaust all questions of schizoanalytic method, as there are still many practices to be carried out and other texts to be written by the multitude of schizoanalysts and schizodramatists that are proliferating on the continent. So, we hope that this book will inspire you to new literary, clinical, academic, institutional, political, and/or artistic productions, in short, for the invention of new devices that produce new possibilities of life.

[4] This book can also be seen as the second part of *Psicologia, Política e Esquizoanálise* [*Psychology, Politics and Schizoanalysis*] (Hur, 2018), but their readings are independent.

Although this book was written by only one person, it results from the inspiration of collective work and reflection, developed in research groups, in activities with advisees, in postgraduate studies at the Federal University of Goiás (Brazil) and at the Pontifical Bolivarian University (Medellín/Colombia), in the lectures given and debates held with companions from the Gregorio Baremblitt Institute (Minas Gerais/Brazil), Pichon-Rivière Institute (Rio Grande do Sul/Brazil), from the specialization course in "Schizoanalysis and post-structuralism" (Paraná/Brazil) and at the events I had the pleasure of being invited to participate in throughout the country, or abroad. Thereby, I register warm thanks to this network of allies and masters for the continuous inspiration and potentiation.

References

Amorim, M., Bichuetti, J., Hur, D. U., Kazi, G., & Oliveira, M. F. (2021). Gregorio Franklin Baremblitt, o guerreiro do devir… cuidado, insurgências inventivas, utopias libertárias. *Revista Memorandum, 38*, 1–11.

Baremblitt, G., Amorim, M. A., & Hur, D. U. (2020). *Esquizodrama: teoria, método e técnica—klínicas*. Ed. IGB.

Bateson, G. (1972). *Steps to an ecology of mind*. University of Chicago Press.

Hur, D. U. (2018). *Psicologia, Política e Esquizoanálise*. Alínea.

Hur, D. U. (2022a). *Esquizoanálise e Esquizodrama: Clínica e política*. Alínea.

Hur, D. U. (2022b). *Esquizoanálisis: Política y Psicología*. La docta ignorancia.

Chapter 2
Schizoanalysis and Schizodrama

Schizoanalysis

To begin this chapter, we briefly introduce the creators of schizoanalysis: the philosopher Gilles Deleuze and the institutional analyst Félix Guattari. Deleuze is considered one of the main Western philosophers of the twentieth century, authoring a vast body of dozens of books and articles that cover numerous topics, such as history of philosophy, cinema, literature, painting, psychoanalysis, politics, etc. It is considered that his intellectual work has three main moments, but does not follow a chronological line (Safatle, 2007): first, as a historian of Philosophy, with books such as *Empiricism and subjectivity* (1953[1]) on David Hume, *Nietzsche and Philosophy* (1962), *Kant's critical philosophy* (1963), the *Bergsonism* (1966), *Spinoza: Practical Philosophy* (1981a), *The Fold—Leibniz and the Baroque* (1988), etc. The second moment is when he becomes the author of a singular, original thought in philosophy, with the books *Difference and repetition* (1968) and *The logic of sense* (1969). In these books, he develops a unique reading on difference, multiplicities, becomings, also having a closer approach to psychoanalysis, or rather, a critique of psychoanalysis. In the third moment, Gilles *transduces* his philosophical work into a social cartography. Obviously, in this migration, he creates new concepts and conceptions. We situate in this moment his partnership with Félix, with five books written together, the works on cinema, literature, and art in general.

Guattari, on the other hand, is the insurgent, creative, chaotic, and unusual counterpart of the duo. With unfinished training in Pharmacy, Music, Philosophy, he was often the great *bricoleur*, the one who connects and transits through knowledge from different fields, always creating the new, like a "theoretical-technical

[1] In this book, we chose to put the year of the original publication of Deleuze and Guattari's books, but with the pagination of the English language editions (online) found in the references. The quotes that were not found in English were translated by us with the support of Artificial Intelligence.

D. U. Hur, *Schizoanalysis and Schizodrama*,
https://doi.org/10.1007/978-3-031-94657-8_2

smuggler," a "praxis trafficker." He was one of the main actors in the International Movement of Alternatives to Psychiatry, being one of the protagonists of the Clinic *La Borde* with Jean Oury. La Borde was a revolutionary psychiatric establishment that, instead of focusing only on curing the "illness" of patients, or on the "poor training" of health professionals, began to analyze the established power relations of the mental health Institution, in which the notion of cure itself was questioned and deconstructed. In *La Borde*, they used alternative psychotherapeutic practices inspired by art, political activism, ambiance management, and various other fields (Oury, 2009). From the precepts of self-analysis and self-management, there was a radicalization of institutional democratic practices, becoming a source of inspiration for the social movements of Psychiatric Reform throughout the West. By maintaining this way of analysis, at the intersection between clinic and self-managed politics, Guattari created Institutional Psychotherapy and Institutional Analysis. Félix was also one of the most engaged intellectuals of the political left in social struggles.

Deleuze and Guattari produced the work *Capitalism and Schizophrenia*, divided into two volumes: *Anti-Oedipus* (1972) and *A Thousand Plateaus* (1980). They also wrote *Kafka: for a minor literature* (1975), *Politics and psychoanalysis* (1977), and *What is philosophy?* (1991), their last joint work. Some historians, like François Dosse (2007), say that Gilles did the favor of putting Félix's name as co-author of the last book more out of friendship, than for effective joint work, due to a supposed intellectual sterility that Guattari was going through at that time. Others disagree with this assumption. Stéphane Nadaud (2016) reminds us that during this period Félix is in intellectual effervescence, for example, publishing *Schizoanalytic Cartographies* (1989a), *The Three Ecologies* (1989b), and *Chaosmosis* (1992).

Both Gilles and Félix were close to Jacques Lacan, the *mainstream* psychoanalyst of the time. Deleuze was invited to be the philosopher of the Freudian School of Paris, directed by Lacan, and Guattari was one of the three main psychoanalysts of the Association. Gilles declined the invitation, not wanting his knowledge subjugated to a "master," and Félix lost this place, but never left the Freudian School, after the publication of *Anti-Oedipus*, which was a major critique of Lacanian structuralist psychoanalysis (Dosse, 2007).

The great philosopher Michel Foucault (1995), a companion and admirer of Deleuze, once said, "Perhaps one day, the century will be Deleuzian," predicting the impact of his colleague's work in the West. This prophetic phrase did not come true, as the twentieth century was unable to assimilate the complexity of Deleuze's thought. His work is still little taught in humanities and health science courses in Europe and America, and it can certainly be said that most scholars in these fields are not familiar with it. This lack of knowledge comes from the theory being quite complex, the difficulty of its concepts, as well as the diversity of intervention devices inspired by schizoanalysis. The twentieth century was not Deleuzian. But everything makes us believe that the twenty-first century is, in the sense of how much his theories are proving to be contributive to an accurate reading of the contemporary, as well as the growing demand and interest by scholars and researchers from several areas of knowledge about his work.

In our case, instead of asking "what is schizoanalysis?" it is more accurate to ask "how does schizoanalysis work?" Unlike most theories, it has an intensely pragmatic character, not restricting itself to the planes of syntax, or semantics. It does not only act in the field of representation, expressing metaphors, or new adjectives, but it is performative. It seeks to elicit processes, to be realizative. Deleuze and Guattari continuously affirm the pragmatic primacy of their theory, which should always be linked to the world and produce effects.

Schizoanalysis works like a machine that incites, assembles, produces, various types of movements aimed at intervening and transforming life. It does not concern itself with a supposed essence of things, or what they are. It seeks to understand how processes work, flow, their movement and configurations, regardless of the materiality they assume. Thus, it is a field of knowledge and practices that analyzes the propagation of flows, connections, and desiring circuits constituted by the interweaving of various materialities of life, whether they are linguistic semiotics, affections, intensities, asignifying processes, machinic, forces, compositions between bodies, etc.

At the same time as schizoanalysis carries out a cartographic labor (see Chap. 3), it commits itself to a pragmatic intervention aimed at giving fluidity to forces previously captured and blocked. Schizoanalysis seeks the liberation of desire and active forces that are trapped in the Oedipal triangulation, in the curtailment of life, in the fiction of lack as a constituent, in the different capturing power arrangements, whether in the social field, or even psychic (see Chaps. 4 and 5). It promotes the eruption of becomings (see Chap. 6), differences, and dissidences, movements directed toward the autonomy of the body, social collectives, peoples, in short, a self-management and self-analysis of life. Schizoanalysis, unlike traditional academic fields, which are committed to constituting an epistemology and ontology, chooses to focus on an ethical-aesthetic-political paradigm aimed at enhancing and producing life in its various modes of actualization (Deleuze & Guattari, 1980).

Deleuze and Guattari seek to map the vectors of forces, their articulations, assemblages, and machines, envisioning that the modes of subjectivation result from multiple connections, that is, from the tension between chaos and cosmos. Thus, they do not focus only on the psychic phenomenon, as they understand that there is an arrangement between desiring investments, relations of forces and social, political, and machinic formations. The human cannot be conceived in isolation without understanding its articulation with the assemblages. Even the psyche overflows from its "bodily envelope," situating itself in the relations and connections it makes with the things and people of its milieu. There is no clear division between internal and external, as the external is constituent of the "internality" (Rolnik, 1997), in which the Self can be understood as the "internalized-externality." Accordingly, schizoanalysis does not restrict itself to the relationship between human and human, as it expands its focus to the connections between human and inhuman, organic and machines, actual and virtual, concrete and abstract, the environment, technologies, understanding them as heterogeneous and hybrid formations that co-function together; then arises a whole *Ecosophy of the mechanosphere* (Guattari, 1989b; Deleuze & Guattari, 1980), a *machinic* of existence. "Inanimate" objects, animals, assume an important psychic and existential function; for instance, the relationship of people with technological devices, or with the *websphere*, which are repositories of great desiring investment. In these multiple combinations, there is a constant production of differences and ways of being. The dizzying development of technology produces a new subjectivity, cyber-human, which is not for us to judge, but to understand and from there, to potentiate the flows of life, against the reigning automatism.

Schizoanalysis performs a methodological turn, privileging new perspectives: (a) It ceases to apprehend processes in the logic of being, predominantly alternative (either... or...), for the logic of becoming, connective, additive (and... and... and...), turning the cosmos into chaosmos, and reality is apprehended as *realterity* (Baremblitt, 1998). (b) Schizoanalysis moves from a structuralist perspective to one that contemplates multiplicities, the flow of duration, articulating the actual to the virtual. Instead of a chronological rememorative line, the block of transtemporal intensities; instead of the primacy of structure, the flows and multiplicities. (c) It opts for a molecular analytics, and not just molar, micropolitics and not just macropolitics, attending to the articulation of relations of forces with desiring investments. (d) Schizoanalysis privileges asignifying logics and modes of composition between bodies, rather than discourse, representation, and the signifier. (e) It analyzes the movements from three distinct types of lines: rigid segmentarity, supple segmentarity, and the line of flight. (f) Therefore, it prefers a geography of affections and displacements, rather than focusing only on the individual's history.

We also highlight a crucial difference in relation to psychoanalysis.[2] If psychoanalysis operates with the model of the family as a determinant social set and neurosis as a founding psychic process, schizoanalysis elaborates another proposition. Instead of working with neurosis, it privileges schizophrenic flows. It refers to the analysis of the *schizo* processes, whether in the psychic, machinic, or social spheres. *Schizo*, or the *schiz*, refers to the discharge of desiring flows in a disordered and chaotic way without a principle of internal structuring or totality, which has a potential for creation, diffusion and are prior to neurosis. It is the movement without image, flow without inscription or psychic representation, which refers more to asignifying logics.[3] Schizoanalysis seeks to map the processes of propagation, diffraction, dissociation, with their distinct actualizations. Schizo flows are not coded by the Oedipal triangulation but rather managed by multiple aspects of the social field. Delirium is not restricted to the family set, to the paternal law, or to the Oedipus complex but it is historical–universal: tribes, races, continents, and galaxies are delirious, and not just family-marital problems. Oedipus is not a founding, phylogenetic structure but rather a subsequent psychic formation (Deleuze &

[2] Throughout the book, some other differences in relation to psychoanalysis are presented, mainly in Chaps. 3, 4, 5 and 7.

[3] Freud himself (1937) opened space for the analysis of asignifying logics when he affirmed that the analyst's work was not only to operate with the repressed material content, but also to provide figuration and figurability to the undiscriminated traces or marks, not inscribed in the psyche, that is to the unrepresented and unrepresentable. Possibly this is the zero mark of the transition from the method of interpretation to experimentation, which Baremblitt radicalized with his transduction procedures (see Chap. 10).

Guattari, 1972). Although schizoanalysis has adopted this singular name for analyzing schizo flows, it does not directly refer to the clinical entity *schizophrenia*, nor does it seek to psychopathologize processes, or make an elegy to madness.

And instead of working with the family as a determinant social set, schizoanalysis operates with capitalism, because it understands that the axiomatic of capital takes precedence in the modulation of forces and conducts (see Chap. 5). The family itself is nothing more than the transmission belt of the functioning of capitalism and the State in a microsphere (Deleuze & Guattari, 1972), where the logic of property, of private and submission is updated. Therefore, capitalism is much more determinant than the family as a diagram of social forces. Consequently, the relationship between psyche and society is no longer read in the classic psychoanalytic pair "Family and neurosis," but with the pair "Capitalism and schizophrenia," which is the title of their main work.

Schizodrama

Schizoanalysis extols the production of rhizomes and the constitution of singular existential territories. Nonetheless, the intellectual of the human sciences in Latin America is closer to Sorbonne (France), than to Rocinha *Favela* (Brazil), or San Miguel Teotongo (Mexico). He dreams more of Paris and London, than of the Amazon and the volcanoes. Even though he knows his material and social situations, such contents do not usually appear in his reflections and publications: academic colonization. It is no wonder that Foucault called the Philosophy department of the former Faculty of Philosophy, Sciences and Letters of the University of São Paulo (FFCL-USP—Brazil) a French overseas department (Rodrigues, 2016), or Claude Lévi-Strauss was surprised by the libraries of Brazilian intellectuals, which resembled the libraries of their French peers.

It is not enough for us to import the philosophical knowledge produced in Europe and "apply" it here without a geographical-historical modulation. Too often the human sciences become Europeanized in Latin America and forget their own context, such as what happened with *mainstream* Lacanian psychoanalysis in the continent. Schizoanalysis must germinate and spread in Latin American territory with all its hybrid, mixed character, and face the prevailing challenges, which is currently the fight against the reactive and death forces, amplified by a right-wing political extremism and by a religious fundamentalism. It is necessary to adopt one's own territory as a starting point, or propagation.

Among the various derivations of schizoanalysis, schizodrama is an example of a singular, creative, and powerful assemblage that constitutes an original Latin American schizoanalysis. It should not be reduced to a mere application of schizoanalysis, as its uncommon knowledge and practices transcend it.[4]

---

[4] It should also not be understood as one of the various traditions of Institutional Analysis, such as the socioanalysis of René Lourau (1975) and Georges Lapassade (1977), or the sociopsychoanalysis of Gerard Mendel (1974).

The history of schizodrama begins long before the creation of psychology as a science in the nineteenth century. It can be said that its beginnings are found in indigenous shamanic rituals in America, in possession sessions and dances in Africa, in meetings and mystics of small communities, in the catharsis of public theater at medieval fairs, in the witches' sabbaths in the clearing of the forests, in the suavity of Buddhist meditation.

So, the creation of Psychology as a discipline is not its original mark but the opposite: it is its decadence. Because it is the moment when it tries to empty the instituting, aesthetic, multiplicitary, and popular symbolic verve of the crowds, for a mechanistic and individualistic logic guided by the rational. The anthropomorphism ceased to draw inspiration from nature, forces, animals, life, to technical machines, the factory, robots, and capitalist production.

Gregorio Baremblitt[5] (1936–2021) was the *medium*, the surveyor of forces, the systematizer of practices of something that was already present in an embryonic form in popular and ancestral knowledge, and which resulted in schizodrama. He was the "pervert of the tribe" (Deleuze & Guattari, 1972), who connects processes, establishes assemblages, provokes becomings. From his clinical-political experience, he articulated in a fabric of bricolages knowledge and practices of the most diverse, reaching the understanding and management of the forces of a molecular and collective unconscious, in which there is no longer isolated individuality, but bodies, atoms, intensities, waves, and energies in connection and resonance, in a *chaosmotic* movement and with becomings that result in the most extraordinary events. Gregorio fostered alterations of consciousness, trances, "psychosis in a laboratory situation," experimental madness. Loose and free delirium, which is not reduced to Oedipus, nor to ideology. Obviously, in this cartography of practices and ancestral knowledge, he did not restrict himself to their mere re-application, but in a theft, in a migration of these knowledge and practices to the clinical-political sphere, for new devices and inventions.

Baremblitt was a psychiatrist, institutional analyst, and Argentine-Brazilian schizoanalyst. He was a member of the Argentine Psychoanalytic Association (APA), a former-student of Enrique Pichon-Rivière and colleague of José Bleger. With the political effervescence of the 1960s and 1970s, he composed a group within the APA called *Plataforma*, which articulated psychoanalysis with other fields of knowledge, social criticism and political activism against State violence. Due to political problems with the APA, Plataforma split from the Association and assumed even more of an interdisciplinary character, radicalizing its Marxist and institutional analysis references. Gregorio migrated to Brazil to escape the Argentine dictatorship, creating with other colleagues the IBRAPSI (Brazilian Institute of Psychoanalysis, Groups and Institutions). This establishment operated with references from the institutional analysis, Radical psychiatry, and schizoanalysis and was one of the main diffusers and trainers of schizoanalysts in the clinical field in

[5] To better understand his history, we suggest the texts of Baremblitt (2021), Amorim et al. (2021), Hur (2014), and Grande & Baremblitt (2022).

the country. He then moved to Minas Gerais and created the Félix Guattari Institute, later renamed, at the insistence of his colleagues, as Gregorio Baremblitt Institute. There he trained hundreds more institutional analysts, schizoanalysts, and schizodramatists. We had the honor of having him as a teacher, clinician and, later, friend.

Baremblitt (1998) uses *klinic* with "k" and not in the traditional use of clinic with "c," with the intention of differentiating his practice from traditional psychology and psychiatry. If clinic, etymologically, has the meaning of leaning over a bedridden patient, in a disciplinary logic, of a clinician who "cures" and "normalizes" his patient; the *klinic*[6] for Gregorio derives from *clinos* and *clinamen*. For the Greek atomist philosophers, *clinos* refers to the movement of subatomic particles. Already *clinamen* refers to the encounter between atoms, which causes a shock that produces a differential deviation in their trajectories. Therefore, for Baremblitt, the *klinic* derives from clinamen, being the art of encounters that produce deviations, that is, the fabrication of differences. Gestation of movements, events, of transformation. Very different from the traditional disciplinary action of psychology, schizodrama pursues the production of deviations and anomalies. The focus of *psy* normalization is even present in Law 4119/1962, which regulates the profession of the psychologist in Brazil, in which one of its exclusive functions is to "solve adjustment problems" (paragraph *d* of article 13), in other words, politically seeks to normalize, adapt, standardize, and harmonize the differences in presupposed patterns. Schizodrama, on the other hand, seeks the opposite path: to incite lines of flight so that insurgent desire can flow and produce other compositions that are not reduced to capitalist subjectivity, or to pre-established disciplines. That's why his *klinics* are understood as "passages," "crossroads."

If Deleuze and Guattari (1991) teach us that philosophy, in this case the schizoanalysis, is the art of creating concepts, Baremblitt affirms that the schizodrama is the art of creating intervention devices, both clinical and political, that dramatize their philosophical concepts. If schizoanalysis is primarily a philosophy, the schizodrama is a smuggling and trafficking machine that operates between borders, and aims to *transduce* its propositions, fabricating new regimes of enunciations and transformative praxis. Thus, the schizodrama is a toolbox that functions as "a fundamentally energetic machine, destined to vibrate and make those who approach it vibrate and engage them in a productive movement, which does not exactly pass through ideas or words, it passes through affects[7]" (Baremblitt, 1998, p. 14).

Schizodrama constitutes a set of practices, strategies, tactics and theoretical and technical tools that map the operation of social machines, both concrete and abstract, taking as constituent elements the forces and desiring investments, whether in "molar" or "molecular" spaces, to foster processes of vibration and transformation. To this end, it acts on the subjective, social, semiotic, and technological aspects of

[6]Throughout the text, we will continue to write clinic with "c," but with the sense of the clinic with "k," that is, of deviation, production of difference. But when it comes to a specific schizodramatic clinic of Baremblitt, we will keep the "k."

[7]This quote refers to the function of schizoanalysis for Baremblitt, but we consider it to apply totally to schizodrama.

its devices to provoke experiences of deterritorialization of established assemblages. It is a minority machine that dismantles unproductive, exhausted, and intoxicated desiring circuits, aiming to give way, circulation and transit to blocked forces and coded flows (psychic, bodily, group, social). It seeks to intensify desiring investments to effect new configurations of forces, other regimes of enunciations, events, processes of creation, singularization and affirmation of life (Baremblitt, 2019). Its operation establishes a shock of materialities, a whirlwind that produces a crack, a fissure, that makes possible flows leak. Like schizoanalysis, it operates in the ethical-aesthetic-political paradigm and secondarily in the scientific one. Its method is dramatic, in the sense of dramatizing an art, philosophical concepts, and performing a more potent life.

Schizodrama brings new clinical frameworks, it does not use only the private office, in the traditional clinical *setting*. It is not closed between four walls; it is not a clinic in the strict sense. It is operated with the schizo walk (Deleuze & Guattari, 1972), and can be performed in the open field, in the streets, in mental health Psychosocial Care Centers, in student occupations. If schizoanalysis has a European origin, schizodrama is Latin American. If Deleuze and Guattari have Nietzsche, Bergson, Spinoza, Marx, etc. as references, Baremblitt's schizodrama also has the popular knowledge of indigenous peoples, ancestors, and social movements as inspiration. Here we are not only occupied by the French of the *Champs Élysées* of May '68, but also by the *xapiris, orixás,* and *shamans* of the Brazilian soil. If schizoanalysis developed in Vincennes, or in the Parisian cafes and libraries, schizodrama arose in the attics, full of pillows (from Rua Herval[8]), in the performances in basements full of people in *Belém do Pará* (Lima, 2014), in Psychosocial Care Centers, as the "Maria Boneca" (Bichuetti, 1999, 2000), in the public squares and, who knows, in the future, in the peripheries, in the crossroads, *terreiros*, and *giras*.

Baremblitt (2014b) "steals" in a theoretical-practical bricolage fragments from several fields for the construction of his machines. He is not inspired only by the precepts of the Philosophy of difference but also by: (a) politics; (b) art; and (c) other psychotherapeutic practices.

Politics

Schizodrama is a clinic of forces and, therefore, it should also grasp the forces of the struggles of social movements, such as the *Movimento dos Trabalhadores Sem Terra* [Landless Workers' Movement] (MTST), the indigenous movements, Zapatismo, guerrilla fights, identity movements, all the minorities that are exploited and not listened to, but that have a lot of power and content to say and teach, to inspire and empower us. Hence, we cannot forget the revolutionary potential of our

[8] Street where the Gregorio Baremblitt Institute is located. It is in the attic where schizodrama training and klinics are held.

Latin American territory. Contrary to what the Marxist "bibles" and their "prophets" advocate, the first proletarian revolution did not start in Europe, it was not the Communist Revolution, nor the Paris Commune. The first proletarian revolution that is even racial and anti-racist takes place in Latin America, more precisely in Haiti (1791–1804) and was made by black and enslaved people (Alliez & Lazzarato, 2016). Enslaved people who updated their active forces and stopped being slaves," becoming warriors, constituting an incredible revolutionary machine long before the bastions of communist parties, such as the Soviet or Chinese Red Army. "Black army was the first proletarian force to profoundly revolutionize the art of war" (Alliez & Lazzarato, 2016, p. 102). They produce a hybrid revolution, singular, in a mix between European militaristic models of army, combined with molecular guerrilla tactics and voodoo rituals. There is a beautiful syncretism between military organization and religious rituals of the territory:

> Carrying torches to light their way, the leaders of the revolt met in an open space in the thick forests of the Morne Rouge, a mountain overlooking Cap François, the largest town. There Boukman, the leader, after voodoo incantations and the sucking of the blood of a stuck pig, gave the last instructions (James[9] cited by Alliez & Lazzarato, 2016, p. 407).

Just like the Colombian guerrilla group M-19 claimed, here it is not the Soviet Union but Macondo. And if one day we are going to make the revolution, it will be dancing *cumbia* with maracas. Or, here in Brazil, singing samba, headbanging to rock, or for the younger generations, dancing funk. Therefore, our references should not only be Lenin and Rosa Luxemburg, but Marighella and Marielle, the Che Guevara's revolutionary love, the Marichuy's indigenous crusade in Mexico. We need to apprehend and actualize all the instituting power of Latin American syncretism in our devices, in this action of resistance and *quilombozation* of minorities. Schizodrama is the Latin American actualization of a decolonial schizoanalysis.

Art

Another important inspiration for schizodrama comes from the field of art. Among the various references, we mention Antonin Artaud's theater of cruelty (1938), which is an artistic modality that intends to escape from the theater of representation, entertainment, and consciousness, to a drama that infects, resonates, the affections and intensities. The French playwright sought with his art to escape from the register of consciousness, the transmission of signifiers, comprehensible words and the rational exercise of each one. He aimed to shuffle the senses, operating mainly in the realm of affections, of estrangement, of the bizarre. Cruelty does not refer to an exercise of violence, understood in the common sense, but in bringing to light sensations, flows, and bodily potentials of an audience today apathetic, almost dead and catatonic. Cruelty here means to intensify and to resonate affects, to deconstruct

[9] James, C.L.R. (1938/1969). *A History of Pan-African revolt*. Oakland: PM Press, 2012, 40.

the presupposed and instituted values in a composition between spectacle and audience that overcomes the barriers of the instituted theater. So Artaud operates an exercise of "violating thought," its instituted images. He does not seek a representational theater, but a theater of intensities, which makes thought and affects collapse in a crazy and dionysiac flow. Orgiastic experience that in Brazil has its actualization in the *Theater Oficina Uzyna Uzona* by Zé Celso.[10]

Baremblitt seeks to actualize the theater of cruelty in the field of the clinic to operate processes of deterritorialization and deconstruction of several aspects, such as identity, stratified social roles, defensive mechanisms, to lead people to get in touch with their molecular unconscious, in an effective production of a body without organs (Artaud, 1947; Deleuze & Guattari, 1980), intensive, fluid, powerful, that escapes from the striated lines of full bodies, from instituted diagrams, for the creation of new possibilities. The schizodrama is configured as a *Diagrammatic*, or *Diagramology*, art (*thike*), science (*logos*), praxis, insurgent, insurrectional, disruptive, which is inspired by the most varied artistic procedures for the creation of its clinical devices and aesthetic expression. But it doesn't just refer to art, because schizodramatic making becomes an Art, the art of knowing how to live and how create new subjectivations.

Other Psychotherapeutic Practices

Gregorio "smuggles" different intervention devices with consignments and mobile settings from different fields, such as psychodrama, body psychotherapy, vegetotherapy, bioenergetics, holotropic breathing, and even from *umbanda*. This unusual reference is inspired in the experience of G. Lapassade (1980) in Africa and Brazil. From his participation in voodoo and umbanda rituals, he took the trance experiences to the clinic, creating the *tranceanalysis* (see Chap. 6).

Schizodrama operates with different machinic-corporeal assemblages in the different devices, such as the face-to-face group situation, or the dramatic performance of the actors on stage and even a dance with tribal drums, which may apparently seem to be a chaotic experience. Baremblitt performed various concepts of schizoanalysis creating several machines that dramatize them and incite the production of encounters and deviations, in an intervention that aims at the transformation of the experienced suffering into change and more potent modes of life. He created devices that foster processes of alteration of consciousness, produced human *rhizomes* in sessions of *Dramatic Multiplicitation*, various *lines of escape* in the psychotherapeutic process, which break with the molar and coded formations, as well as also uses the softness of the expression of affections and good humor. There are so many devices that he and his team created what we can call *A Thousand Klinics*, both those that exist and those that are yet to come.

[10] José Celso Martinez Corrêa (1937–2023), important Brazilian playwright.

Hence, if Deleuze extracted from different philosophers the question of difference and singularization, Baremblitt, with an original philosophical-clinical transduction, extracted from these different references the issue of deterritorialization and invention. Thereby, the schizodramatic devices perform the destructive and positive tasks of schizoanalysis (Deleuze & Guattari, 1972):

> Schizodrama will criticize, attack and act against: a) the stratified, coded, overcoded, subjectivized and individualized, repetitive and standardized; b) the instituted, organized, established, habitual and consecrated, power equipments etc. In its second task (always immanent and synchronous with the first), Schizodrama proposes to "open the way", ally and support, intensify and trigger the "positive forces and affirmative wills" (as Nietzsche would say) of the different types of participants and collectivities for the production of production, their domain and management over the production of reproduction and antiproduction. It is about the invention, always unique, of new modalities of composition and potentiation of nature (Baremblitt, 2014a, p. 21).

The first moment, destructive, of deterritorialization, aims to detect the resistances and instituted desiring circuits that the Self, or the collective, encounters, to deconstruct the coercive strata of desire, the molar and Oedipal formations, whether in the psychic or social instance of the register-control surface. It seeks to map what stops the movement and desire and causes some kind of suffering that disempowers life. The scraping seeks to dilute the armors that become oppressive to both the social and individual body. Morality, norms, the superego, the Oedipus complex, or even psychology and psychoanalysis can have this function of blocking desiring investments, converting into modalities of psychopolitical armors. That is why the clinical devices of schizodrama are configured as a guerrilla machine that aims to deconstruct the repressive equipment that tends to “repress, eliminate or capture productive-desiring singularities” (Baremblitt, 1998, p. 55). The war machine[11] (Deleuze & Guattari, 1980) is a concept that expresses an arrangement that assumes instituting potential of deterritorialization linked to a nomadic movement, which in its propagation transforms and metamorphoses itself, updating a diagram of operation distinct from the capture and conservation of the State apparatus. Marighella, Che Guevara, and Jaime Bateman personify it in the realm of political struggles.

The second moment refers to positive tasks and has a cartographic and connection character. It seeks to map and understand the functioning of the desiring assemblages involved in the process, whether they are abstract, social, technical, or psychic machines: the cartography of the configurations and compositions of forces. With the scraping of what blocks, and the understanding of how the machines work, it aims to connect the flows to social assemblages, that is, to create new desiring circuits, other machines, enabling their fluidity, mitigating the person’s alienation about his body, his vectors of forces and the milieu where he is inserted. It seeks to intensify the chaotic productive-desiring processes, which Baremblitt (2004) names as *Schizoonte*. The production refers to the intensification of the circulation of flows

---

[11] The concept created by Deleuze and Guattari (1980) is named *war machine*. But in this book, due to its molecular effects, of deterritorialization and escape in the face of large strata (and the State), we chose to name it as *guerrilla machine*.

and the creation of new lines and possibilities of life. In brief, this method uses the Triad cartography—scraping—production. First, map the blockages and functioning. Second, scrape and demolish. Third, production–creation.

Then, schizodrama aims to operate on the production surface, by intensifying desiring flows, becomings and events, bringing to the surface asignifying intensities that go beyond any discursive formation. It seeks to map the assemblages and diagrams to dismantle them and disconnect the desire from depotentizing circuits. To raise the desire to its potential to question the established order and make the lines of flight and active and desiring forces flow for the establishment of new paths and territories. It is worth noting that the irruption of a line of flight is not mere escape, or metaphor, but rather the dismantling of an enclosed circuit for the promotion of new possible desiring circuits. It is the propagation of becomings and maps of intensity, agitation of particles and degrees of force of a plane of consistency. In schizodrama, the line of flight is always a line of struggle.

To illustrate this process, we cite the "Faciality" device of Baremblitt (2019; Baremblitt et al., 2020), created from the criticism of the coding processes of the face, in the plateau called "Faciality" (Deleuze & Guattari, 1980). It criticizes how the face overcoded the body, turning its "identity" and reducing its multiplicity of affections and possibilities to the semi-static facial configuration. Currently, there is a greater accentuation of this facialization with social networks, selfies, digital meeting applications (*zoom*, *meet*), which crystallize the face even more, as representative, or sovereign of the body. However, for Baremblitt, there is no primacy of the face but of the powers of the body. From a social point of view, Deleuze and Guattari also criticize the constitution of a standard face, which becomes a model: the pictorial representation of Jesus Christ, a face that expresses the dominance of the civilized-Aryan-male-man of fine features. A psychopolitical capture of faciality is established.

Due to such understanding, Gregorio created a klinical device that aims at the deterritorialization of the coded and instituted face, from a game with mirror, images, and luminosities. He uses a special mirror that at the same time reflects and refracts the image. First, in a semi-dark room, he places pairs of people face-to-face with the mirror between them. According to the variations of lighting on the mirror, it results in the astonishing imagetic effect of conjunction of faces with various configurations. Second, he seeks to intensify the different affects of strangeness that emerge from the most bizarre facial imagetic configuration for the pair, bringing to the surface an affect not yet signified, or rather, an asignifying aspect. The consign is that the emerging stranger must be further intensified. Third, later, the intensified bizarre affect must be object of a figuration process, either through dramatization, wordplay, poetry, drawing, etc. Baremblitt seeks to produce multiple senses for the lived experience, which are sometimes verbalized, other times not, always opening to the field of indeterminacy and novelty. It is emphasized that one never knows what forces will emerge from experimenting with some schizodramatic device. There is the production of a vibration, of events, which can acquire several regimes of figurability and which are inextricably related to problems experienced by the people in question, not only referring to the past, but also to the future.

We understand that the Faciality device is a modality of actualization of a cruelty clinical-political theater, as its machinery incites processes of deterritorialization of the face itself, or the emergence of the head itself (Deleuze, 1981b), in an exercise of intensification of the strange and the unknown in us. The cruelty in not recognizing ourselves and finding our own face strange, or better: it is only through the strangeness of the face that we can get to know the face and the body. Deconstructing the codified in order to perceive it in movement, in flux.

Therefore, the different devices worked on in schizodrama seek to incite processes of deterritorialization for the propagation of flows and the affirmation of desire, which inspire new problems, adventures, practices, and knowledge. Zones of intensity, fantasies, delusions, and affects are elicited, initially in an unordered way, but which in their experiencing undergo a process of production of senses. A new logic of sensation, vibration, makes the body and subjectivity leak into other configurations and intensify the empowerment of thoughts, affects, existential possibilities, and virtues of the collectives (Baremblitt, 2014b).

In addition to the cognitive, affective, existential transformations of people and collectives, Baremblitt emphasizes the political character of schizodrama, aiming for singularities to be able to connect and act as a collective, linking desire to the social and the social to the desiring processes. Gregorio (1998) supports the project of affirming the power of desire, for the production of what he calls "dionysian" energies and acts of creation. One of his goals is the protagonism of the participants, the *actants*,[12] who, in the processes of affectation, of affecting, and being affected, may intensify the assemblages and encounters. The actants should not remain in a passive position, or subjugated by the hierarchy of the *psy* professional, but assume all their potential of forces. The schizodramatic method is eminently clinical-political, as its intervention inevitably culminates in changes in power relations, whether of a collective in relation to the social, or even of a person with himself. Baremblitt envisions schizodrama as a critique of Integrated World Capitalism, neoliberalism, and the various fundamentalisms that plague the world. Therefore, he considers that his molecular action may resonate in the large strata, also promoting macropolitical transformations. Revolutionary micropolitics, as Gregorio Kazi maintains. And we remember that micropolitics is never a politics of small spaces but an analytic of the articulation between desiring assemblages and forces relations in any social set, whether in a "micro" sphere, or even "macro."

Schizodrama dramatizes the concepts of schizoanalysis, but does not restrict itself to mere experimentation. The performative actualization of schizoanalytic concepts in devices is not reduced to the field of technique, to reproduction, or application. Its praxis creates new enunciations, propositions, concepts, and a singular cosmology (or *chaosmology*). That's why Gregorio uses various neologisms to express other phenomena and events. The concepts now receive the name of schizoemas, which are the "semiotic units of schizoanalytic discourse and action" (Baremblitt, 2004, p. 201). The safe and determined cosmos in which one lives

---

[12] We use the term "actant" in the same meaning attributed by Bruno Latour (2008).

becomes Chaosmos, which operates more by processes of differentiation and continuous variation, instead of identity and stability. Reality, or *realterity*, is defined more by heterogeneity, than a supposed and idealized homogeneity, now divided into three surfaces where different processes occur: production, register-control, and consummation. The being gives way to the becoming (Baremblitt, 1998).

Another philosophy is configured, a new world, with other people and territories, hybrids, migrants, minorities, and dissidences, who allow themselves to be affected by the whirlwind of the real and who seek to make themselves heard, to act, to take action. New tools and abstract machines that foster processes of deterritorialization, transformation, and subjectivation (Baremblitt, 1998, 2019; Baremblitt et al., 2020). That's why it's not a "schizoanalytic psychodrama" and not an "applied schizoanalysis," but rather a field that has been singularizing with its experiments and new propositions.

The invention of schizodrama marks Baremblitt's work as the moment when he assumes a "proper name," when he becomes an "author in fact" and begins to speak for himself, as he creates a new regime of enunciations and original and singular practices. With his theories and practices, he figures as a guerrilla machine. Schizodrama is certainly the most untimely invention produced from schizoanalysis. However, it does not worry about the construction of a "School," of a dogmatized field and reproduced by a retinue of faithful. Its purpose is not to be academic, bureaucratized, or fundamentalist. But rather a theoretical-practical field of thought and critical interventions that are directed to the pragmatic production of new possibilities of life, that can be actualized in several areas, such as a practice linked to health and care, in an educational, labor, cultural, artistic establishment, in a social movement, in the community, in a civil association, etc. Baremblitt understands that schizodrama is not taught or transmitted orally, but is dramatized and "contagious" in its making. That's why, in the process of affectations, the participants themselves become schizodramatists, in the proposal that one acts as one lives and lives as one acts.

Gregorio considers that the rescue and study of his work "makes sense in the midst of the struggle between the revolutionary diffusion of schizoanalysis and its recovery by the *establishment*" (2013, p. 3), because he denounces that there are theoretical-practical positions that appease the disruptive potential of schizoanalysis for economic purposes and the capture of its insurgency, in short, that corroborate with the capitalist axiomatics. Baremblitt is the expression of a nomadic thinker and clinician, always in motion, committed to transformation, libertarian desire, a new world, other subjectivations, and the realization of an Active Utopia. Therefore, if Paulo Freire created the Pedagogy of Liberation, Enrique Dussel, the Philosophy of Liberation, Gutiérrez, the Theology of Liberation, Martín-Baró, the Psychology of Liberation, Gregorio Baremblitt invented the schizodrama, as a set of *klinics of liberation*.

Baremblitt gives us a conceptual and clinical-political intervention machinery that is not delimited as a discriminated field of techniques with fixed and demarcated consignments and settings; is much more as continuous variation and an invitation to create new devices, practices, and knowledge. He always encouraged his friends, colleagues, and students to intensify their own creative potential. Consequently, the schizodramatic practice should be productive and not merely technical and reproductive, being characterized more as experimentation than application, more as an instituting doing than a presupposed and given knowledge. To do schizodrama is always an invitation to a movement that corresponds more to the margins, minorities, differences, and dissidences, to exercise the power of thought for the invention of new praxis and possibilities that are articulated to the dear principles of schizoanalysis of scraping and production (Deleuze & Guattari, 1972; Baremblitt, 1998; Baremblitt et al., 2020). It is a call, path, clearing, to the experimentation of new ways of affecting oneself, thinking, acting, existing, enunciating, and subjectivating, in which consciousnesses rise up and the unconscious is decolonized. More than a theory, it must be experienced, but with the audacity and prudence of every traveler who opens himself to the deterritorializing experience of converging in new lines and crossing borders. Following these paths is to actualize and keep the active forces of Baremblitt alive, in a sowing of new fields and production of other possible worlds.

References

Alliez, E., & Lazzarato, M. (2016). *Wars and capital*. Semiotext(e).

Amorim, M., Bichuetti, J., Hur, D. U., Kazi, G., & Oliveira, M. F. (2021). Gregorio Franklin Baremblitt, o guerreiro do devir… cuidado, insurgências inventivas, utopias libertárias. *Revista Memorandum, 38*, 1–11.

Artaud, A. (1938). *O teatro e seu duplo*. Max Limonad, 1987.

Artaud, A. (1947). Para acabar com o juízo de Deus. In C. Willer (Ed.), *Escritos de Antonin Artaud*. Porto Alegre.

Baremblitt, G. (1998). *Introdução à Esquizoanálise*. Instituto Félix Guattari.

Baremblitt, G. (2004). *Psicoanálisis y esquizoanálisis (un ensayo de comparación crítica)*. Asociación Madres de Plaza de Mayo.

Baremblitt, G. (2013). Personal communication to the author (mimeo.).

Baremblitt, G. (2014a). Presentación del esquizodrama. *Teoría y crítica de la Psicología, 4*, 17–23.

Baremblitt, G. (2014b). Dilemas de los aprendices de hechiceros (dudas en la pragmática auto-inventiva de los jóvenes esquizoanalistas y esquizodramatistas). *Teoría y crítica de la Psicología, 4*, 24–50.

Baremblitt, G. (2019). *Esquizodrama: 10 proposições descartáveis*. Instituto Gregorio Baremblitt.

Baremblitt, G. (2021). Posfácio. In A. Rossi (Ed.), *Formação em esquizoanálise: pistas para uma formação transinstitucional* (pp. 151–164). Appris.

Baremblitt, G., Amorim, M. A., & Hur, D. U. (2020). Esquizodrama: teoria, método e técnica—klínicas. Ed. IGB.

Bichuetti, J. (1999). *Lembranças da Loucura*. Instituto Félix Guattari.

Bichuetti, J. (2000). *Crisevida: outras lembranças*. Instituto Félix Guattari.

Deleuze, G. (1953). *Empiricism and subjectivity: An essay on Hume's theory of human nature*. Columbia University Press, 1991.

Deleuze, G. (1962). *Nietzsche and philosophy*. Columbia University Press, 2006.

Deleuze, G. (1963). *Kant's critical philosophy: The doctrine of the faculties*. University of Minnesota Press, 1984.

Deleuze, G. (1966). *Bergsonism*. Zone Books, 1988.

Deleuze, G. (1968). *Difference and repetition*. Columbia University Press, 1994.
Deleuze, G. (1969). *The logic of sense*. Columbia University Press, 1990.
Deleuze, G. (1981a). *Spinoza: Practical philosophy*. City Lights Books, 1988.
Deleuze, G. (1981b). *Francis Bacon: The logic of sensation*. Continuum, 2003.
Deleuze, G. (1988). *The fold: Leibniz and the baroque*. University of Minnesota Press, 1993.
Deleuze, G., & Guattari, F. (1972). *Anti-Oedipus: Capitalism and schizophrenia*. University of Minnesota Press, 1983.
Deleuze, G., & Guattari, F. (1975). *Kafka: Toward a minor literature*. University of Minnesota Press, 1986.
Deleuze, G., & Guattari, F. (1977). *Política y psicoanálisis*. Terra Nova, 1980.
Deleuze, G., & Guattari, F. (1980). *A thousand plateaus: Capitalism and schizophrenia*. University of Minnesota Press, 1987.
Deleuze, G., & Guattari, F. (1991). *What is philosophy?* Columbia University Press, 1994.
Dosse, F. (2007). *Gilles Deleuze et Félix Guattari: Biographie croisée*. La Découverte.
Foucault, M. (1995). *Theatrum philosophicum*. Anagrama.
Freud, S. (1937). Construções em análise. In *Edição standard brasileira das obras completas de Sigmund Freud (1937–1939)* (Vol. XXIII, pp. 289–304). Imago, 1976.
Grande, A., & Baremblitt, G. (2022). *Conversaciones implicadas con Gregorio Baremblitt: psicoanálisis, subjetividades y Revolución*. Ed. Herramienta & Contrahegemonía Web.
Guattari, F. (1989a). *Schizoanalytic cartographies*. Bloomsbury, 2013.
Guattari, F. (1989b). *The three ecologies*. Athlone Press, 2000.
Guattari, F. (1992). *Chaosmosis*. Indiana University Press, 1995.
Hur, D. U. (2014). Trajetórias de um pensador nômade: Gregório Baremblitt. *Estudos e pesquisas em psicologia, 14*(3), 1021–1038.
Lapassade, G. (1977). *Grupos, Organizações e Instituições*. Francisco Alves.
Lapassade, G. (1980). *Socioanalisis y potencial humano*. Gedisa.
Latour, B. (2008). *Reensamblar lo social*. Manatial.
Lima, W. (2014). *O teatro ao alcance do tato*. UFPA.
Lourau, R. (1975). *A análise institucional*. Vozes.
Mendel, G. (1974). *Sociopsiconálisis*. Amorrortu.
Nadaud, S. (2016). Los amores entre una avispa y una orquídea. In F. Guattari (Ed.), *Escritos para el Anti-Edipo. Textos agenciados y presentados por Stéphane Nadaud* (pp. 9–24). Cactus Editorial.
Oury, J. (2009). *O coletivo*. Hucitec.
Rodrigues, H. d. B. C. (2016). *Ensaios sobre Michel Foucault no Brasil: presença, efeitos, ressonâncias*. Lamparina.
Rolnik, S. (1997). Psicologia: subjetividade, ética e cultura. In *Saúdeloucura, 6: Subjetividade*. Hucitec.
Safatle, V. (2007). *Curso Introdução à experiência intelectual de Gilles Deleuze - (mimeo.)*. Filosofia - USP.

Chapter 3
Cartography of Intensities: Device and Haptic Dimension

Schizoanalysis has a unique approach to analyzing and intervening in different social phenomena, moving away from the classic positivist and disciplinary matrix of traditional knowledge. It assumes a constructivist and pragmatic perspective, arguing that theories should not constitute as a rigid, dogmatic, or totalized foundation; on the contrary, they should be used as toolboxes, with a perspective that Baremblitt calls "Superior Eclecticism."

In the famous dialogue with Foucault, titled "*Intellectuals and power*," Deleuze emphasizes this pragmatic character, where theory is not reduced to representation. For the philosopher, theories must work, assemble with the phenomenon, producing more senses about the investigated problem. If a theory, or a concept, does not prove useful for analyzing a certain problem, it should be changed, or even a new theory should be invented: "treat my book as a pair of glasses directed to the outside; if they don't suit you, find another pair; I leave it to you to find your own instrument, which is necessarily an instrument for combat[1]"(Foucault & Deleuze, 1972, p. 208). The theory should not totalize, nor reduce the phenomena, that is, it cannot format reality to its set of codes and signifiers, but should multiply the senses arising from reality, in a rhizomatic movement of construction.

In this chapter, we intend to discuss on how the schizoanalytic research approach is operated. We present some methodological changes of schizoanalysis that offer unique contributions to the clinic, intervention, and research in the human and health sciences. We provide clues to the researcher about the types of traces to map in his work, on how to guide the search for intensive elements, which can produce more senses and complexify the situation, instead of reduction and formatting.

[1] In this book, we chose to put the year of the original publication of Deleuze and Guattari's books, but with the pagination of the English language editions (online) found in the references. The quotes that were not found in English were translated by us with the support of Artificial Intelligence.

D. U. Hur, *Schizoanalysis and Schizodrama*,
https://doi.org/10.1007/978-3-031-94657-8_3

Among the various concepts of Deleuze and Guattari's work, we selected four: the device, the cartography, the logic of intensities, and the haptic perspective.

It is worth noting that the activity of research and thought is also a clinical activity. "The thinker is first of all a clinician, a sensitive decipherer and a patient of the regimes of signs that existence produces, and according to which it itself is produced" (Zourabichvili, 2012, p. 170). Because research can also be the art of encounters that produces enunciations and differential senses about what we experience in relation to the investigated phenomena.

Device

A fundamental element that must be had prior to an intervention and research is the device. Schizoanalysis provides rich theorization, contributing to the elucidation of its various effects for the clinic and investigation. The device is a machine that creates a connection, gathering, articulation, between heterogeneous components (Deleuze, 1989). It is a disposition, bond, that keeps the different elements provisionally in a "circuit," which generates a functioning, machination, with various consequences. It can be taken as the concrete machine, the actualization, of the assemblage (Baremblitt, 1984).

Deleuze (1989) makes a unique reading of the device, understanding it as a machine that even synthesizes Foucault's own philosophical work, assembling the lines of (a) knowledge; (b) power; and (c) subjectivation. He discusses how the device is: (a) a machine for making speech, which produces regimes of enunciations; (b) a machine for making visible, creating regimes of visibility; and finally, (c) a machine for production of subjectivation. That's why when we participate in devices, we come out different, in some way, changed, transformed, or the opposite, even more formatted. For instance, psychotherapeutic, pedagogical, military, devices, etc. are heterogeneous machines that produce different ways of being, that mobilize power relations and that modulate enunciations in unique ways.

Baremblitt hypertrophies the pragmatic and transformational facets of the device, understanding it as an assembly of a novel artifact that articulates elements of different materialities, such as social machines, techniques machines, and even microscopic subpersonal functions, being the vehicle of "deterritorialization" (1984, p. 55). The use of the device in the Baremblittian approach does not aim to foster adaptation and normalization but the opposite: movements of deterritorialization, that is, transformations in the cognitive, affective, and social realms. The clinical-political devices in schizodrama are always taken as disruptive and enhancers of desiring flows and lines of flight, in a commitment to change, and not with stereotyping and formatting. Therefore, the device is a concrete machine that incites the "psychopolitical work" of the person/collective, managing forces related to thinking, affecting, enunciating, and subjectivating, seeking to foster movements of vibration and transformation.

In *A Thousand Plateaus*, there is another reading about the assemblage that allows us to understand the functioning of the device in a new perspective. Deleuze and Guattari (1980) teach us that the device (assemblage) has four distinct polarities which are very operative for clinical-interventional work. There is a *tetravalence* divided into two axes, horizontal and vertical; thus, each valence refers to one of the four poles.

There are two polarities on the horizontal axis. On the left pole, the *machinic assemblage of bodies*, and on the right pole, the *collective assemblage of enunciation*. The machinic assemblage of bodies are related to the content regimes, articulating bodies, affections, actions, and spatial relations. In turn, collective assemblage of enunciation refers to the regimes of expression. They handle associative, expressive, enunciative, and discursive processes. It is not about separating the two processes but proposing that they are two inseparable and irreducible planes to each other, a "matter" of content and a "matter" of expression.

On the vertical axis, two other polarities appear. At the lower pole are the *territorial sides*, and at the upper pole are the *cutting edges of deterritorialization*. The lower pole provides the operations of fixation and stratification, that is, the processes of deceleration that foster sedimentation and territorialization. On the territorial sides, rigid segmentation lines, stability, and constancy are produced, that is, a striated space, the setting of the device. The cutting edges of deterritorialization refer to another functioning. They propagate the lines of flight, the unbound energies, the intensive peaks and the operations of rapture. They refer to the processes of transformation, in relation to the virtual and with the vectors of abstract forces, being the polarity of a smooth space, of the body without organs. Consequently, there is a pole that provides the territory, with its anchoring processes, and another, of fluidity, transmutation, and creation (Hur, 2018).

The enunciations, affections, and intensities are the result of the operation of this concrete machinery, connected to the actualization of an abstract machine, virtual, which operates by a magmatic, rhizomatic, logic. Knowing the functioning of the tetravalence of each intervention device allows us a greater understanding and handling of its effects.

We systematize the tetravalence of the device in Fig. 3.1, which should be treated dynamically and not statically. The functioning of each clinical-interventional device transits in the different positions of this schematization, being able to situate itself in one of the valences, or in one of the various intersections. For example, in the psychoanalytic intervention device, what is its main operating machine?

Sigmund Freud invented the couch-divan device to solve a problem faced at the time, which was not the fatigue of sustaining the face-to-face of psychoanalytic sessions, as is propagated by common sense. Psychiatry of the late nineteenth century failed to create a therapeutic device to effectively treat the pathology known as hysteria, which mainly affected women.[2] Let's remember that Freud was a great

[2] Here we add the criticism of some feminist authors that psychoanalysis with hysteria operated as a power device to maintain domination between sexes, as a mechanism to maintain social subjection in traditional sex-gender domination. In psychoanalysis, hysteria is not apprehended from its political point of view but as a disease. The libertarian, independent woman should thus be controlled, psychopathologized, psychoanalyzed.

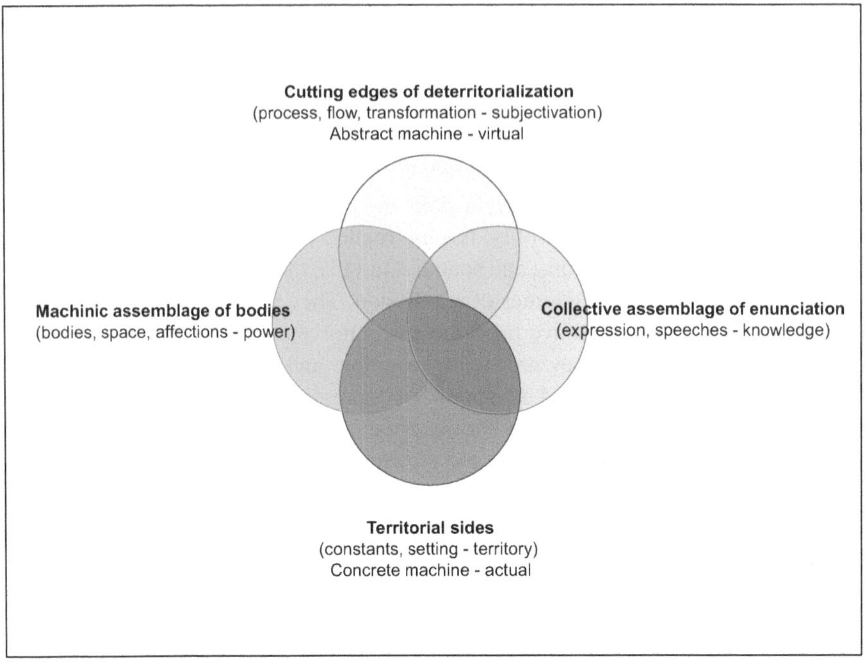

Fig. 3.1 Tetravalence of the device

experimenter of techniques in his work. From a neuroanatomical method, the belief in psychotropic drugs such as cocaine, in ill-fated experiences with suggestion and hypnosis, he arrived at the technology of the couch-divan. To reduce the transferential load of the "hysteric" to the analyst, the Austrian doctor aimed to operate in a different way in the machinic assemblage of bodies. He experimented with subtracting the analyst from the patient's field of vision, creating a very artificial spatial situation, where the analysand had to lie on his back to his doctor. He placed the patient lying on a divan and his doctor sitting in an armchair, or sofa, behind him. And to optimize the "cure," the elaboration processes, he adopted a collective assemblage of enunciation quite unusual for Vienna of the Austro-Hungarian Empire, with the so-called method of free association. The patient would have to express everything that associated with the doctor, even contents considered taboo at the time, such as sexual fantasies and of destruction directed at the analyst. (Fernandes & Hur, 2022; Kaës, 1997). That is, on the horizontal axis, he operated with an "almost" immobilization of the body, added to the primacy of discursive productions. On the vertical axis, the cutting edges of deterritorialization were reached when the so-called manifestations of the unconscious occurred, or processes of association and elaboration. On the other hand, the psychoanalytic device of the couch-divan is of low intensity, often provides experiences that remain more in the stratification of the territorial sides, than in the opposite pole. If we locate most of the psychoanalytic interventions in Fig. 3.1, these are predominantly located in the lower right quadrant, at the intersection between collective assemblage of enunciation and the territorial sides, having small peaks that momentarily cross the line of the "equator."

Like many institutions, the psychoanalytic Institution has bureaucratized the couch-divan device, combating other machinic assemblage of bodies, such as the face-to-face worked in group psychoanalytic sessions, or even when the pathologies to be faced are others, very different from hysteria. It is now known that *borderline* experiences, of disaggregation of the Self, of problems of psychic boundaries and panic are treated more effectively when there is a work of production of figuration of the body and of oneself, which is often catalyzed in a face-to-face situation. So, one of the consequences of the institutionalization of traditional psychoanalysis was the rejection of other clinical intervention devices, such as group psychoanalysis (Kaës, 1997).

The psychodrama device has another machination. The machinic assemblage of bodies places the different actors, patients, on the "stage," interacting in the scene, where often their body movement and affective expressions are more significant than verbal enunciation. The psychodramatic device can be considered of medium intensity, being located on the meridian to the left of Fig. 3.1. Other devices like holotropic breathing (see Chap. 8), considered of high intensity, reach the cutting edges of deterritorialization, possibly being in the upper left quadrant. Schizodrama also operates more with the valence referring to the peaks of deterritorialization, as it seeks to foster the production of asignifying processes and other associations from medium and high intensity devices. It aims to produce cuts and fissures to foster new desiring circuits. On the other hand, a psychodiagnostic device, like the famous psychological tests, seeks more to territorialize people and collectives, instead of providing change and transformation. It is located at the lower right extreme of Fig. 3.1, normalizing and formatting people according to the pre-established norms of its discipline of knowledge.

With this description, we do not seek to compare one device with another to say if one is better or worse. The question for the clinician and the researcher in schizo-analysis is to know how their device mobilizes desiring regimes, forces, and production of enunciations and subjectivation. What are the discourses, affects, and intensities mobilized in interventional clinical work? What are its virtues and limitations? And if it is capable of managing them, because an experience of radical deterritorialization, or of intense delusions, is often difficult to handle. That's why we must know the modes of functioning of our machines, to assume an attitude of prudence, before putting them into operation.

Cartography as a Method

There are many books, articles, theses, and dissertations that adopt cartography as a privileged method of investigation in the Brazilian literature referenced by schizo-analysis, especially in the area of psychology. Among them, the collection *Pistas do Método da Cartografia [Clues of the cartography method]* (Passos et al., 2010), which influenced many subsequent researches. In these studies, cartography is considered as a method of investigation and analysis created by Deleuze and Guattari (1980), from their discussion on the logic of the rhizome. It is noteworthy that practically all these researches allude more to the methodological approach of cartography, instead of Guattari's (1989) later reflections on the *schizoanalytic cartographies*, in which he outlines the four "categories" of *machinic phylum*, incorporeal universes, existential territories, and economy of flows, fundamental components for the production of subjectivation. In this topic, we also treat cartography only as a method.

In *Rhizome* (Deleuze & Guattari, 1980), cartography can be taken as a method that does not refer to reproduction, reduction, or tracing of the real. It functions more like a map that constitutes an open system with multiple entries and exits, having a connection and intertwining with the real. An open map to its tracing, to the construction of processes, an a-centered, non-hierarchical, and asignifying system. It is a mapping that produces reality and not merely represents it.

To trace the lines of cartographic investigation, it is necessary to follow the processes (Barros & Kastrup, 2010; Rolnik, 1989). To carry out a constructivist and pragmatic movement of tracing lines with the displacements of the investigated phenomenon. In this way, cartography is not restitutive, or regressive, it adopts a perspective of construction that is made with the walking of the investigator. That's why the method of schizoanalysis gives up interpretation, in favor of experimentation. Instead of reproducing the traditional interpretative method of psychoanalysis, of regression to an imagined or experienced past, cartography is constructivist; it is prospective and not regressive. Instead of excavating the "pharaoh's tomb," it prefers to follow and map the movements of drift, of displacement, of the continents (Deleuze, 1993). Instead of digging the root and looking historically for an origin, the supposed cause of the problem, it follows the movement of propagation in the channels (Deleuze & Guattari, 1980). Therefore, it is not an archaeological, genealogical, historical task, but above all, geographical and geological. Cartography does not reproduce the past, but produces the future and the present, that is, it is situated in a paradoxical coexistence between multiple temporal planes (Deleuze, 1966). It does not seek idealized and transcendent essences, but the production of senses in the investigated phenomena. It is worth noting that, evidently, cartography does not ignore history but it is not only restricted to it. Cartography prefers a geography of affects and nomadism, concerned with the movements and displacements of bodies in the territory, rather than an individual history of the person.

Thus, cartography in research and in the clinic is undertaken with walking, following, tracking, the investigated phenomenon. The aim is to map the field, the territory, its elements, the desiring investments, like a surveyor, or even a hunter, who scratches and traces contours, limits, paths, and clearings, producing multiple senses and non-senses. The clinician is situated, implicated, in the field, where his actions influence the investigated collectives, producing a modality of research-intervention (Passos & Barros, 2010). In the mapping of the territory, of the phenomenon, we are inspired by the method of nomadism, of decentralization, which traces lines in movement, follows the fluxes of the field, the city, the body, desire.

The aim is to propagate like the movement of the rhizome, without center, beginning, limits, or end, in drifts in the territory. The investigation plane is always an open field, in continuous variation, and is only constituted when traced.

In cartography, the objective is not only to analyze the matter, the reified substance, the stratified and the concrete machines. We search to investigate the dispersion of flows, of desire, their trajectories, coordinates, directions, and senses. It does not focus only on what is at rest, but rather the movements, the vectors of forces, their speeds, and slownesses. Cartography focuses on what is in continuous variation, the virtualities and the abstract machines. It does not only adhere to the logic of being, but also to the logic of becoming (Deleuze, 1969), or rather, it understands being as the being of becoming (Baremblitt, 1998), being as duration, change, and self-alteration (Deleuze, 1966). From this perspective, it does not only research what appears as similarity, pattern, identity, and constancy, but dissimilarity, deviations, differences, dissonances, variations, and especially what erupts as an event.

Thus, cartography is a kind of *diagrammatic* (Hur, 2018). It analyzes and follows the vectors, the configurations and diagrams of forces, always mobile, plastic, and mutant. Cartography investigates the desiring circuits constituted, the forces that make flow, as well as those that block, pressure, and coerce movement, both of abstract and concrete machines. It draws the networks of forces that involve the investigated phenomenon (Barros & Kastrup, 2010). We highlight that a diagram is always accompanied by its concrete machines (Deleuze, 1986), that is, by its updated formations.

Even though it is open, it is worth emphasizing the importance of a territory of anchorage for the development of cartography. Clinical prudence is necessary. Therefore, we do not consider that cartography is a laissez-faire activity, which is done in any way at the investigator's pleasure. As Deleuze asserts on several occasions, the task of thought starts from a problem, which often needs to be produced. So, the cartographic activity is a result of the problem investigated and developed by the researcher. A clinical, political, and research problem that produces an axis and territory for subsequent investigation. That's why the investigator, before going to the field, must establish a "cartographic program," which is his portion of firm ground, the understanding of the management of his devices. Obviously, his program is not based on a fixed framework, but on the contrary, it is structured in *mobile settings* (Lans, 2003), or as it is said in schizodrama, "*vibratile settings*," where it is possible to make curves and deviations in the course of the process, derivations of the problem, according to the events of the outside.

Logic of Intensities

In schizoanalytic research and clinic, the thinker does not only adhere to discursive materiality. Cartography does not restrict itself in search of what is represented, in the signifier, it does not reduce the multiple data from the field only to the text, or to the visible. Representation, writing, is a movement among many others, like walking, swimming, hunting, making a bow (Krenak, 2015), feeling, desiring, affecting oneself. The cartographic method operates with other materialities that go beyond representation: it seeks to grasp the extralinguistic and the distinct components of expression (Tedesco et al., 2013). It is a research procedure that opens up to asignifying materialities, to vectors, and configurations of forces, apprehending a new element: intensities, which for Deleuze (1968a), should be the focus of thought.

For the conduct of cartographic investigation, we use a *sui generis* method. Our attention is guided by all the emerging and collected information, though we select those that are more related to the problem of the research itself and that present greater intensity. Unlike traditional research methods, we do not seek what has the greatest appearance, but another "index" totally different from the frequency register and that assumes a higher degree of power, that is, what is intensive: the intensities.

As we do not prioritize a quantitative analysis, we do not restrict ourselves to the "frequency" indicator. Because it is known that not necessarily the "frequency," an important quantitative measure, is the most relevant for a certain research problem. It is not because it appeared more times that it will always be more important. Sometimes, even a high frequency of appearance can be related to a stereotype, established habit, presupposed discourse, empty and bureaucratized speech, that seems to spin in vain (Guattari & Rolnik, 1986), an *as if*, either from interviewees, or even by the bias, or suggestion of the researcher. Therefore, it may not bring new senses to the investigated problem, staying in the repetition of the same already known and recognized. It's very common to come across surveys with a large sample size and data collection technology, which, after long statistical procedures, conclude the obvious. The logic of frequency is a machinic index of how a certain desiring circuit is functioning, but it is generally more related to its constancy, stability, than to its variation and differentiation. It may even configure itself as a black hole (Deleuze & Guattari, 1980), with all its centripetal forces, obscuring the differential expressions of the investigated phenomenon, in which even the clinician can get his thought and analysis captured by the logic of frequency of appearance.

The intensities figure practically in all books of Deleuze and Guattari, mainly in the work resulting from the philosopher's doctoral thesis, *Difference and Repetition* (Deleuze, 1968a). A first aspect to be highlighted is that intensities do not refer to the field of signifier and of the represented, but allude to particles and asignifying processes (Deleuze & Guattari, 1975). A second aspect is that intensities are not subjugated by the planes of quantity, nor of quality, they express a third aspect that becomes independent.

Intensities receive various conceptions in his work, as synonym for forces (Deleuze & Guattari, 1975), a quantity, or degree, of power (Deleuze, 1968b), and mainly as difference, differential relationship. They update the difference, differential relations, being "the form of difference in so far as this is the reason of the sensible. Every intensity is differential, by itself a difference" (Deleuze, 1968a, p. 222). Thus, referring to difference and intensity in the same expression can be considered as a redundancy, as "intensities comprehend in themselves the unequal or the different" (Deleuze, 1969, p. 297). Their expression produces disparity, which is the state of infinitely redoubled difference, the successive unfoldings of difference.

We consider that intensity is a degree of force, a degree of power, which expresses a differential relationship, a leap, a kind of "tonic accent" that carries another process, in another logic of sense that is not restricted to identity, equality, and similarity.

> On the contrary, tonic and intensive values act by creating inequalities or incommensurabilities between metrically equivalent periods or spaces. They create distinctive points, privileged instants which always indicate a poly-rhythm. Here again, the unequal is the most positive element. Cadence is only the envelope of a rhythm, and of a relation between rhythms (Deleuze, 1968a, p. 22).

Thus, intensity produces differences, inequalities, both on metric, measurable planes and in the continuous flow and variation of duration. It is related to rhythmic events, which produce a stretching of processes, and not to the logic of the cadence, which is a kind of organization of rhythm. Intensity and rhythm are consequent and creators of events, while repetition–cadence can be associated with the logic of frequency and coding. Intensity expresses the unequal in itself, affirms the difference and implication. It is implicated, involved, "embryonated," by extensions, evidently in different degrees of distension and contraction. That's why "intensities are implicated multiplicities, 'implexes', made up of relations between asymmetrical elements which direct the course of the actualisation of Ideas and determine the cases of solution for problems" (Deleuze, 1968a, p. 244).

But how to map the intensities in the clinical-investigative work? How do they express themselves? How to operationalize this tracking?

Deleuze affirms that we must read the processes in intensity, because it establishes a new logic of sensibility. "It is intensity or difference in intensity which constitutes the peculiar limit of sensibility. (...) The point of sensory distortion is often to grasp intensity independently of extensity or prior to the qualities in which it is developed" (1968a, pp. 236–237).

There must be a twist in sensibility, its own distortion, in order to be able to apprehend the processes of irruption and differentiation. Because intensity is not extension, it is the virtual of what is presented actualized, in the relationship between *intensio* and *extensio* (Deleuze, 1968a; Hur, 2018). That's why "intensity is not the sensible but the being of the sensible, where different relates to different" (Deleuze, 1968a, p. 266), it is pure difference, the perceived quality, the intensity of sensation.

In the investigation, we seek to track the intensive indicators or tensors (Deleuze & Guattari, 1975) of the process, the lines of escape, fissures, and ruptures. Intensity can refer to the irruption of a new association, a fold of the sensible, to the emergence of a crisis, or new movement. "Intensity, being already difference in itself, opens onto disjoint or divergent series" (Deleuze, 1969, p. 299), unfolding in new planes and vectors, producing disparities.

Therefore, intensities are fundamental indices, as they trace openings to becomings. They have a high degree of forces, with a disruptive poignancy. The intensive, the line of flight, appears as a differential element that provokes fissures in the established desiring circuit. The cracks and crevices can lead to the rupture of stereotypy, to decoding and deterritorialization. Crisis and movement that incite the production of lines for the construction of a new desiring circuit. It is what crosses the established thresholds and is determinant in the processes of actualization: it is the intensity that dramatizes. It can foster the production of events, the processes of haecceity, which are possible events resulting from the intervention. Intensity refers to processes of singularization, which are not reduced to the Self. "Between the intensive and thought, it is always by means of an intensity that thought comes to us" (Deleuze, 1968a, p. 144).

We seek elements that carry a quantum of forces that express the difference, new lines, and another configuration for the lived, that is, the production of events. Often, they appear only once, in contrast to another element that appears with a higher frequency. Nevertheless, they can be much more expressive for the lived problem, since it is more important to see how a particular theme appears as an event than to quantify its occurrence. If we draw some parallels with authors of institutional and group analysis, in the terminology of Enrique Pichon-Rivière (1983), tracking intensities is analogous to mapping the *emergents* in the group associative chain. For the Argentinian social psychologist, these emergents do not refer only to discursive formations but also to symptoms, dreams, and affections. In the terminology of René Lourau (1975), tracking intensities is to look for the *analyzers*.[3]

We cite as an example the interview of Rodrigo Pimentel for the documentary *News from a personal war* (Salles & Lund, 1999). He is a former captain of BOPE (Special Police Operations Battalion) from Rio de Janeiro (Brazil), whose story inspired the creation of the character *Captain Nascimento* in the movie *Elite Squad* (Padilha, 2007). Throughout his interview[4] he proudly praised, several times, the armed actions in which he regularly participated, and only once questioned what he was doing and its effectiveness, but was deeply moved by this new association made. So, if we follow the logic of frequency, we will conclude that there was a positive representation of police militarism, without mentioning his moment of questioning, because it was an "isolated," unexpected speech. However, in the logic of intensities, we give more space to the new differential association, both for its unique content and for the emotional overflow of the moment. Such content only appeared once, but it had a very strong intensive quantum, to such an extent that shortly after this interview Pimentel left BOPE and dedicated himself to other activities, including those related to human rights issues. Therefore, the intensive indicator was much more decisive, and "accurate," than the frequency indicator, for his existential trajectory.

Intensities can be seen as propelling indices of movements, becomings, passages (Deleuze & Guattari, 1972), and the production of alterities. Their emergence

[3] Guattari (1989) states that he invented the concept of analyzers in the 1960s and criticizes the way it was recovered by the institutional analysis of Lourau (1975) and Lapassade (1977). Despite possible differences between both authors, we consider that the concept of analyzers used by Lourau is close to our conception for the tracking of intensities.

[4] The extra DVD material includes interviews with all participants, which were obviously summarized for the documentary.

causes a ripple, resonance, which incites new processes, another rotation, centrifugal force, which fosters differential repetition. That's why "the true subject of eternal return is the intensity and singularity" (Deleuze, 1969, p. 300), for it is the intensity that has the strength to return and removes repetition from its established orbit, producing an abstract line that shifts the body's center of gravity to new routes. Refrain[5] (Deleuze & Guattari, 1980), the repetition of difference, the repetition of novelty.

Thus, in the logic of intensities, instead of reducing data into broad and general categories, the aim is to complexify the phenomena, find differences and not just equalities and similarities, highlight anomalies and not norms. To travel in zones of intensity, in the *continuum* of intensities. That is, to track intensities from the problem, from the emerging and differential elements and dilemmatic and crisis situations. To follow the flows, the eruption of differences and the *multiplicitation* of phenomena, in other words, to understand identities and structures as multiplicities. To operate not with organization, signification, and subjectivation, but with disarticulation, experimentation, and nomadism (Deleuze & Guattari, 1980).

Haptic Dimension

There must be a new movement and a change in the clinician's sensitivity in order to grasp the logic of intensities. We have to change the perspective of the gaze, with a transition from a merely visual and auditory perspective to a kind of vision that touches. To exchange the distance of optical vision for the proximity and touch of a *haptic vision*, that is, a tactile vision, which does not refer only to the visual but to a gaze that is linked to tactile functions. Deleuze (1981c) uses the term haptic from Alois Riegl, a philosopher of aesthetics, to deal with the assemblage between vision and touch, in a form of synesthetic sensitivity. "Optical vision would be the distant perspective, relatively distant. On the contrary, the haptic exercise, or haptic vision, is the close perspective that grasps the form and the background on the same plane, equally close" (Deleuze, 1981d, p. 205). Thus, the haptic perspective is a mode of sensitivity that apprehends not only syntheses, figures, but also movements, schemes, the relationship between figure and background, the contour, intermediate processes, molecular vibrations and oscillations, corporeality itself, and resulting affections. It is a modality of vibratile gaze (Rolnik, 1997) in which we are affected by what surrounds us, by the forces and oscillations of the territory.

There must be a self-suspicion in relation to traditional ways of seeing, feeling, and acting in order to reach the haptic dimension. Thereby, it is not intended to codify processes with the established perspective of gaze and listening, with images

[5]The concept of *ritornello* is translated as *refrain* in English. We consider that it is not the best translation, as ritornello is closer to the idea of a musical phrase, which in its repetition, opens up to differential processes. The refrain can bring the idea of the repetition of the same, which is not the meaning that Deleuze and Guattari want to attribute to the concept.

of thought or established norms. The eye translates thought as technique, and the guilt of morality transforms thought into servitude. But affects go beyond functionalism and morality to a connectivity with others and differences. Thus, a deterritorialization and a process of unfolding of the being is sought as a method of a cartography of intensities. A scraping of the Self, of clichés, a decolonization of consciousness, which can be provoked by different forms, such as self-analysis, schizodrama, or other undisciplining practices, resulting in a reinvention of oneself and the collective. Because the act of scraping the gaze, to achieve haptic sensitivity, modulates and transforms our working tools, which are not only cognition but mainly affects, the body, and collectivity.

This change in the perception of life and reality makes us perceive processes in a different way. As Deleuze (1994) talks about the Japanese: instead of seeing the world from their Self, to extend to their street and then to the neighborhood and the horizon, they perceive the contour first. They first apprehend the horizon, the world, the continent, then arriving in the neighborhood and in the Self. This perceptive perspective is the same as that of Brazilian indigenous peoples. Krenak (2015) states that indigenous collectives apprehend the cosmos, before the country, humanity as a universal Tribe, in which the individual should not be the main focus. In these two cases, there is a perception of the tip, of the other, from a look of a social minority. From what is to our left and not from our own navel. It is a perception that places collectivity as a principle, and does not close itself to the opportunistic and competitive selfishness of the Self. So, it is the opening to difference, the intrusion of a becoming-other and not always staying in the logic of being, of the narcissistic, such as the neoliberal logic, or the neofascist. Therefore, for this deconstruction and reworking to the haptic dimension, there must also be a scraping of the old models in which we were formed. To stop prioritizing unmeasured hyperproduction, or the morality of obedience, for a sensitivity to (self)transformation. Open up to the processes of sensation and vibration (Deleuze, 1981c).

In the haptic perspective, of the method of multiple affectations, we do not just focus on the search for the signifier, on discursive materiality, we seek to trace and map the becomings, affects, and intensities. We seek to make "the sequences vibrate, to open the word onto unexpected internal intensities—in short, an asignifying intensive utilization of language" (Deleuze & Guattari, 1975, p. 22). To escape from significant formations, because we know that expressive processes do not only occur in the realm of verbal language, but also in its suprasegmental characters, such as height, timbre, rhythms (Baremblitt, 2019), which are also referred to as paralinguistic, as well as body iconic expressions, that is, its kinetics[6] (Bateson, 1972). It is also necessary to escape from normalizing semantics, such as psychoanalytic codes, Oedipus, phantoms and dreams, which can occupy this same reducing function, operating as tourniquets that block desiring flows and lines of flights

[6] It should be noted that there are many branches of study in linguistics, not only semantics and syntax, but also pragmatics, phonetics, phonology, prosody, metalanguage, etc.

(Deleuze & Guattari, 1972). We should take them only as indicators, traces, of the process, but not the final goal. Therefore, it is necessary to change the way of apprehension and jump such coded formations to make the flows run, map how the desiring investments work in the social field and what shapes/models/modulates this movement.

In this investigative modality, we also aim not to fix ourselves in our conscious field. As Spinoza says, consciousness can be a place of illusion (Deleuze, 1981a, 1981b), which often reduces and formats the power of the body and its compositions. Consequently, we seek to de-totalize consciousness, understanding that it is a result of processes, of the tension and composition of the forces of the body, and not the other way around. We also emphasize that there is no primacy of consciousness, of the cogito, over the data (see Chap. 8). That's why we seek to move from the Self, to other perspectives and angles of analysis. We operate a decentering of the Self in order to ascend to an experience of the contour, of edges that are always stretching, spreading out, as in the film *Dreams* by Akira Kurosawa (1990). To contemplate the painting of Van Gogh, but when we realize, we are inside it. And when looking at the edges, to return to our previous *locus*, we realize that the contours, the limits, always expand, following our perception, in which we are already swept away by what we contemplate. In other words, the aim is to scrape away one's own gaze and feelings in order to move away from the primacy of consciousness toward movements. It is worth noting that scraping refers to the first task of schizoanalysis: the destructive one (Deleuze & Guattari, 1972). It is also worth noting that this movement of decentering has nothing to do with a position of neutrality, but rather with an attempt to access the investigated phenomenon from its various angles, and that goes beyond the biased and formatted look of the investigator: a search for the experience of contours and dissolution of the observer's point of view (Passos & Eirado, 2010). As a result, we seek to trace a movement more impersonal than personal, pre-subjective than subjective, in a displacement more geographical than temporal that articulates anonymous singularities to the multiple and material context of the phenomenon. This mode of apprehension operates as the opening of a new sensitivity that maps the forces of movement, of the incorporeal, the invisible that does not appear in narratives and figurations, and that results in a mix between figure and background.

We also use the body as a data collection instrument, opening it to affectations of the most different species. Affects, sounds, noises, smells, movements, displacements, and tiredness become investigative indices of the process. It is the mode of apprehension that opens up the potential for affections that the field of investigation imposes on the researcher, who is implicated and situated in the territory. It is the sensitivity to the power of being affected by the multiple undulations and vectors of forces of the field. So, we do not only actualize narratives but also forces and affects, displacements, speeds, and slownesses. Cartography investigates the routes of desire and its machines, its constituted desiring circuits, the vectors of active and reactive forces (Deleuze, 1962). For example, why desire desires its repression, or even its self-abolition? In an approach with institutional analysis,[7] we affirm that cartography accompanies the instituting and instituted movements, in a process of self-analysis that seeks self-management (Baremblitt, 1992).

Several research devices result from this conception of cartography, such as: clinical cartographies, cartographic drifts through the territory, cartographic visits to the community, organization of events and workshops, observational cartographies, schizodrama, and various other clinical-investigative devices that the researcher may come to invent.

After the implementation of these devices, we can make a written or even graphic record of some of the percepts experienced in a field diary (Hur, 2024). After the production stage, we move to the connection and reterritorialization stage, the register-surface (Baremblitt, 1998), fundamental for the elaboration of figurations and narratives. The record is usually made after the intervention-research and is not restricted to people's speeches, but extends to the affections, perceptions, and sensations of both the participants and the researcher himself. The emerging intensive indicators are configured as the analyzers of the process and can produce more senses about the phenomenon. From the diffracted and apparently chaotic material, the intensive emergents are connected to strata, such as distinct narratives, visibility regimes, statements, etc. We make this articulation using the criterion of intensity, and thus we derive other interventions and even the general categories of analysis, which are evidently discussed from the concepts of schizoanalysis.

Hence, a schizoanalytic[8] "clinical and research methodology" operates more like a plane of opening, under construction, with a twist of sensitivity and the intensities that erupt, rather than totalized and formatted systems and the frequency indices of the appearance of a given element. It expands the way data is apprehended, moving from the merely visual or even auditory dimensions to the haptic dimension, in a tactile vision modality.

Therefore, the result of the investigative work is also in continuous variation and interrelated with other research and knowledge. Schizoanalytic research and clinical practice are always a mixture of intervention and investigation, in which the theory not only acts on the empirical data, transforming it, but also the new production of senses about the phenomenon can modify its conceptual tools. As theories are taken as toolboxes, concepts are always stretched, articulated with concepts from other fields, resulting in conceptual bricolages that generate a theoretical hybridism. And if possible, the proposal is that the research/intervention process should always be participatory, in a horizontal work between clinician and actants, which can foster zones of intensity, zones of common power to the collectives investigated.

---

[7] In Brazil, there is a tradition of working with concepts of schizoanalysis and institutional analysis in parallel, even though they have distinct conceptual origins.

[8] Evidently, this investigative perspective is part of the so-called qualitative methodologies and not the quantitative ones. Even if, at a certain stage of the investigation, there may be quantification of some data, the development of a broad discussion and analysis in the logic of intensities is maintained, and not in the mechanistic or positivist logic.

From this perspective, the research is a praxis, dramatization, intervention, clinical-political, activist-analysis, because it is production of life and processes of potentiation. That's why we seek to link such theoretical tools to our context and realities, where we have to translate, or rather, transduce, these concepts to Latin American reality. In a knowledge that mobilizes both cognitive, affective, and political aspects, instituting an *ethos* body-affective-political. Finally, research and clinical practice in the logic of the cartography of intensities show us that schizoanalysis should not only be called a philosophy of difference or multiplicities, but also a *philosophy of intensities*.

References

Baremblitt, G. (Ed.). (1984). *O inconsciente institucional*. Vozes.
Baremblitt, G. (1992). *Compêndio de Análise Institucional*. Rosa dos Tempos.
Baremblitt, G. (1998). *Introdução à Esquizoanálise*. Instituto Félix Guattari.
Baremblitt, G. (2019). *Esquizodrama: 10 proposições descartáveis*. Instituto Gregorio Baremblitt.
Barros, L. P., & Kastrup, V. (2010). Cartografar é acompanhar processos. In E. Passos, V. Kastrup, & L. Escóssia (Eds.), *Pistas do método da cartografia* (pp. 32–52). Sulina.
Bateson, G. (1972). *Steps to an ecology of mind*. University of Chicago Press.
Deleuze, G. (1962). *Nietzsche and philosophy*. Columbia University Press, 2006.
Deleuze, G. (1966). *Bergsonism*. Zone Books, 1988.
Deleuze, G. (1968a). *Difference and repetition*. Columbia University Press, 1994.
Deleuze, G. (1968b). *Spinoza et le problème de l'expression*. Minuit.
Deleuze, G. (1969). *The logic of sense*. Columbia University Press, 1990.
Deleuze, G. (1981a). *Spinoza: Practical philosophy* (p. 1988). City Lights Books.
Deleuze, G. (1981b). *Cursos sobre Spinoza* (3rd ed.). EdUECE, 2019.
Deleuze, G. (1981c). *Francis Bacon: The logic of sensation*. Continuum, 2003.
Deleuze, G. (1981d). *Pintura: el concepto de diagrama*. Cactus, 2007.
Deleuze, G. (1986). *El poder: curso sobre Foucault (Tomo 2)*. Cactus editorial, 2014.
Deleuze, G. (1989). Qu'est-ce qu'un disposif? In *Michel Foucault philosophe* (Rencontre internationale. Paris 9, 10, 11 janvier 1988). Paris, Seuil.
Deleuze, G. (1993). *Essays - Critical and clinical*. Verso, 1998.
Deleuze, G. (1994). *Gilles Deleuze's alphabet book*. Vídeo.
Deleuze, G., & Guattari, F. (1972). *Anti-Oedipus: Capitalism and schizophrenia*. University of Minnesota Press, 1983.
Deleuze, G., & Guattari, F. (1975). *Kafka: Toward a minor literature*. University of Minnesota Press, 1986.
Deleuze, G., & Guattari, F. (1980). *A thousand plateaus: Capitalism and schizophrenia*. University of Minnesota Press, 1987.
Fernandes, M. I. A., & Hur, D. U. (2022). Psicanálise, grupo e teoria da técnica: conselhos ao jovem coordenador de grupos. *Revista Psicologia USP, 33*, 1–8.
Foucault, M., & Deleuze, G. (1972). Intellectuals and power. In *Language, counter-memory, practice: Selected essays and interviews*. Cornell University Press, 1977.
Guattari, F. (1989). *Schizoanalytic cartographies*. Bloomsbury, 2013.
Guattari, F., & Rolnik, S. (1986). *Micropolítica: cartografias do desejo*. Vozes.
Hur, D. U. (2018). *Psicologia, política e Esquizoanálise*. Alínea.
Hur, D. U. (2024). Diário de campo, poder e análise da implicação. In F. L. C. Freitas (Ed.), *Algumas intercessões epistemológicas e metodológicas entre as Ciências Humanas e os Saberes Psis* (pp. 251–276). EDUFMA.

Kaës, R. (1997). *O grupo e o sujeito do grupo: elementos para uma teoria psicanalítica de grupo*. Casa do psicólogo.
Krenak, A. (2015). *Encontros*. Azougue.
Kurosawa, A. (1990). *Dreams* [Film].
Lans, A. (2003). *El esquizoanálisis: una clínica en movimiento*. Multiplicidades.
Lapassade, G. (1977). *Grupos, Organizações e Instituições*. Francisco Alves.
Lourau, R. (1975). *A análise institucional*. Vozes.
Padilha, J. (2007). *Elite Squad* [Film].
Passos, E., & Barros, R. B. (2010). A cartografia como método de pesquisa-intervenção. In E. Passos, V. Kastrup, & L. Escóssia (Eds.), *Pistas do método da cartografia* (pp. 17–31). Sulina.
Passos, E., & Eirado, A. (2010). Cartografia como dissolução do ponto de vista do observador. In E. Passos, V. Kastrup, & L. Escóssia (Eds.), *Pistas do método da cartografia* (pp. 109–130). Sulina.
Passos, E., Kastrup, V., & Escossia, L. (2010). *Pistas do método da cartografia*. Sulina.
Pichon-Rivière, E. (1983). *O processo grupal*. Martins Fontes.
Rolnik, S. (1989). *Cartografia sentimental: transformações contemporâneas do desejo*. Estação Liberdade.
Rolnik, S. (1997). Psicologia: subjetividade, ética e cultura. In *Saúdeloucura, 6: Subjetividade*. Hucitec.
Salles, J. M., & Lund, K. (1999). *News from a personal war* [Film].
Tedesco, S. H., Sade, C., & Caliman, L. V. (2013). A entrevista na pesquisa cartográfica: a experiência do dizer. *Fractal, Revista de Psicologia, 25*(2), 299–322.
Zourabichvili, F. (2012). *Deleuze: A philosophy of the event together with the vocabulary of Deleuze*. Edinburgh University Press.

Chapter 4
Desire as a Force: Clinic and Politics

What forces are at play? What desiring investments are circulating in the social field? What desiring circuit is constituted when the force desires its own abolition? For any clinical or political activity, it is fundamental to analyze "the libidinal investments in the economic and political spheres, and thereby to show how, in the subject who desires, desire can be made to desire its own repression" (Deleuze & Guattari, 1972, p. 105[1]). A cartography of the forces related to the psychopolitical phenomena should be made, such as investigating the dimensions of paralysis in situations of abuse and oppression, capitalist and neofascist desires, the success of extremism through desiring assemblages, the weight of morality and guilt, the feeling of loneliness, fatigue, and exhaustion in the present, etc.

If, at every moment, we are taught that we are only one thing, or that we are good for few things, that we are weak and powerless, this does not mean that it is *the* truth, *the* reality. It is a narrative produced to disempower, to bring sad affections into a condition that makes it easier for us to be dominated, governed, by a political representative, a boss, a spouse, a friend or even the psychologist himself. So, we should not always trust what is told to us, but rather try to develop our own potency, that is, not to fixate on what they say we should be and desire, but to affirm and produce what we can become, to give way to lines of flight and desiring investments.

Desire is one of the most discussed terms in psychology, psychoanalysis, and schizoanalysis. Yet, it is used in a mix of common sense with conceptual issues. In the natural attitude, and even in some of Deleuze's early texts, desire can take on the meaning of wanting, of will. But this changes quickly, schizoanalysis creates an original definition of desire, which is linked to the question of forces.

[1] In this book, we chose to put the year of the original publication of Deleuze and Guattari's books, but with the pagination of the English language editions (online) found in the references. The quotes that were not found in English were translated by us with the support of Artificial Intelligence.

D. U. Hur, *Schizoanalysis and Schizodrama*,
https://doi.org/10.1007/978-3-031-94657-8_4

Schizoanalysis intends to analyze the force in itself; thus the allusion to Nietzsche permeates all of Deleuze's work. The forces are constituents of all processes, power, the Law, concrete Institutions. Rather than being the possession of something or someone, they are exercised (Foucault, 1976a; Deleuze, 1986a). Consequently, the forces, as well as power, should not be seen as stagnant, static things, but rather in motion, like a kind of flow, such as the propagation of becoming.

Addressing forces and desire in parallel may seem redundant to the schizoanalysis scholar; because in the limit, desire is force. In this book, we seek to further reinforce this relationship. The approximation between forces and desire appears in various ways in Deleuzian thought, but without this relationship being developed categorically. Possibly the most substantial clues to this articulation can be found in Deleuze's dialogues with Foucault. In the text *Desire and pleasure* (Deleuze, 1977), there is a direct connection between desire and power. In differentiating his thought from Foucault, after the publication of *The Will to Knowledge* (Foucault, 1976a), Gilles does not see the primacy of power devices in this intertwining, but rather of desiring assemblages. He understands that power is not first, but is a result of desire, being "an affection of desire"(Deleuze, 1977, p. 125), one of its resulting processes, that is, one of its actualizations.

At another moment, Deleuze (1986b) states that power is equal to relations of forces, or rather, power is a result of relations of forces. It is noticed that in these two cases, the philosopher is discussing the relationship between the virtual and the actual (1966), between intensities and their extensions (1968). In the virtual plane are the desiring assemblages and the forces, and in the actual plane, power and the concrete machines. So, desire, like force, is on the plane of intensities, of the virtual, while power and the concrete machines are the formations derived from their process of actualization.

It can be seen that in the different periods of schizoanalytic work, the movements and flows that occupy the virtual plane are called in different ways, for example: vectors of forces, desiring investments, degrees of potency. We consider that both are "configurations" of the intensities and can be actualized, materialized, in different ways; they have different extensions. Therefore, we understand that there is a direct correlation of immanence between forces and desire.

By taking desire as a force, we can see why desire is never worked on in schizoanalysis in the logic of negativity, or as an absence, but as the expression of a productive, creative, multiple power (Deleuze & Guattari, 1972; Deleuze, 1962). Desire "appears neither as a power of negation nor as an element of an opposition, but rather as a questioning, problematising and searching force which operates in a different domain than that of desire and satisfaction" (Deleuze, 1968, p. 106). It is always taken in its affirmation and positivity, being apprehended as a process, propagation, and not as an entity, substance, or opposition and negation to something.

This perspective makes desire not restricted to pleasure (Deleuze, 1973; Deleuze & Guattari, 1980), hedonism, nor is it a party, form, intentionality, or the will, of a person. Because it constitutes itself as a polyvocal flow of forces, "and its polyvocality makes of it a single and unique desire that flows over everything" (Deleuze & Guattari, 1975, p. 57), operating in the expression of multiplicities:

"desiring-production is pure multiplicity" (Deleuze & Guattari, 1972, p. 42). It is configured as flows, a whirlwind of particle and wave emission, which "the objectivity of desire itself (...) is the system of a-signifying signs out of which unconscious flows are produced in a social-historical field" (Deleuze, 1973, p. 81).

Understanding desire as forces, flows, produces a change in the conception of the unconscious, which shifts from a representative model, to a pragmatic scheme. Unlike psychoanalysis, the unconscious does not function as a figuration, representation, restitution of a family theater. It is seen as the plane of emission of forces, that is, particles of desire, functioning more like a power plant (Deleuze & Guattari, 1980), in a machinic logic that propagates desiring flows. The unconscious operates as a factory producing asignifying elements, in which its intensities cannot be reduced to representation. An industry that assumes a pragmatic operation that pulses and produces magma, forces, affections, desiring investments. Then, the unconscious is a pure productive process, it is not figurative, nor symbolic (Baremblitt, 1998), it operates more by a "magmatic" logic, which overflows and does not cease to deterritorialize.

So, desire, like force, unlike structuralist psychoanalysis, is never taken as lack, restitution of a lack, or of an original mythical fantasy. It does not start from a supposed constitutive lack, nor seeks to restore a lost whole, an oceanic sensation. And neither is it constituted by fixation on ideal images and representation. Desire is the expression of life's own potency, being positivity that presents itself in different ways: movement and self-alteration. Desire overflows, it is excess and affirmation of an intensive process. The double allusion to forces and desire also serves to make a counterpoint to critical theoretical perspectives that leave affections, the intensities, and desire out of their field of analysis, in which they usually privilege "consciousness," and stereotype them in a reductionist way, in the logic of negativity, as "irrationalism."

Therefore, force is desiring, and desire expresses forces. In schizoanalysis there is a relationship of immanence between desire and production (Baremblitt, 1998), in which desire is always production, as well as all production is always desiring, it actualizes forces. Desire is the expression of the potency of being, of affecting (oneself), of acting, of agency. And like the forces, desire can also undergo capture processes, become reactive, fed/intoxicated by resentment. At this point it is worth asking, what are the different modalities of desire, of forces, in schizoanalysis?

Typology of Forces

In Deleuze's early texts (1953, 1955), there is a description of two modalities of forces: one of interdiction and another of attraction. The forces of interdiction refer to limitation, repulsion, to the negative bond that forms between one and another. These relations of opposition and coercion have their actualization in Law and the State, which are concrete machines that govern by repression. The logic of negativity is predominant, operating through antagonism and opposition (Deleuze, 1962).

The perspective of the negative is widely used in Hegel's dialectic, as well as in psychoanalysis itself and in common sense, from dichotomies, reductive binary oppositions and with conceptions widely propagated socially, such as "man is the wolf of man," the "hell is others," etc.

However, Deleuze points out that the negative logic of the forces of the State does not express itself in all social formations. Instead of operating only with the forces of prohibition of Law and the State, he makes visible a second modality of forces that operates with attraction, association, to the bond that is constituted between different elements. This connective model, which has another type of coupling, has its actualization in the *institution*. Accordingly, the French philosopher jointly treats the terms instinct and institution to "designate procedures of satisfaction" (1955, p.19), or the association between an impulse and its social formation. Therefore, the "tendencies find satisfaction in the institution" (1955, p. 19), such as the will to know in educational establishments, aggression in fighting academies, sexuality in conjugal connections, whether perennial or temporary, closed or open, etc. Desire always connects, links, forming sets and maps. So, connections, and consequently, institutions, present a logic of associativity. They refer to a positive model of action directly related to association. Thus, in the case of institutions, one must understand the processes by sympathy and not by selfishness, with the social not being a restrictive space regulated by antagonistic individual interests, but a composition and invention plane of association models. That's why "tyranny is a regime which there are many laws and few institutions; democracy is a regime in which there are many institutions, and few laws" (1955, p. 20).

In *Nietzsche and Philosophy*, still at the beginning of his work, Deleuze (1962) presents another typology of forces, no longer based on attraction and interdiction but based on two poles: active and reactive forces. In summary, they present the qualitative characteristics shown in Table 4.1 (see Hur, 2018).

From the idea of desire as forces, one can derive a conception of desire modulated by its activity, as well as by its reactivity. The proposition that there is an active and a reactive desiring investment does not imply entering into the logic of lack or negativity. If the active desire refers to the forces of creation and production, the reactive desire refers to another qualitative mode, another vector: to the forces of decomposition and antiproduction. It is as if the desire, previously active, undergoes a molecular mutation, in which it begins to assume characteristics of subtraction, of boycott and depreciation of processes, and which also cannot be reduced to the death drive.

Table 4.1 Characteristics of forces

Active forces	Reactive forces
Affirmation and action	Denial and reaction
Composition	Decomposition
Addition	Subtraction
Creation	Capture
Production	Antiproduction

The established state of affairs, the modality of relations that is assumed, is an expression, an update, of the configurations of forces and desiring investments. Nietzsche maps that in contemporary times, there is the triumph of reactive forces, in which the logic of the slave is predominant. Instead of the propagation of active forces, of an affirmative and liberated desire, we live in a period marked by excluding logics, explicit authoritarianisms, hostility against differences, and death. This configuration of forces is incorporated in the State, updating to the maximum what Foucault (1976b) calls the racist State (see Chap. 5). In all these contexts, hatred, the depreciation of the other and a lack of care for life are preached. They are the symptoms of a certain modality of forces, in which the reactive desire, resentment, bad conscience, the ascetic ideal, nihilism, the will to nothingness, and the hatred of life predominate (Deleuze, 1962). And our challenge is to prevent the active desire from continuing to be contaminated by these forces and to perpetuating itself as reactive.

It should be noted that Guattari does not share this conception between force and desire, and even reproached Deleuze for his references to forces in Nietzsche, an author he does not like at all (Uno, 2016). This is possibly why they give a certain prevalence to desire over forces, in addition to Felix's psychoanalytic past. Nevertheless, in this book, we choose to make the direct articulation between forces and desire, understanding their relationship of immanence; then, when we address one, we are simultaneously talking about the other. It is also worth noting that in the initial works, desire still appears in a bipolar form, but with its execution in machines there will be a pluralization of its vectors and configurations (see Chap. 5), in which binarisms are abandoned.

Transmutation of Forces and Desire: Klinic of Difference-Repetition

Nietzsche does not get stuck in a fatalism of reactive forces and he seeks to theorize how their transmutation can occur, the qualitative transformation of the desiring investment (Deleuze, 1962) that refers to the affirmation of life. He advocates the constitution of a new movement that does not reproduce reactivity and resentment, yet arduous and difficult the task may be. How can one not be saddened and not act reactively to the state of affairs in which we live? How can we not hate who hate us? If we breathe death, how can we breathe life? So, a fundamental movement must be the effectuation of a torsion, a bending, of desire (Deleuze, 1986c).

We believe that schizoanalytic clinic can contribute to this twist. Baremblitt (2019) lists some crucial klinics[2] of the schizodrama: Difference-repetition; Production of production, reproduction and antiproduction; Chaos, Chaosmos,

[2] Baremblitt uses klinic with a "k" to differentiate it from the traditional sense of the established clinic (see Chap. 2).

Cosmos; Event-becoming and Dramatic multiplicitation. These klinics refer to axial *schizoemas* of his work and actualize five axes of the schizodrama, interdependent, transversal, which often merge and fuse. In this chapter, we work with the first.

The klinic of difference-repetition of Baremblitt seeks to update all the power of repetition, for the production of differences, simulacra, and the transmutation of forces. Unlike the history of philosophy and common sense, difference is not apprehended as subjugated or subordinate to the identical. It is not its negative, or secondary in relation to identity or representation. The difference is seen in schizoanalysis as first and pure positivity, whether the difference of the infinitely small, or the infinitely large (Deleuze, 1968). A difference without concept, which is not reduced to similarity, analogy, the same, or opposition, and which refers to the universality of a singular against the Law. A difference that actualizes all the plurality of the plane of immanence and of a convulsing multitude. It also does not reduce to the conciliation of the *beautiful soul*, because it is acted upon by relations of force and tension: difference is aggressive, violent, and creates the dimension of the problematic. "Only difference gives rise to problems" (Deleuze, 1968, p. 235) and it is what drives thought and life.

In a convergent way, repetition is also not apprehended as a category of identity and similarity. But rather as an action scheme, with its own space–time dynamism, a movement that is the process of dramatization itself. Rather than a reflective category, repetition is an operating mechanism, an assemblage that operates in a nomadic distribution, with a rotation of centrifugal vectors, inciting the production of differences. *Refrains*. Repetition that goes beyond imitation, as it incites the tracing of an abstract line that escapes from the centripetal point of gravitation.

Repetition is always a "throw the dice," a new move, a "stroke in the sea" and not a reproduction. It is more guided by the forces of chance, than by a pattern. Hence, this klinic operates from the "theater of repetition," the rotation of the scheme, which actualizes differential forces and intensities. It starts from mimesis but assumes a positive productivity, or a productive positivity, which fosters a very intense rotating movement of centrifugal vectors. This rotation expels reactive forces, resentment, hatred, and weak forms. From this operation only "return" the active forces, which insist, subsist, and have the power to return. This process follows the same movement of the device of the eternal return of Nietzsche's Zarathustra. In it, what repeats is not the same, but the difference. Only the extreme, the excessive, the unequal, returns (Deleuze, 1968).

In this twist of forces, it is encouraged that the experienced nihilism gives way to the desiring production of life. The negativity of selfishness, antipathy, gives way to the associativity of sympathy (Deleuze, 1953) and altruism. Regardless of which device is adopted, one should seek the effectuation of this fold, a flexion of force, which results in the transmutation of reactive to active desire.

In the context of the theory of the technique, we request to repeat in forms of scenes, dramatizations of experiences, affects, and traumatic and highly complex events. Each repetition of the "triggering" scene updates different forces, returning those that insist the most. Each rotational cycle implies a distension of the margins, a flow of intensities that leads to an expansion of the borders. The centrifugal force causes a development by the edges, which can constitute new surfaces (Deleuze, 1969). Thereby, the repetition of the same scene produces differential performativities. And it is precisely these differential forces that we want to map, so we seek to incite what is not yet crystallized, organized, or what wants to escape: the lines of flight, the deviations, the lines of flexibility, or even the compositions. They form arrangements that are always disaggregating, in an unstable balance. The rotation of the dramatization, its repetition as a mechanism of action, refers to the propagation of new lines, in other words, the production of difference.

As a result, this rotation actualizes a virtual that makes us differ from what we are, in a composition of forces. An orgiastic joy that makes us move and jump, move from one affection to another, in which we repeat space–time dynamics and not just appearances; movements and not just identities. Action schemes that are operated by people, or collectives, and that become part of them, taking them even further.

This recourse to repetition in forms of scenes also seeks to map and create visibilities and sensitivities both for the clinician and for the participants. Images, schemes, affects, and intensities that transversalize and cross are dramatized, repeated, and transformed. It aims to affect and make visible the lived, with the concomitant production of new affections, senses, experiences, and implications with the problematized and experienced performativity. It is the intensity that dramatizes, that makes the pulleys of repetition ignite. It can also be seen that the transmutation of forces produces a transition in affective modes, an affective fold that can lead to the transition from sadness to joy, from power to potency.

As a procedure of conduction, we try to move away from narratives, meanings, illustrations, presupposed figures, *clichés*, in short, figurative data. It does not seek to reproduce articulated language, but rather the inarticulate, the iconic and the non-linguistic, the scream, the voice that transcends words, its height, the rhythm of breathing, the tones, intonations, including inaudible sounds. To bring out the figural from the figurative, the goosebumps, the bristling of hairs, the facial grimace, the movement itself. It aims to grasp the dramatization of forces, the eruption of the pictorial. And from them, produce events.

The different dramatized scenes are intermittent masks, disguises, which are assumed at a certain space-time moment. The mask is the true subject of repetition (Deleuze, 1968), being a localized and temporal production. It seeks not the *representation* of something, but the dramatization of a *presence*, of the movement of forces, of an image without similarity (Deleuze, 1981). It is not to imitate, but to become. A dramatization that is not restricted to the production of a figure, but that merges, spreads across the plane, the scene, surpassing, or diluting, its own contours, in a conjunction between lines and stains. In a performance that is not subjugated by the gaze and the visible, but that is guided by the movement, by the corporeality, in a tactile-optical articulation, haptic dimension, that manages and produces visibilities and invisibilities.

Therefore, the klinic of difference-repetition aims for a change, the propagation of lines, the repetition of difference. It is a clinic-politics, because at the same time that it delves into the agitation of molecules in the psychic and desiring scope, it analyzes and acts on the vectors of forces. The *clinic-politics* is a practice that manages the relations of forces and desiring investments in an instituting movement, being committed to the production of lines of flight and the emission of desiring particles with a new qualitative vector. It is eminently micropolitical, because it aims for a transmutation of forces that is not reduced to the individual and psychological plane, but is assembled to the social and political. It fosters the insurgent difference that repeats itself in change, transformation, project of autonomy, and active utopia. Finally, the clinic-politics is an intervention guided by the insurgent desire (Gondar, 2004), because its desiring expression is an eruption of power that can break with the established models and release the previously blocked, channeled, or axiomatized flows, producing new configurations of forces and modes of being and positioning oneself in relation to collectives and the world, in other words, configuring new sensitivities and existential possibilities. That's why Baremblitt bets on new devices, whether in the field of the clinic, in art, and in social movements, for the production of this other quality of forces and desire. Lines of flight and desiring guerrilla machines in their different contexts of action. To create new assemblages, apparatuses, machines, for the potentiation of life and the transmutation.

References

Baremblitt, G. (1998). *Introdução à Esquizoanálise*. Instituto Félix Guattari.

Baremblitt, G. (2019). *Esquizodrama: 10 proposições descartáveis*. Instituto Gregorio Baremblitt.

Deleuze, G. (1953). *Empiricism and subjectivity: An essay on Hume's theory of human nature*. Columbia University Press, 1991.

Deleuze, G. (1955). Instinct and institutions. In *Desert Islands and other texts - 1953-1974* (pp. 19–21). Semiotext(e), 2004.

Deleuze, G. (1962). *Nietzsche and philosophy*. Columbia University Press, 2006.

Deleuze, G. (1966). *Bergsonism*. Zone Books, 1988.

Deleuze, G. (1968). *Difference and repetition*. Columbia University Press, 1994.

Deleuze, G. (1969). *The logic of sense*. Columbia University Press, 1990.

Deleuze, G. (1973). Four propositions on psychoanalysis. In *Two regimes of madness - Texts and interviews 1975–1995* (pp. 79–88). Semiotext(e), 2006.

Deleuze, G. (1977). Desire and pleasure. In *Two regimes of madness - Texts and interviews 1975–1995* (pp. 122–134). Semiotext(e), 2006.

Deleuze, G. (1981). *Francis Bacon: The logic of sensation*. Continuum, 2003.

Deleuze, G. (1986a). *Foucault*. University of Minnesota Press, 1988.

Deleuze, G. (1986b). *El poder: curso sobre Foucault* (Vol. Tomo 2). Cactus Editorial, 2014.

Deleuze, G. (1986c). *La subjetivación: curso sobre Foucault* (Vol. Tomo 3). Cactus editorial, 2015.

Deleuze, G., & Guattari, F. (1972). *Anti-Oedipus: Capitalism and schizophrenia*. University of Minnesota Press, 1983.

Deleuze, G., & Guattari, F. (1975). *Kafka: Toward a minor literature*. University of Minnesota Press, 1986.

Deleuze, G., & Guattari, F. (1980). *A thousand plateaus: Capitalism and schizophrenia*. University of Minnesota Press, 1987.
Foucault, M. (1976a). *The history of sexuality: The will to knowledge*. Penguin, 1998.
Foucault, M. (1976b). *Society must be defended: Lectures at the Collège de France, 1975–1976*. Picador, 2003.
Gondar, J. (2004). A clínica como prática política. *Lugar Comum, 19*, 125–134.
Hur, D. U. (2018). *Psicologia, política e Esquizoanálise*. Alínea.
Uno, K. (2016). *Guattari—Confrontações: conversas com Kuniichi Uno e Laymert Garcia dos Santos*. n – 1.

Chapter 5
Desire and Political Machines: Coding, Neoliberal and Neofascist

A clinical-political cartography from the perspective of schizoanalysis must assume a singular approach. The analysis of concrete machines, such as the State, capitalism, fascism, or contemporary pathologies, like depression, panic, resentment: first, should not be restricted to a negative critique of these social machines, no matter how much we radically criticize them; and second, should not only be an analysis of their concreteness, no matter how much we discuss their concrete machines.

It is necessary to analyze their vectors of forces, the desiring investments, the diagrams, in short, their abstract machines. Thus, we do not want to investigate the State, capitalism, fascism and symptoms only as entities, substances, with their laws, ideologies, histories and norms. Rather, they are modes of operation, machines that produce certain types of desiring flows, with their gears for connecting, damming up, blocking, and constituting systems, closed or open, which result in the production of subjectivities.

This chapter seeks to discuss the different movements of desire, which culminate in distinct desiring circuits and subjectivations. It seeks to investigate how desire constitutes and is constituted by several machines, as well as to map the different assemblages in vogue. In contemporaneity, the operation of three hegemonic modalities of machines that agency desire is observed: coding, neoliberal, and neofascist. In this book, we do not seek to make their genealogy, or the Universal History (Deleuze & Guattari, 1972) but to discuss their couplings and current modes of operation.

Desire and Machines

Schizoanalysis shows that desire, like force, a becoming, transits and passes. It is not a substance that is limited to a person, group, or object but to circuits, "that it traverses, the vibrations and flows of every sort to which it is joined, introducing

D. U. Hur, *Schizoanalysis and Schizodrama*,
https://doi.org/10.1007/978-3-031-94657-8_5

therein breaks and captures—an always nomadic and migrant desire" (Deleuze & Guattari, 1972, p. 292[1]). It is not possession of someone, being, or only of some stratum. "Desire is what animates a process that is not proper to an instance, system or territory of the subject, but of reality itself and its realization" (Baremblitt, 1998, p. 85).

Desire is conceived as a propagation of flows, lines, that produce realities and connections. "Never consider a flux all on its own" (Deleuze & Parnet, 1977, p. 121), because there are not only free forces, they always create new paths, meeting points. Its proliferation opens passages, weaves lines, makes circuits. The forces, the desiring investments, connect to each other, constituting maps of forces, couplings that configure gears, systems, and machines. They are assembled in the coexistence of various levels, assuming a consolidation in *desiring circuits*. In this sense, desire refers to an assemblage; its diffusion manufactures a map that does not preexist its tracing, which elaborates its own plane of consistency:

> a field of immanence, a 'body without organs', as Artaud put it, criss-crossed by particles and fluxes which break free from objects and subjects... Desire is therefore not internal to a subject, any more than it tends towards an object: it is strictly immanent to a plane which it does not pre-exist, to a plane which must be constructed, where particles are emitted and fluxes combine (Deleuze & Parnet, 1977, p. 89).

In this sense, it is by navigating that we produce the route, the paths, the territory, and perhaps even the body itself. Desire assumes different vectors, with various connections and conjunctions of flows, continuous of intensity and particle emissions. In its proliferation, it supposes voids and deserts, but in its tracing they are populated, territories that are demarcated and occupied, a reality that is constantly produced. The void should not be seen as lack, or negativity, because empty and full are positivities that differentiate by their degrees of intensity: "void and fullness are like two demarcations of intensity"(Deleuze & Parnet, 1977, p. 110).

This circuit manufactures configurations of forces, several types of desiring assemblages (Deleuze & Guattari, 1975), such as a rural social movement that mobilizes hundreds of workers in the struggle for access to land, or even the machine formed by the baby's mouth—mother's breast, with the flow of milk transmission. Thus, desire is a force that assembles and is assembled by various components that articulate it to the social field and to things, forming circuits and machines. "Desire and its object are one and the same thing: the machine, as a machine of a machine" (Deleuze & Guattari, 1972, p. 26). Its propagation uninterruptedly forms connections and gears, machines that are always desiring circuits, in other words, desiring machines. Desire establishes a set with the gears, being inseparable from the connections, from the circuits and the new resulting machines. It is emphasized that when the machines work, they disassemble, produce flows, including other machines

[1] In this book, we chose to put the year of the original publication of Deleuze and Guattari's books, but with the pagination of the English language editions (online) found in the references. The quotes that were not found in English were translated by us with the support of Artificial Intelligence.

and gears, new frontiers, other thresholds of intensity: desire is inextricable to a machine, because there is no machine without desire, it is desire itself diagrammed.

Even with this terminology, it is worth reinforcing that the machine is not mechanical, technical, or organic. It is a circuit of desire, a set of human-tool-animal-thing neighborhood, among independent heterogeneous terms. Propulsion and flow-cutting system, connection and disassembly gears, which incites a co-functioning between the distinct elements, tracing a line that transversalizes and makes them operate together. It is noteworthy that machinic assemblages do not only work in a closed circuit, as their operation incites "the shift of a centre of gravity along an abstract line" (Deleuze & Parnet, 1977, p. 117), which provides an opening to new processes. Desire is the crossing of becoming in a desert that is incessantly populated.

The desiring assemblage produces and circulates through different types of abstract, virtual machines, which are updated in concrete machines, technical machines. This circulation orbits between two coexisting poles, the paranoid and the schizo. On the one hand, it can be segmented in a space, in a concrete institution, with a specific modeling of desire, where it is fixed in machines that constitute closed systems, forms that dam it, but at the same time, it can be swept away as a free force, in the production of becomings and events that stretch the borders for exits and new possibilities (Deleuze & Guattari, 1975). In the assemblage, there is a coexistence between the territorial sides and the cutting edges of deterritorialization (Deleuze & Guattari, 1980), in a desire that is rebutted, but also raised (Deleuze & Guattari, 1975). Therefore, desire is a flow that forms a collective assemblage, where the person is just a point, or a resultant, of its connections.

Due to the virtual and multiple character of the intensities, desiring machines are polyvocal. Consequently, there is no overdetermination of one modality of flow over another. Unlike psychoanalysis, sexuality itself becomes just another flow among others. So, there is no idealizing sublimation that would generate other flows (for instance: art, work, culture), but an interpenetration between them. Later, Deleuze and Guattari, to distance themselves even further from the psychoanalytic bias of desire, abandon the term desiring machines and choose to work with the proposition of desiring machinic assemblages (Deleuze & Parnet, 1977).

In the final period of Deleuze's work, the circuit resulting from the connections of the desiring flows receives another name: *diagram*, a term we use extensively in this book. The diagram is the connection of mobile forces, a configuration formed by vectors of forces in motion, fluid and unstratified (Deleuze, 1986). It not only represents the processes, but also produces them. It is an exposition, combination of relations of variable forces, with an emission of singularities that refer to a movement, a "stroke in the sea," a "throw of the dice," of unformed matter and unformalized functions. It is the map of forces in itself, unstable, in perpetual movement, but which denotes different types of functioning.

The diagram operates as a modulation matrix, being "the operative set of asignifying and nonrepresentative lines and zones, line-strokes and color-patches" (Deleuze, 1981a, p. 101). And its function is to "suggest," or, more rigorously, "it is to introduce 'possibilities of fact'" (1981a, p. 101). In this operation, the philosopher distinguishes the modulation of the diagram, from the mold and the model. Broadly speaking, the *mold* follows the reference of the crystal, being what produces a molding, in fixed and rigid configurations. The *model* refers to the plane of the organic, is what models, which produces processes of mimesis and imitation from norms. The *modulation* does not refer to fixity, nor to the reproduction of a model, but rather to a dynamic movement that refers, for example, to the old electronic tube of the television, which modulates the movements of the electrons inside it, or currently, the transmission of digital television signals. "A modulator is a continuous temporal mold" (Simondon quoted by Deleuze, 1981b, p. 156). Therefore, the diagram can be understood as an abstract machine, the map of the relations of dynamic and unstable forces that continuously modulates the processes. It does not exist by itself, independent, isolated; there is always a direct relationship between mobile and virtual forces and the actual and consolidated structures that result from them. There is always a singular diagram related to a certain social formation, even if "precarious forms" are generated. The diagram is also correlated to the idea of a full body without organs of a society (Deleuze & Guattari, 1972), which Baremblitt chooses to call as full body. Thus, there are different social diagrams, such as those referring to the State machine, the capitalist machine, or even the neofascist machine. We worked extensively on these diagrams in a previous book (Hur, 2018), but we present them here with another theorization.

Coding Machine: State, Discipline and Psychoanalysis

Social machines, the *socius*, always seek "to codify the flows of desire, to inscribe them, to record them, to see to it that no flow exists that is not properly clammed up, channeled, regulated" (Deleuze & Guattari, 1972, p. 33). The existing social coding mechanisms intend to format and reduce the whirlwind of difference and reality. As an example to visualize this movement of reduction, the philosopher Lalande states "that reality is difference, whereas the law of reality, or principle of thought, is identification" (quoted by Deleuze, 1968, p. 226). So, the difference is subsumed to identity, even in thinking.

Another example to distinguish the production and reproduction processes can be found in *noology*, that is, the science of thought (Deleuze & Guattari, 1980). Just as the denunciation of the poor treatment given to difference in the history of philosophy, Deleuze (1968) criticizes that there is not enough reflection on thinking. He denounces the fact that there is no method for analyzing thought, in which thinking in common sense is totalized by its apparent and static form: *the image of thought*.

The reproduction of images of thought subsists in the identity of the synthetic image, which is a mere decal of the magma of thinking. The criticism is that thought should not be taken only by its figures, in its syntheses, to be reduced to instituted and static images, as apprehended on the surface of the control-register. Thinking refers to a contrary movement, not to an image, but a spark (Foucault, 1973), ignition, combustion, which produces a new process. To think, according to Artaud, one must disarrange the image of thought, because it only works in its collapse (Deleuze & Guattari, 1972). A corrosion that refers to a flux of flows that generates a movement in the territory. Thinking is movement, or the opposite of the image of thought: it is a thought without image. Therefore, for its effective exercise, one must escape from centripetal forces, from white walls and from the territories constituted by reproduction (Hur, 2018).

Nevertheless, a movement of capture of the chaotic flow operates: its coding. This formatting occurs from a process of inscription of the desiring flow in certain symbols, signifiers, in short, codes. If there are two distinct series (series A—desiring flow or real; series B—instituted codes), the social machine always seeks to take the series A and translate it, decal it, to series B. It results in the reduction of multiplicity to structure, from thing to signifier, from unconscious to language, from real to known codes.

From this perspective, social machines are the actualization of desiring circuits, which, coded, form closed systems, where desire must circulate. The coding of flows occurs in two main ways: by molding and modeling processes. The first type, *mold*, corresponds to the operations of inscription of flows in the rites of the tribe, of the primitive territorial machine, or to the overcoding through the imperatives of the sovereign, his Laws, in the despotic imperial formation (Deleuze & Guattari, 1972), of the diagram of capture/sovereignty (Hur, 2018). The second type, *model*, refers to the normalization of conducts operated by disciplinary knowledge and norms, that is, by the disciplinary diagram (Foucault, 1975; Deleuze, 1986). These procedures mix and update in a variety of social instances, such as Law, institutional norm, ideology, as well as in psychic formations, fantasies, the super-ego, the Oedipus complex. Such social and psychic formations can encode, fix, and channel desiring investments, reducing them to exclusive conjunctive syntheses.

The State is an example of a coding and coercive machine that shapes the diffusion of flows, from the logic of sovereignty, of the desire of the despot (Deleuze & Guattari, 1972), being one of the oldest apparatuses of governmentality. It constitutes a diagram of capture that *molds* and formats the forces and desire with an intense gravitational power, of centripetal vectors. This diagram resonates forces of stabilization and conservation, and desire forms a circuit with the sovereign and patriarchal logic, having to adapt to this stratified mold.

In the disciplinary diagram, desire is channeled by norms, for example sexuality, which is dammed up in heterosexuality, what is considered "normal," and what deviates from the rule is seen as deviant, "a-normal." There is a *modeling*, and not a molding, as in the sovereign diagram. However, the two diagrams operate with the dichotomous logic of negativity: what adapts to the mold/model is positivized, and what escapes is negativized. Therefore, in the disciplinary logic, the sexual flows must be propagated within the patriarchal and heteronormative desiring model, and those who escape the norm are reduced, or suppressed. We can exemplify the sovereign logic with the case of Islamic fundamentalist countries that prohibit homosexuality by Law, condemning such conduct to punishment and, in some extreme cases, even death. In this example, it would not be a sexual model, but a sexual mold, a heterosexual patriarchal desiring imperative that must be strictly followed. It can be seen that such organizations of forms incapacitate desire, subjecting it to the negative, to lack, to the norm and to the Law (Deleuze & Parnet, 1977). So, there is a paradox of desire, which is lived in its propagation, enjoyment, but also in its confinement, capture. At the same time that the code forms a mold/model of reference, it also configures a despotic signifier that binds the entire chain. Due to this second function that there is a prevalence of desiring circuits governed by reactive forces, by a desire that seeks to fix itself, in many cases, in its own repression. It is worth noting that it is the desiring circuits that form the bonding configurations, and their stratification is what keeps us trapped, for example, to the Oedipus.

Psychoanalysis itself is a disciplinary knowledge and technique that creates a register of translatability, of coding, of desire. Far from being a revolutionary and insurgent practice, it is a transmission belt of the power of the State and the capitalist logic (Deleuze & Guattari, 1972). Schizoanalysis makes a harsh critique of psychoanalysis, understanding it as a disciplinary machine that "stifles the production of desire" (Deleuze, 1973, p. 79), always trying to reduce and format it to presupposed images. "Psychoanalysis unhooks and reduces every connection and assemblage. That is its job. It hates desire, and it hates politics"(1973, 81–82). On the other hand, the propagation of desire is the opposite; it is the production of the unconscious, formation of enunciations and matter of intensities. But psychoanalysis tries to reduce the intensive and polysemic flow of desire to the logic of castration and Oedipus, with a conservative force regime, which, instead of liberating desire, the forces, crushes it (Deleuze & Guattari, 1972). The truth of desire for this discipline is castration and Oedipus (Deleuze & Parnet, 1977). And even the method of free association and the consignment of the production of enunciation are criticized:

> Psychoanalysis impedes the formation of utterances. (...) The flows of desire are now dominates by an imperialist signifying system; they are reduced to a world of mental representations where the intensities lose their steam and the connections are broken (Deleuze, 1973, p. 83).

Psychoanalysis is considered as a mode of expression that prevents people from speaking, in which the free association of the analysand is coded only "with readymade collective utterances, Oedipal in nature" (Deleuze, 1973, p. 84). It constitutes a machine of interpretation, an apparatus of subjectivation and translation at the same time, which provides a signifier to the symptom (Deleuze & Parnet, 1977). Here the coding of one series over another appears again. The "produced" statements are only what psychoanalytic grammar allows, leaving out everything that is not consigned by it. If someone raves about races, worlds, cosmos, the psychoanalytic translatability device converts such contents to Oedipus, to castration, to the Law, to the mother. All assemblages are overcoded "in order to subject desires to signifying chains, utterances to the status of subjective examples—all of which reconcile them with an established order" (Deleuze & Parnet, 1977, 88–89). If free desire operates a pulsation of centrifugal vectors, to the outside, psychoanalysis, like every coding machine, establishes a closed desiring circuit, with centripetal vectors, as made visible in Fig. 5.1. There is no transduction of the real, only translation and reduction (see Chap. 10).

The Oedipus complex is an emblematic example of desiring capture. It is not a phylogenetic psychic formation, inherent to the human species, as some psychoanalysts defend. Oedipus is not the constitutive figure that determines the whole of reality; on the contrary, it is a construct resulting from the actualization of the State logic of codification of desire within the family triangle, in which its "resolution" is directly associated with the elaboration of castration and the internalization of the phallocratic Law. "In short, it's not Oedipus that produces neurosis; it is neurosis—that is, *a desire that is already submissive and searching to communicate its own submission*—that produces Oedipus. Oedipus, the market value of neurosis" (Deleuze & Guattari, 1975, p. 10, italics in the original). It is not the father who is transferred to the State, but the State that is actualized in the father. So, family and Oedipus present the force diagram of the State, the mold as a new model. They are concrete machines, social and psychic formations, that assume a function of State capture apparatus (Deleuze & Guattari, 1980) in the local, family, psychic coding, and colonization of the unconscious. Therefore, Oedipus is a form of domestication and channeling of desire, previously plural, rhizomatic, and which results in the depotentiation and government of the individual or social body. It is a coercive

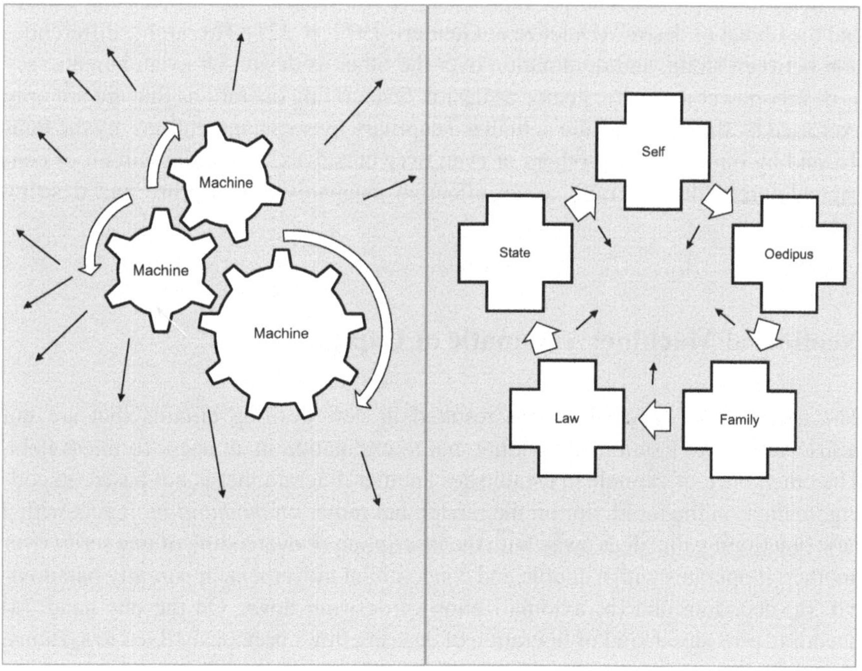

Fig. 5.1 From desiring assemblages to the coding of the desiring circuit

psychic formation that must be scraped off. By basing itself on the perpetuation of the order and the established hierarchy, psychoanalysis does not take into account the assemblages, the geography of displacements but only the history that legitimizes the Law. That is why "psychoanalysis is the murder of souls" (Deleuze, 1973, p. 85), as it instills lack, absence and the Law in desire, in which psychoanalysts teach infinite resignation, being the last priests (Deleuze & Parnet, 1977).

Thus, psychoanalysis operates in the same system of overcoding of the State, but with a disciplinary semantics, added to an aura of initiation, like a parable, mixed with science. In the analytic session, people have to "discover themselves," but from a pedagogy that adopts the configuration of State forces, with their hierarchies, Laws and normalizations, covered by an "academic-scientific" discourse. In this way, they discover the State desiring machinic assemblage that reverberates in their bodies, but judging that it is their secret, essence, intimacy. They naturalize the State and hierarchy as desire and mode of subjectivation. They accept the norms, the disciplines, the regimes of subjection and servitude, and learn to desire and legitimize them, articulating them with their own homeostatic movement, of search for regulation. They find the diagram of sovereignty, but do not open it to new desiring circuits, more flexible, less capturing. "Oedipus is always colonization pursued by other means, it is the interior colony" (Deleuze & Guattari, 1972, p. 170), being the result of the State force diagram.

In this case, we do not see the desire for the State, but the State as desire. A desiring circuit that establishes the damming of forces, their formatting. "A State desire, the most fantastic machine for repression, is still desire—the subject that desires and the object of desire" (Deleuze & Guattari, 1972, p. 221). Hierarchy, differentiation between strata, and domination over the other as desire. Or even, bureaucracy as desire, power as desire, justice as desire. Overcoding operations that are not only exercised by the State, but are actualized capillary by social institutions, by the family, and by ourselves over others or even over ourselves. A desiring circuit of centripetal forces that operates as an effective mechanism of capture and desiring colonization.

Neoliberal Machine: Axiomatic of Capital

The transition of force diagrams resulted in new desiring circuits that are not restricted only to fixation and coding, but to circulation in an open, formless field. The emergence of capitalism establishes another diagram that is not based on coding, neither on the mold, nor on the model, but rather on *modulation*. It acts with a new functioning that does away with the inscription or overcoding of one series over another. It operates with a double and concomitant movement, apparently paradoxical: (a) decoding and (b) axiomatization of desiring flows. On the one hand, (a) decoding provides a kind of liberation of desiring flows previously fixed to systems, giving the impression that desire becomes free, like an unbound energy, configuring what some authors call liquid modernity (Bauman, 1999). On the other hand, (b) axiomatization ensures that there are no free, or "liquid," flows, as it constitutes a distinct circuit in which there is *modulation* of the decoded desiring flows according to the logic of capitalist functioning. This second movement does not correspond to the formatting, fixation, of desire in a closed circuit, whether by the mold or model, but rather by its resonance and agitation in the open field. It does not generate a new code, but rather a maxim, the axiomatic of capital (Deleuze & Guattari, 1972), the abstract machine of capitalism.

This double movement operates as a kind of equation, formula, in which the elements are variables. It constitutes a machinic assemblage of semiotization that is actualized in the most distinct materialities, such as in economy, politics, architecture, subjectivity, sexuality, in the body (see Hur, 2018), which modulates conducts in the open field. It seeks the maximization of the production of any object, as it is the "relation between creative activity of wealth without determination and any object of abstract labor" (Deleuze, 1979, p. 256). The desiring circuit of the capitalist machine diffuses a mode of functioning that is related to a generalized acceleration, always directed toward the production of wealth, which becomes subjective (Deleuze, 1979). The imperative to accelerate the frequency of rotation, the emission of particles and ripples is established in all technical processes and machines: a performance diagram is created, as a desire for hypertrophy of production (Hur, 2018).

The axiomatic of capital produces a universal equation of regulation to the different logics and institutions—it universalizes local logics by the primacy of the hypertrophy of performance. The codes remain as desiring circuits, but lose their primacy to this new modality of immaterial circuit, which is actualized as acceleration of production in any instance. The desiring flows are modulated by a quantitative logic of more-production that has as its correlate financialization, always aiming at the highest yield. Bifo (2018) highlights how financial abstraction sharpens the impersonal operations of automatisms, as if a logical-mathematical chain were established, based on the algorithms of capital, which every day replace human management.[2]

The result is the progressive decoding of the State, as well as of other institutions, the decline of the great strata and ideologies such as socialism, in favor of Mafia Capitalism (Hur, 2018). Unfortunately, socialism, like communism, in the power of the State failed to create a new desiring circuit, another diagram of forces, alternative to capitalism. In its attempt, it even reached the point of reverting to the capture machine of the diagram of sovereignty, expressed by the fateful Stalinist model, tarnishing, in practice, the libertarian and egalitarian ideals of communism.

It is noteworthy that the acceleration of the frequency of production of the any object is not just centrifugal, as the desiring flows do not direct themselves to an outside, to the edges, propagating chaotically, or rhizomatically. There is a

[2] Bifo (2018). We highlight that Lazzarato (2021) criticizes this statement by Bifo, considering it depoliticized for ignoring the Mafia Capitalism, that is, the corporations, groups, and people who manage the flows of capital (Hur, 2018).

modulation that causes a semi-centrifugal propagation, from its emission poles, which propagates concentrically, following the same operation of increasing the hypertrophy of production (see Fig. 5.2). Thus, desire is not incited to propagate nomadically, nor to constitute closed circuits, but rather to an expansion of its circulation in mobile and floating states, never free, but always seeking to increase its borders. There is the promotion of forces of destabilization and acceleration, so crises are constituents of its functioning, its engine (and perhaps, downfall).

In this diagram people believe that they live in a period of freedom, progressive in relation to previous ones. Because they are not primarily governed by norms and are situated outside the walls of institutions, they posit neoliberalism and its justifying ideologies. "Their" desiring flows make a circuit with this machine, no longer primarily molded by the State or modeled by disciplinary norms. Desire is no longer blocked, but incited to the maximum in its operation of acceleration, stimulated to run and produce more connections. However, not in a free and anarchic enjoyment. There is a composition between reactive and active forces, and if there's any freedom, it would be the freedom between working more, or working even more.

The ingenuity of the capitalist machine is the elaboration of ideals of transcendence that create the myths of meritocracy and the *self-made man*; the belief in common sense is: the harder everyone works, the more successful they will be. Nonetheless, this is just a fallacious discourse that conceals systems of individualized accountability and blame (Guattari, 1989). The axiomatic of capital refers to a collective-political–social system that creates its scapegoats on an individual level.

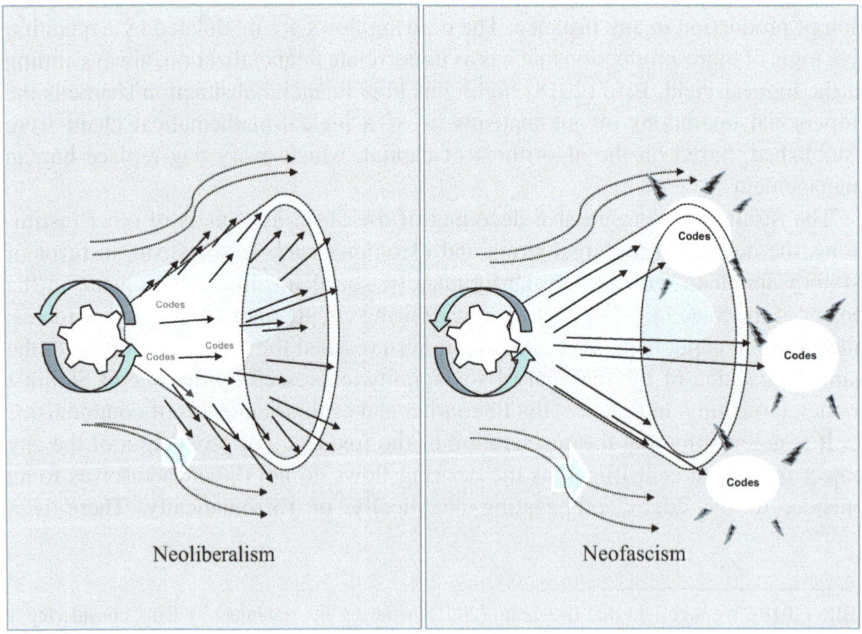

Fig. 5.2 Axiomatic of capital in two moments

For example, the population that is condemned to poverty, instead of attacking those who caused this condition, internalizes poverty and economic failure as if it were their own fault, individual. Thus, the creation of self-blame is a very effective mechanism of neoliberal management. In the disciplinary diagram, if one fails, they are excluded by the concrete Institution. In the performance diagram, those who fail can be annihilated not only by others but also by themselves, by their own demands.

The configuration of this desiring assemblage makes this political machine much more legitimized than the previous ones. Its modulation provides an immaterial, molecular, impersonal governmentality, very effective in managing populations in the open field, outside State and institutional walls. It provides a desiring self-regulation in microspaces, diffused and capillarized in the city. It governs not by social totalization but by a management via the calculation of probabilities that uses as its main tool the government of affects, which is currently greatly optimized by algorithms and artificial intelligence.

As much as the axiomatic of capital operates by equations and algorithms, inexorably it ties itself to the different relations of forces at play. Its emergence and consolidation were intimately coupled with imperialism and wars (Alliez & Lazzarato, 2016). Hence, capitalism itself operates with colonialist traits, as much as its neoliberal equation wants to consign the opposite. Because, concretely, "the apparatuses that depersonalize power relations (money, wages, etc.) cannot function without personal relations of power"(Lazzarato, 2021, p. 88). And history has shown us that capitalism is built on a founding violence, such as the dictatorships of the 1960s and 1970s, in the extermination of left-wing groups and opponents, who were replaced by the *Chicago boys* (in Chile), or now with neofascist governments.

At this point, the crucial question to ask is: how do social forces reverberate in the human body and psyche? In the relationship between people and political forces, how is the correlation between bodily pulsations and the modes of governmentality of everyday life? It is naive to believe that the diagram of capitalism, or its discourse, reverberates *ipsis litteris* in the human, because the body is not a technical machine. There is capitalism from a sociopolitical-desiring point of view, but it is distinct from the functioning of capitalist subjectivity.

Capitalist pragmatism has become the primacy of action, of the ideal, of belief, and even of utopia for many people. But the human body has not been able to keep up with its functioning. Its actualization may have resulted in super-efficient, hyper-productive, hypertrophied, and tireless capitalist human-machine assemblages. However, these automaton behaviors are in the minority.

Its movement of crisis and decoding, in addition to fostering incessant production, stimulates negative competitiveness (zero-sum) and produces insecurity, causing people to behave more aggressively and dichotomously. Consequently, there is the emergence of a contradictory phenomenon, that "*the more the productive forces were developed*, the more archaism was reinforced (or had to be reinforced)" (Guattari, 2012, 66, italics in the original). Thus, the processes of capitalist decoding also led to hyperterritorialization in new social codes.

There is a subjective modality that results in its own contradiction. Rolnik (2018) calls this subjective form the colonial-capitalistic unconscious. It articulates two apparently disparate processes, both the production and actualization of the axiomatic of capital, as well as archaic, conservative behaviors that refer to a colonized-colonizing subjectivity, historically grounded on the Latin American colonial experience.

Within the neoliberal diagram, there is a modulation of forces that refers to decoding-modulation and incessant production, but from the perspective of a bodily subjectivity there is a zigzag, or a coexistence between capitalist discourse, of hypertrophy of production, with practices of conservation and fixation, which refer to fundamentalist beliefs, or even feudal ones. As if the body could not withstand radical acceleration, and this hinterland zone and crisis for productivity always led people to a closing movement for stabilization.

The result of this equation is that capitalist subjectivity operates in these two modes: (a) acceleration of the hyperproduction of any object and (b) reterritorialization in any sets of codes. Possibly the fixation on archaisms may even be the *rest* of the operation of deterritorialization. "(...) But out of the pressure of always new and always harder segments, he will accelerate the speed of segmentalization, this speed of segmental production" (Deleuze & Guattari, 1975, p. 58). That is why the regimes of assumed codes constitute themselves as temporary territories, constantly being replaced by others that prove to be more effective, or profitable, but always maintaining the functioning of acceleration and momentary grasping. For example, in the religious sphere, neo-Pentecostalism has replaced Pentecostalism, by directly intensifying the axiomatic of capital, but also updating even more archaic beliefs and conducts.

As a result, we have the *boomerang-subject*, who always goes and comes back, or the *elastic-subject*, who stretches, extends himself for the production, but always wants to return to the starting point, to the comfort zone, territorialized and feudalized. However, he never returns the same, because every stretch of the elastic frays, little by little, his substance, to such an extent that a series of fissures appear, reaching the limit of not being able to stretch anymore, until he breaks.

As a result, this functioning that operates through incessant and infinite acceleration collapses, causing its opposite: the crisis of the subjectivity and the machine capitalist. In the diagram of sovereignty, there was the slave worker, already in capitalism there is a "free" worker, who with his acceleration of production aims to constitute a new sovereignty, unattainable. Instead of wealth, he achieves its reverse, debt (Lazzarato, 2013, 2014), instead of happiness, depression, in not reaching the expected ideals. Instead of power, exhaustion, and fatigue (Han, 2012). Neoliberal forces do not produce wealth and fulfillment, but illness, indebtedness, and depression. They keep us in an unpayable debt (renamed as "financing"), in which we have already sold our tomorrow (Krenak, 2020b), in which we reduce the plurality of life's possibilities only to its principle of utility (Krenak, 2020a). Hence, there is a rearrangement of the capitalist machine to a somewhat bizarre and deadly desiring configuration.

Neofascist Machine: Necroliberal

Since the 1970s, many sociology and political science books allude to the return of neoconservatisms, neofascisms, neoarchaisms. This repeats in the 1990s, and recently, after the crisis of 2007. It is noted that there is an outbreak of extremist and neofascists waves concomitant to the crises of capitalism. That is, as mentioned above, the system of generalized decoding of the axiomatic of capital, which refers to individualizing perspectives, contradictorily doubled in identity reterritorializations, such as nationalisms, fundamentalisms, and conservatisms (Guattari, 1989): in the neofascist machine.

In modernity, there was a separation between *logos* and *pathos* as a way to transform people into productive machines in the service of the logic of capitalism: the primacy of reason was sustained for more production. Nevertheless, with neoliberalism and the crisis of capitalist subjectivity there is a reconstitution of *pathos* as apparatus of the new governmentality. As technical rationality is no longer enough as a justification for hyperproduction, the dimension of affect is explored. Affective forms are incited that implicate the individual for the maximum production, be it joy, well-being, pleasure, the ideal of "vocation" and "satisfaction" at work, the "American dream," etc. Affect becomes fundamental in the apparatus of contemporary governmentality. Its management is what may contain the crisis of capitalist subjectivity and of capital itself. But as the idealized models of happiness, well-being, ideals, are no longer so effective, hatred, sadness, and resentment are currently managed.

If there is a crisis of the economy and capitalist subjectivity, which produces the subject of debt, exhaustion, fatigue, and neoliberal rhetoric no longer convinces and persuades collective and individual reason, the desiring investments are managed in a way to maintain their adherence to neoliberalism, even if unconsciously. The desiring flows in collapse, unrewarded, exhausted, indebted, are incited to suffer another type of modulation.

Another form of governmentality is fostered, based on generating anxiety, in the culture of insecurity, uncertainty about the future, and social helplessness. There is an affective and desiring management that leads the population to a state of persecutoriness, generating a mode of cognition that works in a binary, dichotomous way, that is, by the logic of negativity, increasing the effect of the *elastic-subject*. The active and reactive forces become only reactivity and nihilism. The desiring flows continue to run in the neoliberal circuit of hyperproduction, maintaining the acceleration of work, but no longer with the expectation of producing wealth and happiness, but with a bitterness, disenchantment, pessimism, in which only the maintenance of survival matters.

Then, contemporary neofascisms do not constitute a new diagram of forces, different from the capitalist axiomatic. They express another polarity of the capitalist machine, its sharpening. It is a more forceful and aggressive mode of desiring management, which aims at maintaining the rotation of the capitalist gears. It is the governmentality based on hatred, on the politics of resentment and of nihilism.

"Neo-fascism results from a twofold mutation: from historical fascism, on one hand, and from the organization of counter-revolutionary political violence, on the other hand" (Lazzarato, 2021, p. 41). And as we saw in the historical experiences of the twentieth and twenty-first centuries, the (neo)liberals and the fascists always got along very well with each other.

In this context, (a) there is a population movement to assume vectors directed to new sets of codes, as a way of creating an existential territory and containment to the felt helplessness. There is a desiring reterritorialization in beliefs and values, in new segments, that function as support to the vertigo of the real and the exhaustion, providing a psychic regulation. Extremist conducts, new beliefs, and political offerings that give containment to the discomfort felt are assumed by people. And to ensure this security, one adheres to these new discourses in a fundamentalist way. For this reason, extremisms can be characterized as a conduct, a way of being, rigid, polarized, and extreme. A categorical positioning that does not accept dialogues, reformulations, any opinion, belief, values, ideologies, different from its own. A rigid and armored structure is adopted, but which maintains the acceleration of the production of any object. We schematize this operation in Fig. 5.2.

The fixation on these new segments creates the logic of antagonism and attack on dialogue and everything that is different. Insecurity, intensified anxiety, and fear activate a surveillance system that turns into a system of repulsion, of rejection, of the other who is not positioned in the same code. In the "fight" for survival, the other becomes more and more an enemy, as they can threaten your job, your beliefs, and identity configurations, constituting themselves as an object of hatred. The desire assumes a reactive and immune configuration, in which it seeks to destroy the difference that threatens, the part that can damage the whole, and to attack the "foreign bodies" that can disaggregate the collective body as a whole.

This desiring circuit is assembled by the paranoid pole of the desiring assemblage and is actualized in a racial biopolitics that produces segmentations that preach: authoritarianisms, excluding logics, a tendency toward domination, self-affirmation, rejection, extermination and destruction of difference, whatever it may be. Foucault describes this characteristic as State racism. Racism that is not seen only from the point of view of ethnic-racial differences, but in a more generalized way, of population differences, characterized by biological factors. For the philosopher, the function of racism is "to fragment, to create caesuras within the biological continuum addressed by biopower" (Foucault, 1976, p. 255). Just like the logic of eugenics, which always seeks to turn the population into white-middle class-behaved-docile-worker. And what was Nazifascism, if not a process of capture and political–economic reterritorialization in the open field?

The segmentations and racisms of several kinds provide a government over life and domination of heterogeneities. They become the markers of differences, the indicators of otherness that must be attacked, that is, the scapegoats of neofascist governmentality. Racism figures as a strategy, a governmental weapon of one group over another, with the purpose of government and domination. There is a construction of the other, the target of racism, as an inferior being, who must be eliminated for the guarantee of population life, as if he was an infectious agent (Deleuze, 1986). "In a normalizing society, race or racism is the precondition that makes killing acceptable" (Foucault, 1976, p. 256). Death, exclusion, expulsion, as well as the supposed right to domination, to enslavement. It is in this sense that Foucault directly articulates racism to colonization. Race "persists as a technique of division, segregation, inferiorization. 'Racism without race' continues to produce its political, warlike, and military, effects" (Lazzarato, 2021, p. 101).

Therefore, in the current sociopolitical context, racism is configured as the main strategic management of the war against the populations, segmented in their differential traits and territorialities (Lazzarato, 2021). Racism, sexism, nationalism, division, and class hatred are not mere social judgments but dangerous strategies of domination. Minority groups, blacks, indigenous people, women, the poor, LGBTQI+, become the receptacle of hostility, resentment, and nihilism characteristic of the neofascist desiring circuit. Desire for abolition of the other, which turns into bad conscience (Deleuze, 1962), self-abolitionist line of flight and hatred for life, which is actualized in this fight against the community itself, to the detriment of the continuity of the propagation of capitalist flows. It results in the production of a generalized civil war (Alliez & Lazzarato, 2016).

In this social mortification, there seems to be a molecular mutation that leads to the growth of blasts that mortify part of its own body, or even an immune system that starts to attack the same organism. Cells that grow rhizomatically, forming microfascist nuclei, "destructive feces," in a great movement of social antiproduction, in a kind of self-intoxication, but which still aim for more profit. A desiring circuit that actualizes itself in the hierarchy of races, ethnic, sex-gender, national, social class, religion, cultural, values, moral, and fundamentalisms of all kinds. Segregationist neofascisms, in which "the political strategy remains neoliberal" (Lazzarato, 2021, p. 56). Therefore, this operation of extermination and destruction maintains the neoliberal management of life, or even radicalizes it. Neofascism = Neoliberalism in its necropolitical intensification = *necroliberalism*.

This is why neofascism is politically effective, because it directly addresses the desire to destroy difference: it provides concrete action. Even if they are expressed in the realm of opinions and values, extremism is more a question of functioning, of conduct, rather than mere discursive content. Consequently, it is more a matter of style than of representation; it is more a pragmatics than a semantics. As a result, one can assume an extremist conduct both on the right or on the political left. Being extremist in values, habits, and customs. That is why it is very difficult to dialogue, or convince, a neofascist, because there is a desiring investment that stratifies his conduct in the mortification of the other. Perhaps it is not possible to "conscientize" a neofascist, but it is possible to work on his reactive desiring investments, his nihilism, his abolition and Self-abolition forces for a desired transformation.

Klinic of Production–Reproduction–Antiproduction

In this chapter, we map three modalities of political machines linked to desire and that produce distinct desiring circuits: the coding, the neoliberal, and the neofascist machine. The first refers to the processes of coding of the diagram of sovereignty, of capture, of the State, or of the disciplinary diagram. It channels desire into closed and coded circuits, such as Laws and norms; molds and models. It also actualizes itself in disciplinary knowledge and practices, such as psychoanalysis. The second, neoliberal, no longer operates by coding the desiring flows, but from an incitement to the acceleration of production, which combines decoding and modulation of flows in the so-called axiomatic of capital. The third, neofascist, maintains the previous diagram, but operates with desiring vectors directed toward a hyperterritorialization in sets of codes. Desiring flows that enter into a regime of antiproduction to what escapes these codes. In the macropolitical scope, these segmentations, as well as racism, become tools of domination and government over the population. We synthesize in Table 5.1 the main characteristics of each social machine and its desiring management, contrasting them with the schizodramatic machine.

One way to work these configurations is with the klinic of production–reproduction–antiproduction by Baremblitt. It performs the distinct processes of constitution of reality and realterity, such as the intensive and instituting production, the instituted reproduction of images and syntheses of the surface of register-control, or even the processes of antiproduction, blockers and restrictors of life.

The klinic of production is closely linked to the notion of machines. But not only technical and concrete machines but also abstract machines, the assemblages that connect different processes and produce forces, energies: their discharge, propagation, and consummation. For instance, as already mentioned, thinking is characterized more by movement, by disorder, and by the logic of flows, but it is encoded by

Table 5.1 Characteristics of the different social machines

	State	Capitalism	Neofascism	Schizodrama
Abstract machine	Apparatus of capture	Axiomatic of capital	(Self)abolitionist, axiomatic of capital	Lines of flight, BwO
Vector of forces	Centripetal	Resonance	Propagation, immune	Centrifugal
Process	Coding, colonization	Acceleration, modulation	(Self)destruction, acceleration	Intensification, creation
Diagram	Capture, sovereignty	Performance	Performance, Antiproduction	Autonomy
System	Stabilization	Crisis	Hyperterritorialization	Transduction, multiplicitation
Forces	Reactive	Reactive–active	Reactive	Active
Movement	Instituted	Instituted-entrepreneur	Instituted-aggressive	Instituting
Desire is:	Formatted, channeled	Incited, linked to acceleration	Destructive, abolitionist	Free, of life

the *image of thought* (Deleuze, 1968). Therefore, placing thought in the sphere of production of production implies using devices to force thinking, stretch it, take it beyond the limits, dilute the established images of thought, make the whirlwind flow and drag. To follow the space–time dynamics, the ripples, flows, and ruptures of thinking. That's why thinking is always an exercise of extrapolation and violence. Thought is an exercise of disarray and creation. So, the klinic of production of production seeks to rescue the intensities of a nomadic thought, mobilized by free energies, and not by the bureaucracies of Western cognitions, colonizing, synthetic, and academic.

It is about inventing various machines that perform these different processes, from the creation of a free energy, unbound, instituting, wild (production of production), through the bound energy, coded, institutionalized (production of reproduction), to self-capturing and self-abolitionist energies (production of antiproduction). These three energies mentioned expand the conception of the three types of lines elaborated by Deleuze and Guattari. The free energy of production refers to the lines of flight, to the forces of the outside, to the diagram of an intensive and deterritorializing body without organs: the active forces *par excellence*. The bound energy of reproduction refers both to supple segmentarity lines as well as rigid segmentarity lines. Lines that refer to the established routine, to the organized and trained body of the individual, his domesticated and civilized consciousness, to structures and channeled ducts, but also to some deviations. They refer more to reactive forces, but can also maintain some quantum of positivity of active forces. But to the energies of antiproduction, self-capturing and self-abolitionist, nothing of affirmation remains: they are reactive forces to the highest degree. Thus, they do not refer directly to the rigid segmentarity lines but to the reactivity and nihilism resulting from the confinement of energy, a cloister that produced a self-intoxication of the lines and the system. Self-poisoning that traces a line that only desires implosion and self-implosion. Will of nothingness and destruction, hatred of life and of difference. Therefore, the production of antiproduction refers to a type of force that manufactures a fourth type of line: the destructive line that seeks the mortification of the social body.

The devices of this klinic have a wide range of variation, especially in these times of political extremism, fundamentalisms, and social polarization. They make explicit the forces and desiring investments at stake, their activity and reactivity, creativity and destructiveness. The actualization of both creative becomings and anxieties and blockages. The dramatization of these processes can lead to the production of an orgiastic body, of an organic-organized body, of an accelerated body-machine and of a destructive-fascist body.

So, there is not only the intensification of the forces of joy and of an anthropomorphic carnival, but also of established habits, stereotypes, hyper-productivism, conservatism, even of fascism and the abolitionist forces that we carry within ourselves. Not only is the difference dramatized and intensified but also what seeks to abolish the difference (see Hur, Amorim, & Teixeira, 2022). We are faced here with our greatest blockages and coercive strata, our own microfascisms. Obviously, the dramatization of these different diagrams does not seek the constitution of life-abolishing energies. Their actualization aims at the tracing and attempt to scrape off such strata and self-destructive desires, the molds, models, and modulations, for the creation of new possibilities of life. According to our ethical–aesthetic–political paradigm, the commitment of schizoanalysis and schizodrama clinics is to autonomy the empowerment of social minorities, peoples, nature, life, encounters, and the invention of commons.

References

Alliez, E., & Lazzarato, M. (2016). *Wars and capital*. Semiotext(e).

Baremblitt, G. (1998). *Introdução à Esquizoanálise*. Instituto Félix Guattari.

Bauman, Z. (1999). *Modernidade e ambivalência*. Zahar.

Bifo, F. B. (2018). Malinche and the automaton. *Alfabeta* 2.

Deleuze, G. (1962). *Nietzsche and philosophy*. Columbia University Press, 2006.

Deleuze, G. (1968). *Difference and repetition*. Columbia University Press, 1994.

Deleuze, G. (1973). Four propositions on psychoanalysis. In *Two regimes of madness - Texts and interviews 1975–1995* (pp. 79–88). Semiotext(e), 2006.

Deleuze, G. (1979). *Derrames II: Aparatos de Estado y axiomática capitalista*. Cactus editorial, 2017.

Deleuze, G. (1981a). *Francis Bacon: The logic of sensation*. Continuum, 2003.

Deleuze, G. (1981b). *Pintura: el concepto de diagrama*. Cactus, 2007.

Deleuze, G. (1986). *El poder: curso sobre Foucault* (Vol. Tomo 2). Cactus editorial, 2014.

Deleuze, G., & Guattari, F. (1972). *Anti-Oedipus: Capitalism and schizophrenia*. University of Minnesota Press, 1983.

Deleuze, G., & Guattari, F. (1975). *Kafka: Toward a minor literature*. University of Minnesota Press, 1986.

Deleuze, G., & Guattari, F. (1980). *A thousand plateaus: Capitalism and schizophrenia*. University of Minnesota Press, 1987.

Deleuze, G., & Parnet, C. (1977). *Dialogues*. Columbia University Press, 1987.

Foucault, M. (1973). *A verdade e as formas jurídicas*. Nau, 1996.

Foucault, M. (1975). *Vigiar e Punir*. Vozes, 1984.

Foucault, M. (1976). *Society must be defended: Lectures at the Collège de France, 1975–1976*. Picador, 2003.

Guattari, F. (1989). *Schizoanalytic cartographies*. Bloomsbury, 2013.

Guattari, F. (2012). *The anti-Oedipus papers*. Semiotext(e), 2006.

Han, B. C. (2012). *La sociedad del cansancio*. Herder editorial.

Hur, D. U. (2018). *Psicologia, política e Esquizoanálise*. Alínea.

Hur, D. U., Amorim, M., & Teixeira, R. (2022). Esquizodrama das máquinas políticas: klínica, estética e formação. *Revista Digital do Laboratório de Artes Visuais, 15*, 1–18.

Krenak, A. (2020a). *A vida não é útil*. Cia das Letras.

Krenak, A. (2020b). *O amanhã não está à venda*. Cia das Letras.

Lazzarato, M. (2013). *La fábrica del hombre endeudado: ensayo sobre la condición neoliberal*. Amorrortu.

Lazzarato, M. (2014). *Signos, máquinas, subjetividades*. Edições SESC; n −1 edições.

Lazzarato, M. (2021). *Capital hates everyone: Fascism or revolution*. Semiotext(e).

Rolnik, S. (2018). *Esferas da insurreição*. n—1 edições.

Chapter 6
The Becomings and Their Clinic

Schizoanalysis operates with another logic of being, of sense, which is not restricted to the instituted, formatted, and identitarian. Being is not grasped only in its static form, at rest, marked by traditional processes of identity, representation, similarity, and analogy. It is seen as flow, continuous variation, and multiplicity. So being is not only marked by its fixed traits, constancy and instituted substance, but also by a *becoming-mad* that snatches it from the same, like points of deterritorialization that always imply the surpassing of oneself to new lands. Being is not taken in its finitude, but rather by the infinity of possibilities and multiplicities, not only by what *is*, but in what can *become*.

In this chapter, we discuss the issue of becoming in three movements. First, a philosophical conceptualization about becoming, in the work *The logic of sense* (Deleuze, 1969); second, the development of the concept *in A Thousand Plateaus* (Deleuze & Guattari, 1980), articulating it to contemporary issues, and third, the proposition of some movements of becomings for the schizodramatic clinic.

Becoming and Event

The question of being divided into two polarities, as fixity, or variation, is already found in ancient Greek philosophy. There is a subdivision between a static state, referring to being (Parmenides), and another, of the movement of flow, which refers to a new figure: becoming (Heraclitus). Plato also operated with these two distinct modalities, in which being refers to the state of affairs, fixed, and becoming to a movement, a whirlwind, to inconstancy. As becoming has this character of movement, of flow, it cannot be codified or reached. Becoming is a coming that is experienced in its flow. It is not a future, because becoming does not "come to be," it operates in a different logic in relation to being. Becoming is an unattainable that is only experienced in its propagation (Deleuze, 1969).

D. U. Hur, *Schizoanalysis and Schizodrama*,
https://doi.org/10.1007/978-3-031-94657-8_6

As a result, two different plans are configured. The plane of being corresponds to the logic of the model and the good copy, of the Apollonian. The plane of becoming, to the simulacra, to the demonic and Dionysian forces of transformation and impermanence. Here, Apollo represents the God of beauty, of perfection, and Dionysius the God of excess, orgiastic. From this dual dimension results a whole discussion between the *good copy* and the *simulacrum*, the pure and the impure, the authentic and the false. Plato seeks to eradicate the second in detriment of the first, understanding the simulacrum as a degraded copy, thereby he operates with a dichotomy of negativity.

Since the logic-ontology of common sense is heir to Platonism, perfect and pure copies are valued, sought after, and considered authentic. But in the philosophy of difference, in *realterity* (Baremblitt, 1998), everything is difference, flow, and movement. There is no reproduction of good copies, but rather the irruption of differences, which always refer to the production of a deviation, to the simulation of experimentations, and which are called *simulacra*. We are all differences, we are all simulacra, however much we want to reproduce, trace the good form, the supposed perfection. We are all multiplicities, even though we seek to adapt-fit to the logic of the one, to the molds and models, in a homeostatic movement of regulation and control.

The simulacrum preexists the good copies, just as becoming preexists being, movement preexists static, intensities preexist extensions and flows preexist the Self. In this perspective, becoming assumes primacy over being, and the simulacrum becomes the conceptual persona protagonist, much more expressive than the Apollonian good copy. Being can be understood as an "image" of becoming, or even its actualization, in a static configuration.

Becoming operates a multiple movement that establishes the figure of paradox, which can be understood as the new grammar of sense. There is a flow of duration, bidirectional, which consists in the affirmation of two contrary senses, which produces "a pure becoming without measure, a veritable becoming-mad, which never rests" (Deleuze, 1969, pp. 1–2[1]). The paradox results in the coexistence of disparate movements, apparently contradictory. It traces a common line between one and the other at the same time. In *The logic of sense*, Deleuze (1969) masterfully works with the issue of paradoxes, using literature as figuration, in this case, with Lewis Carroll's books, *Alice in Wonderland* and *Through the Looking Glass*.

Deleuze (1969) portrays the numerous paradoxes of Alice. She grows and shrinks at the same time. Becomes larger than she was and becomes smaller than she is now. She moves from the present to the past and future in a simultaneous movement. A series of inversions are traced in Alice, such as growing and shrinking, the eve and the tomorrow, the more and the less, the active and the passive, the cause and the effect. Alice slides in an intensive becoming that transversalizes the dimensions of size, temporality, degrees of intensity, of positions, of causality, at the same moment.

[1] In this book, we chose to put the year of the original publication of Deleuze and Guattari's books, but with the pagination of the English language editions (online) found in the references. The quotes that were not found in English were translated by us with the support of Artificial Intelligence.

From the Stoic philosophers, Deleuze affirms that the paradox refers to becoming one and the other at the same time, to the production of a kind of zone of indifferentiation, a space in between. Thus, being is conjugated with becoming, in other words, it produces another type of being: "the being of becoming" (Baremblitt, 1998).

The French philosopher argues that becoming does not support separation, nor the distinction of before and after. It advances between points, in two directions. Becoming does not form points, nor lines, but blocks of intensities. In its propagation, it produces paradoxes, destroying good sense as a single sense and common sense as the designation of fixed identities. Becoming traces the tip of deterritorialization, being a border phenomenon, of the extrapolation of the contour and the limits, which establishes the unequal, the anomaly. In schizoanalysis, the anomaly is not pathologized, it is seen as a configuration that surpasses itself, a differential production, and that is evidently different from the abnormal. Anomalies are not negativity, but singularities.

The emergence of becoming carries pure difference, the transformation, the production of events, in a whirlwind movement. From the processes of connection and mixture, distinct effects result. It abandons the depths to propagate on "the plane of facts, which frolic on the surface of being, and constitute an endless multiplicity of incorporeal beings" (Deleuze, 1969, p. 5). Multiple trails and clearings open for the production of new possibilities: the eruption of events.

Becoming brings a displacement, in which the attribute ceases to be taken as a predicate to be understood as a verb, that is, not as concept, but as an event (Deleuze, 1969). For example, it is not to say that a person is brilliant, but to grasp their *shining*. Similarly, it is not to see that the pepper is red, but to grasp its *reddening*, or even its *stinging*. The blowing, the swinging, the vibrating, the striking, the lifting… Adjectives that become verbs in the infinitive, that is, events.

The event is the irruption of becoming, the pure movement, the pure sliding: it is a block in between. The event happens between beings, but does not belong as possession to any of them, maintaining a certain quantum of incommensurability. Therefore, it establishes the paradox and moves in two, or more, disparate directions, following a rhizomatic flow, just like becoming. "Events are like crystals, they become and grow only out of the edges, or on the edge" (Deleuze, 1969, p. 9). They are the flow of a flux, in a movement without prior sense, but to which senses are attributed, always with new "masks," different strata: "is not what occurs (an accident), it is rather inside what occurs, the purely expressed. It signals and awaits us (…), it is what must be understood, willed, and represented in that which occurs" (Deleuze, 1969, p. 149).

The event is not a noun, nor an adjective, but a verb in the infinitive, pure potency. That's why it's not an accident, but the emergence of a creative becoming. It forces the suspension of space and time, asserts itself against the image of thought, in a violent irruption within our forms of life. As a result, its objective structure is personal uncertainty and the propagation of lines. Alice, who no longer knows right who she is, makes lateral movements and slides in this new world populated by card-men, prototypical beings of this territory. The event-becoming produces a zone of indistinction, indiscernibility, and ambiguity:

> between two terms, as if they reached the point immediately preceding their respective differentiation: not a similitude, but a slippage, an extreme proximity, an absolute contiguity; not a natural filiation, but an unnatural alliance. It is a "hyperborean", "arctic" zone. It is no longer a question of Mimesis, but of becoming. Ahab does not imitate the whale, he becomes Moby-Dick, he enters into the zone of proximity [*zone de voisinage*] where he can no longer be distinguished from Moby-Dick, and strikes himself in striking the whale. Moby-Dick is the "wall, shoved near" with which he merges (Deleuze, 1993, p. 78).

The irruption of events refers to the production of becomings that crack the Self leading to zones of contiguity with difference. In this intermediate zone, of indifferentiation, incorporeal transformations can occur that are not reduced to mere relations of imitation and mimicry. And one of the tasks of schizoanalytic clinic is to be able to map, trigger, the event-becomings, distill their potency and life, to leave the depth and go to the surface. "It is by following the border, by skirting the surface, that one passes from bodies to the incorporeal" (Deleuze, 1969, p. 10). Not to seek the roots, but to propagate in the channels (Deleuze & Guattari, 1980). Or as Paul Valéry proclaims: "what is most deep is the skin" (quoted by Deleuze, 1969, p. 10). The propagation of flows on the surface always refers to the production of new possibilities, other affections, new worlds, realities and ways of being. For didactic purposes, we indicate in Table 6.1 the main characteristics related to being and becoming.

Becomings-X

In *A Thousand Plateaus*, Deleuze and Guattari expand the notion of becoming to think about it in the "applied" scope, of how becoming can be visualized in different instances and assemblages. So becoming is not only portrayed as a pure virtual

Table 6.1 Distinct characteristics of being and becoming

Being	Becoming
State of affairs	Movement—becoming-mad
Limited, measured, fixed things	Unlimited, flow, fluid
Rest, static	Movement, speed, dynamics
Point	Line
"Photo"	"Film"
Identity, similarity	Difference, transformation, event
Noun, adjective	Infinitive verb
Actual	Virtual
Bodies	Incorporeal
Agents, patients	Result of actions and passions
Good copy, (ab)normal	Simulacrum, anomalous
Present	Infinitive
Chronos	Aion
Physical qualities and properties	Logical and paradoxical attributes
Deep and real being	Plane of the surface, incorporeal beings

movement of the irruption of difference, but a flow covered with modes that generate numerous types of configurations as movement, such as: becoming-animal, becoming-molecular, becoming-woman, etc.

Becoming-Animal

Becoming-animal is the modality of becoming most explored in this plateau, such as the becomings-animal that warriors, witches, and sorcerers actualize, or the composition of becomings that animals establish with nature. For example, the famous becoming relationship between the wasp and the orchid (Deleuze & Guattari, 1980). The wasp assumes a becoming-orchid, at the same time as the orchid actualizes a becoming-wasp, both deterritorializing and reterritorializing in each other. There is a composition between these heterogeneous elements, in which the wasp deterritorializes itself by acting as an independent piece of the orchid's sexual organ, and the orchid deterritorializes from its functions and reterritorializes itself in the image sought by the wasp. Both enter a coupling relationship that refers to a parallel evolution between two beings very different from each other, in an evolution between heterogeneities, or better, an involution, which in no way is regressive, and that generates a productive pollination of life.

Becoming-animal, becoming in general, is considered as a process between. It is a rhizome (Deleuze & Guattari, 1980), block of intensities, pack, bands: it is an *intermezzo*. Becoming-animal is not a phantom, dream, metaphor, nor is it reduced to the signifier, it is a movement, flow. There is the production of a becoming that connects us with pets, the malts, the animals to be hunted (in the case of hunters). Its propagation is the emission of particles that refer to their singularities, being able to effect events.

Animals can both express their becomings, as well as be traced in human logic. This diagrammatic difference can be seen in the opposition between pack animals and familiar domestic animals (Deleuze & Guattari, 1980). The first type actualizes its singularities, its forces, its becomings, and affects as animals. Such as the three affects of the tick. *Vision*. The tick seeks a point with greater luminosity, thus it tries to climb a tree. *Smell*. Upon smelling blood, the tick lets itself fall on the prey. *Touch*. On it, from its tactile function, the tick seeks the point with fewer hairs to attach itself and feast. Only three affects, but it is the production of an entire world, which "its value lies exclusively in the intensities, the singularities, and the dynamisms that it presents" (Zourabichvili, 2012, 170). Animals owe countless powers that also do not reduce to the being of their species, for example, the difference between a wild horse, running free through the steppes, or a draft horse. It is the same "flesh," but the affects and movements actualized are totally different, which make them very distinct from each other. They are individuals of the same species who have very different worlds and realities, which make them totally strange to each other. Domesticated animals are those that are coded by a significant set, like that of the family. In the family assemblage there is a blockage of their own becomings-animal in which the little dog becomes the "baby" of the family and the kitten, the "rebellious child." An entire coding and oedipalization is generated in which their becomings, their desire, are reflected in the figure of a familiar being. And what remains is the insistent barking of the dog, which often seems like an annoying lamentation, or when he escapes, traces his line of flight toward the street, leaving his "Stockholm syndrome." Possibly street dogs can actualize more joyful powers than domestic dogs, even though they are more vulnerable too. Due to this differentiation, Deleuze (1994) makes his unusual criticism of domestic animals, which we can even extend to people, who have their animality, their becomings-animal, always refuted, codified, domesticated, in favor of neoliberal machinisms of hyperproduction. Perhaps laughter can be a line of escape in relation to domesticated consciousness, being a possible way of connection to our animality.

In ancient societies, witches occupied this place of becoming. They were located in border regions, on the outskirts of the village, between two towns, at the edge of the woods, or in the forests, just like where the witches' sabbaths were located. In their devices, their programs, there is an entire production of becomings-animal, an entire molecularization with the forces of nature. Conjuring of unnameable forces that became incomprehensible to the dominant powers, and which unfortunately was a justification for their extermination.[2] In Brazil, Kopenawa (2015) dancing with his xapiris, several wise men relating to their enchanted ones. An anthropomorphization that is not to imitate, but to actualize the animal forces, of nature, geological, in their ritual-machines. There is an entire connection with these forces that make them the intermediaries, the *medium*, between the known and the unknown, the material and the spiritual. They create a gap in the visible, actualizing unnamed and unknown forces, considered divine. In a relationship that is no longer of filiation, like traditional imperial societies, but rather of alliance.

There is an alliance with an unknown supernatural entity, the "pact with the devil," represented anthropomorphically in a hybrid composition between human and goat. To establish the contract, the alliance, with the demon, one must, at the sabbath, kiss his anus, to establish a desiring circuit. And the frontier man seeks to obtain from the devil his desires. The demon becomes the vehicle, the transporter, of what he wants, of what he desires. And he marks him for the rest of his existence.

The devil occupies this place of *intermezzo* in various cultures. Symbiosis between human and animal, between divine and fallen; in the Marseille tarot, he is depicted as a hybrid trans between man and woman, possessing penis and breasts. He assumes various animal forms, being an intermediary between these planes. But not only the devil, there is a whole parade of different hybrid beings, coming from the composition of humans–animals.

[2] In this discussion, it is worth mentioning the work of Silvia Federici (2010), who brought to light the relationship between the extermination of women carried out by the dominant powers with the emergence of capitalism. As justification for the tortures, murders, and appropriation of territory, the State and the Church attributed to women the exercise of witchcraft, as if they were the "terrorists" of the time. It was the annihilation of becomings, of difference, of women, by the hegemonic logic of the dominator.

Animals like the goat, the bull, the wolf, the horse, the fish, the snake, compose the most spectacular beings, represented by Beelzebub, minotaur, werewolf, centaur, satyr, the mermaid, the dragon. All beings of the border, or of labyrinths, caves, crossroads, woods, seas, of fire, which refer to a mythological composition between heterogeneous elements and that do not reproduce biologically with the other.

It is noteworthy that all are beings that make the passage, the intermediation. In *candomblé*, the medium, the one who is possessed by a spiritual entity, is called a horse (Lapassade & Luz, 1972). He receives this term because he is the transporter of something, of a divine spirit. In his state of possession, he carries affections, becomings, and other messages that enter into a composition regime with his body and with the people who participate in the ritual.

Becoming operates in block, horizontally and not vertically. By contagion and not by filiation. It does not act by analogy, or similarity, but by degrees of speeds and slownesses. Due to this character *between*, of propagation and connection, there is an intrinsic relationship between becoming, multiplicity, and symbiosis, that is, between resonance, affectation, mixture, and multiplication of the Self. "Each multiplicity is defined by a borderline functioning as Anomalous, but there is a string of borderlines, a continuous line of borderlines *(fiber)* following which the multiplicity changes" (Deleuze & Guattari, 1980, 249).

Becoming-Molecular, Possession, and Psychedelics

All becomings-x lead to a molecularization, to a molecular dimension that erupts from the large molar strata. This production of events also receives the name of *haecceity*, which is a mode of individuation that is not reduced to the person, to subjectivity, to an entity, or substance. "Nothing subjectifies, but haecceities form according to compositions of nonsubjectified powers or affects" (Deleuze & Guattari, 1980, p. 266). The eruption of intensities constitutes becomings-other, which also refers to the construction of a plane of consistency, or immanence.

Let's take as examples the devices of consciousness alteration and trance (see Chap. 8). Both express the eruption of a becoming-molecular and as possible paths for deterritorialization and production of new senses.

Davi Kopenawa (2015) describes his program to become a shaman. He seeks to connect himself to the different elements and forces of the planet. Davi must distance himself from the pleasures of the flesh (in his development), to relate to these other forces. To catalyze his molecularization, he takes *yãkoana*. Kopenawa opens up and connects with the invisible forces, carrying out his transduction to his own semantics. He makes the xapiris dance and sing. And with that, heal. The shaman is the one who hallucinates and sees the imperceptible, and with his delusions is the one who guides an entire population. His *guerrilla machine* comes from sharing two different worlds. He is the one who makes the passage between the virtual and the actual, the one who migrates between the borders. Becoming one and another, always traveling, materially and spiritually; extrapolating thought far away. Davi is not only the bridge between the xapiris and his tribe but also between white men and the Yanomami. Because he was already in this strategic position, his father-in-law, like the "perverse of the tribe" (Deleuze & Guattari, 1972), set up a game of alliances, in which he "gifted" him his daughter, in order to arrange Davi for himself. The indigenous who was at the service of the white men of FUNAI (National Foundation for Indigenous Peoples), became a Yanomami infiltrated in FUNAI, a product of his father-in-law's machinations, a man perhaps even wiser than Davi himself.

We consider the trance of possession as another experiment in the production of a becoming-molecular. Like the schizodrama, it is more a lived theater, than an acted theater. It is embodied, incorporated, and not merely represented. It is noteworthy that the rite of possession does not seek to domesticate the trance, nor to normalize the body into presupposed norms and standards. The trance "activates the expressive possibilities inscribed in the body" (Lapassade, 1980, p. 244) and is the process of crossing (Lapassade & Luz, 1972) in its various senses, material or immaterial. It expresses unnameable forces and leads to a moment and zone of indiscernibility between bodies, temporal and spatial planes, wakefulness and delirium.

Thereby, the dance of possession "is a therapeutic party" (Lapassade, 1980, p. 249), because it does not seek to extirpate the spiritual entity that occupies a certain body, in an intended cure. It does not aim to extract the "symptom" to achieve a supposed normality. It does not discipline, nor domesticate, but establishes a kind of agreement, contract, machine, so that the entity can express itself, gets what he wants, and satisfied, calms down. Thus, parties, offerings, sacrifices are given to him, which free the movement and the powers of this entity, and "possession becomes a blessing" (Lapassade, 1980, p. 249). It is noted that this rite is not performed merely in the dimension of the verb, but in the passage to the act, with the dance, screams, body movement, which results in energy discharges and numerous processes of sense production. Instead of the spoken verb in a private and intimate office, there is the chaotic spinning in a public arena, where *Pombagira* can be loose. We know that the significant narrative often can cover the tension and the body forces (the "blah blah blah" of the neurotic). So, it is not aimed to operate in the resentment of the memory and the trauma, but in the joy of the intensity of the movement. Scraping of the identity-conscious self and incitement of the energies that extrapolate the body. Hence, the therapeutic space is not the one of guilt, but of overflow and the feast of intensities. *Exu* is not eliminated, but he is freed and put to "work," in a production of a molecularization in which one contracts with one's own "madness" from its flow and fluidity. A "madness" that is not extirpated, but that is put to spin, dance, pulsate, potentiate, and produce events and becomings. "And when we talk about freeing the trance, it is emphasized that it is about freeing it as a dance of the body, as circulation of energy throughout the body, and not as contraction" (Lapassade, 1980, p. 254). Therefore, it consists in the production of intensities of a body without organs, with its circulation and energy discharges, with orgiastic forces, a program that undoubtedly can potentiate the realizations and affections of this "possessed" body. It is to bring to the surface the production of events and all the power of chaos.

The experiment with "drugs[3]" can also enable this becoming-molecular, although we have to distinguish their various types. Among the stimulating, narcotic, and hallucinogenic drugs, we consider that mainly the third type, the psychedelics, can catalyze the irruption of becomings and lines of deterritorialization. But among the various types of psychedelics, such as Carlos Castañeda's peyote and datura, Timothy Leary's LSD, Kopenawa's yãkoana, we only mention ayahuasca in this book, widely used by Brazilian Amazonian religions such as *Santo Daime* and civil associations, with a religious profile, like the *União do Vegetal* (UDV).

Ayahuasca is a drink that comes from the fermentation of the juice extracted from two compounds, a vine, called *jagube*, and a leaf, known as *chacrona*. Of ancient use in indigenous rituals, it began to be widely used by "civilization" when the rubber tapper, Master Irineu, took the compound and had a vision, an enlightenment with the Virgin Mary. From this experience he created a religion, Santo Daime, which results from the syncretism between several others, such as Catholicism, Spiritism, Candomblé, and the knowledge of the forest.

The active principle of ayahuasca, N-dimethyltryptamine (DMT), acts on the central nervous system causing delusions, intense affections, and self-analytical modes. Unlike LSD, it is impossible to imagine that someone could take ayahuasca and go partying at a *rave*. Ayahuasca users report that there is an expansion of consciousness, the irruption of intense affections related to their life experience, a series of *insights*, a strong sense of connection with nature and the cosmos, and *visions*. We consider that there is established a program of deterritorialization in an experimental situation, a molecular becoming where forms and strata begin to vibrate and the person moves from the actual to the virtual, from identity to multiplicities, experiencing intense molecularization of processes. From the existential territory of departure, one accesses incorporeal universes and a journey to the *machinic phylum* (Guattari, 1989). Some have delusions and visions of divine and extraterrestrial entities, many are invaded by anguish and crying due to a self-analysis of themselves. There is a scraping of the identity ego. An immeasurable force transpasses the bodies, now molecularized, taking them far away. In this experience of becoming-molecular:

> experimentation replaces interpretation, now molecular, nonfigurative, and nonsymbolic, the unconscious as such is given in microperceptions; desire directly invests the field of perception, where the imperceptible appears as the perceived object of desire itself, "the nonfigurative of desire" (Deleuze & Guattari, 1980, p. 284).

The deterritorialization can be so intensive that the Santo Daime Institution has created a series of reterritorialization anchors, where the molecularization of processes can quickly be molarized into a stern discipline, rules of conduct, clothing, diet, sexual regime, spatial separations between sex/gender, etc. The rigid signifiers of the Santo Daime Institution aim to provide a portion of solid ground to those who are traveling on the journey of molecularization. Obviously, one must avoid that this molarization turns into the gravitation of the centripetal forces of an institutional

---

[3] We emphasize that it is not an apology for its use, just reflection on its effects.

ideology fundamentalism, or more fatefully, when it results in a great emptying and depotentiation of the body, falling more into the black hole, "down, instead of high" (Deleuze & Guattari, 1980, 285). Black holes that have a high coefficient of territorialization that start to block becoming, and give space only to being, or to an emptying that makes the body without strength, without energy, turning it into a lugubrious, vitrified, and petrified body, and not full and Dionysian body. It is important to remember the fatal outcome that culminated in the murder of Glauco, famous Brazilian cartoonist, and also godfather of Santo Daime.

Becoming-Woman, Becoming-Trans, Music

Another becoming quite worked on in schizoanalysis and schizodrama is becoming-woman. There is the process of molecularization that actualizes forces referring to a feminine singularization, but it is not about appearing like a woman, nor "imitating or assuming the female form, but emitting particles that enter the relation of movement and rest, or the zone of proximity, of a microfemininity, in other words, that produce in us a molecular woman" (Deleuze & Guattari, 1980, p. 275).

It is a journey of becoming that not only men can go through, but women themselves can becoming-woman. Thus, the issue is not being as substance, identity, and similarity but the irruption of forces of singularization and affection that are not compromised with the coding of what is considered to be a woman in today's society. Hence, becoming-woman is a device that makes the person create lines of flight in front of the codes and standards that represent and normalize the woman today. To deconstruct the molds and models that constitute capture regimes, that result in a political position of submission, of standardization of facial and body beauty, of the reproduction of the logic of what Suely Rolnik (1989) calls *brides*, those who *spoil and stick*. The aim is to escape this molarity and achieve a molecularization so that one can become another. In this sense, not only men should go through a becoming-woman, as well as women can become-woman, or even the black person can go through a becoming-black, actualizing their powers and escaping the subjugation and coding of the majority, as a power regime, over the minority. And currently with the development of the discussions of the theories and movements of gender all people *cis* and *trans* can also go through a becoming-trans.

We take the *trans* journey as the expression of a becoming-trans that can lead to the creation of a body without organs, when a seemingly *cis* young person starts to produce something in himself, actualizing forces he is unaware of. But forces that cause ignition when assembling a new machine, for example, when he secretly wears his mother's high heels, and reach another plateau of intensities. A mix of astonishment and excitement, until more elaborate machines start to be experimented with. *Lingerie*, feminine makeup, the risky idea of going out dressed up on the street. A new circuit is set up with the walking in the city streets, which is an authentic clinic-politics (Preciado, 2008). A horizon of ineffability begins to project ahead. New positions in the world and types of relationships are established, other friendships, new partners and allies, other desiring circuits. Something moves, passes through this body, until it is decided that it must be anatomically transformed, either by the use of hormones, or through surgeries. The ends are stretched, the borders are crossed. How far can the body go? A true "pharmaco-biological engineering" is produced there. It is possibly during this period of the trans journey, of transition, when these different thresholds of intensity are crossed, that the greatest overflow of power occurs in this body in transmutation. See, for example, the power of thought and the affections in the production of Paul Beatriz Preciado (2008) in *Testo Junkie*, with his pharmaco-pornographic regime. Insurgent, critical, radical, acidic, and sarcastic, which exceeds the thresholds of intensity.

Often the trans journey is overcoded by the Apollonian ideal images, which result in the virile trans male, or in the trans woman, in the hypersexualized transvestite, more feminine than the cis woman. The expression of a becoming can result in an extremely Apollonian copy, a full body. Such bodies can stratify in the logic of being, flattening the becoming. But even so, they do not restrict themselves to being a good copy. They are not imitations, they produce a simulacrum, in the sense of an inexorable fabrication of a novelty. Another gender is created, not a third, but countless genders, countless sexes, or *intermezzo*. Another body, perhaps cyborg (Haraway, 1985), or not. An anomaly is produced, in its most miraculous and differential sense. Thus, the denominations are multiple, not only the transvestite, but also the transsexual, the drag queen, the transformist. Not only related to trans people, hence the LGBTQI+ movement, in recent years included the *queer*, the +, always changing its acronyms, that is, its modes of expression, of actualizing, in multiple sexes.

Consequently, the transvestite is by no means a man who wants to copy being a woman. She is a woman, or a differential type of woman, a trans woman. She is not *fake* at all, but she is the incarnation, actualization of an intensive journey of the real. We quote the dialogue of the characters Stan and Angel, from the television series *Pose* (Murphy, Falchuk, & Canals, 2018). Angel asks Stan why he wants to be with her, a trans, Latina and black person, since he apparently is not gay and has no interest in her penis.

> I am none of those things. I am not gay. I'm no one. I want what I'm supposed to want… I wear what I'm supposed to wear and I work where I'm supposed to work. I stand for nothing. (…) I can buy things I can't afford, which means they're never really mine. I don't live. I don't believe. I accumulate. I'm a brand, a middle-class white guy. But you're who you are, even though the price you pay for it is being disinvited from the rest of the world. I'm the one playing dress-up. Is it wrong to want to be with one of the few people in the world who isn't, to have one person in my life who I know is real?

Here we have a great inversion in relation to common sense, or to what the mechanisms of social and capitalist coding consign. The cis hetero white man, successful, executive of a large company, perceives the social forces that drive him. And he states that he is a great fraud, a fiction, he lives a farce. This character denounces the financier and capitalist logic, in which he buys things he cannot afford and is merely an accumulator, a brand. But he considers that Angel is the opposite, she is the expression of the power of the real. That's why he wants to be with her, for expressing her being, her becoming, and all her transfeminine power. So in this passage, the transvestite is not a distorted figure of the feminine, but rather the authentic desiring expression of gender embodied in a new body: an anomaly, a simulacrum, the pure difference of the real. The capitalist, on the other hand, is the one who is modulated by a whole social logic, but who is always empty, lost.

It is emphasized that every becoming is a minority. One cannot becoming-man, or becoming-white, because man is a majoritarian configuration, a standard, a dominant majority. One never becoming-majority, because already is or seeks to be majority, one is already present in the logic of stratified being. The majority is an ideal, which follows a logic of transcendence, and even the oppressed minorities may yearn for, or are captured by, the ideals of the majority; which is impoverishing and depowering.

It is also emphasized that there is a becoming-old, which paradoxically mixes with a becoming-child. "Knowing how to age does not mean remaining young; it means extracting from one's age the particles, the speeds and slownesses, the flows that constitute the youth of that age (…) It is Age itself that is a becoming-child" (Deleuze & Guattari, 1980, p. 277). That is, aging is not to follow the Apollonian image of youth, the supposed ideal image, to be in debt with it, but to extract the particles of the singularity of what one lives, the movements and speeds and slownesses of one's own age, constituting a breath of life and freshness, in a fruition of a becoming-child, with lightness and without guilt.

Art is also a device for the incitement of becomings. Music, singing, implies a deterritorialization of the voice and the signifier. With singing one accesses another regime of resonance. In the collective sphere, common waves propagate in which they resonate to the same rhythm, in which bodies are arranged in a rhizomatic way, by contagion. It is a way of leaving the closure of the self, to share collective pulsations, the creation of a collective body in common. Collective *ritornellos*, in which the music itself deterritorializes the refrain.

We cite the example of melodic *heavy metal* as a process of deterritorialization of the voice, and of the music itself. Heavy metal[4] emerged in the 1970s as a form of cultural contestation and criticism of *mainstream* music. It adopted lyrics with social criticism, distorted guitars, beats, and rhythm at high frequency and an aggressive, shouted, and torn vocal, or even grave and gloomy. Some of its derivatives were the *thrash metal* and the *death metal* that extrapolate the aggressiveness in music. They are musical styles that assume a guttural vocalization, which often do not escape the stereotype of the man–macho–virile and that were modulated by the phonographic market. Or even those Norwegian bands of *black metal* that traced a suicidal escape line, burning historical churches, committing crimes, expelling all resentment and nihilism in the other and in the world. Euronymous (Mayhem) paid the price with his life (see movie *Lord of Chaos* [Åkerlund, 2019]). And it is not surprising that today the murderer and arsonist Varg Vikernes assumes an extreme-right ideology.

[4] Some sources attribute to William Burroughs the invention of the term heavy metal.

However, in melodic heavy metal, there is a deterritorialization of the voice in which it seeks to hit high notes with great intensity. We cite the example of the Brazilian singer André Matos (1971–2019), vocalist of bands like *Viper*, *Angra*, and *Shaman*. With his high-pitched singing, he updates a becoming-woman that in no way relates to imitating the singing of a woman. But it reaches another level, a border plane, which is no longer the traditional aggressive vocal, or guttural, or "full of testosterone" of traditional heavy metal. With his interpretation of *Wuthering Heights*, Matos achieves a becoming-woman, an *intermezzo* zone, in which he accesses a feminine molecular potency that transcends the original author of the song, the British Kate Bush. The peaks and the sound that the "Maestro's" voice reaches in this song are singular and impressive. It is emphasized that it is not a question of being, nor imitating, or becoming a woman, but a composition between, which produces a neighborhood zone and unusual and unspeakable compositions. A border zone in which the voice is freed from sex–gender dichotomies, which can produce a new gender, or continue to inhabit this interstitial field of becoming: a trans zone. It is worth mentioning that the Maestro always sought to go beyond the borders, leaving a consolidated career in Viper for new musical projects, often not commercially successful. It is highlighted that animals also make music, according to their singularity, be it the songs of the "voices" of the birds, the screeches of the monkeys, or the instruments of the insects, with their percussions, violins, trumpets (Deleuze & Guattari, 1980).

Thus, speaking of becoming-x implies the simultaneity of a double movement, in "which a term (the subject) is withdrawn from the majority, and another by which a term (the medium or agent) rises up from the minority" (Deleuze & Guattari, 1980, 291). It traces a block of intensity between heterogeneous and disparate elements, in a process of creative involution, an incorporeal fusion, in a zone of creation of compositions and assemblages. Possibly speaking of becoming-trans is a redundancy, since every becoming creates a zone, a process, trans.

Klinic of Becoming

The klinic of the event-becoming of Baremblitt is the one that incites the experiencing of flows and becomings that make the Self other, that open to movement and alterity. It operates in the decoding of the staticity of being, in the enjoyment of a crazy flow that updates other events. In its operation, it fosters a Self that cracks, and from its fissures, rhizomatizes.

It seeks to provide encounters, connections, conjunctions, approximation between bodies of heterogeneous natures, material or immaterial, actual or virtual, that constitute a regime of neighborhood and composition. In the relation of encounter–connection, there is a kind of mixture and fusion between bodies: "incorporation." The playwright Zé Celso, from *Oficina Theater*, teaches us that every actor incorporates Exu, actualizes other beings, forces, in his body. This makes us think that Deleuze himself incorporates other authors in his reflective–creative method, and makes his body, his pen, speak for them. He is a spokesperson, the *horse*, who actualizes their powers for the production of differences. In the connections fostered by the klinic of becoming, we seek to incorporate in our devices these different intensities. Forces of nature, of animals, of technology: machinic forces. Free forces that are updated in processes of contraction and distension and result in incorporeal transformations.

This process is lived in a paradoxical way, because at the same time that it connects, establishes a regime of symbiosis, there is the sensation of deterritorialization. Multiple events, multiple affections, imperceptible becomings, waves of forces, intensities, and incorporeal transformations are generated that maintain a double quantum of discernibility-indiscernibility. Flows and percepts, on which senses are produced. Lines of flight that can fissure the diagram of hegemonic forces, providing other desiring configurations. There is a production of incorporeals, and or corporealities, in a connection with new territories and forces, as well as with ancestries, other races, species, and peoples, in an invention of a cosmos that transcends the Oedipal and family issues. Delirium and molecular becomings are forces of chaos that actualize continents, worlds, constellations, divine and profane energies that are far beyond processes of conscious representation.

The interventions aim to create blocks of childhood, of becoming-child, becoming-trans, becomings-molecular, of various becomings, and not just a successive chronological line, striated and significant of remembrance. To make people vibrate on what passes over them, to surf, slide, over "a zone of intensity or flux, which is common to our enterprise" (Deleuze & Parnet, 1977, p. 112), on the blocks of becoming, the emissions of flows and particles. In this plane, "the series become intensive, the journey reveals itself as an intensity, the map is a map of intensities, and the moving frontiers are themselves thresholds (blocks of intensity)" (Deleuze & Guattari, 1975, p. 78). And just like the movement of becoming, "transmutation is never recorded by the conscious subjective of the empirical participants in the process, their expressions are always recorded afterwards, or act without registering" (Baremblitt, 2019, p. 31), because there operates another logic of sensation.

The encounters between bodies can also generate regimes of composition and mutual and collective potentiation with the presence of joyful affects. Joy is an affection that refers to a positive composition between bodies, where this encounter suits both, forming a collective production denominated as *common notion* by Spinoza (Deleuze, 1981). This composition makes the person and the collective take possession of their power, producing active affections and achievements. Connections that aim at production and events and not the decomposition and depotentiation of the bodies in relation. That's why this clinic is accompanied by joy, empathy with the other, erotic energies, production of life.

As a result, enjoyment and creation are inalienable dimensions of this klinic, which eminently results in aesthetic productions. *Autopoiesis* that does not follow an instituted model, a norm, or copy. Therefore, the schizodramatic klinics seek to produce events and encounters that result in regimes of composition and potentiation and that never close in totalizing meanings and interpretations. They seek to maintain the coexistence between connections that generate a creation of senses and an unnamed becoming, to open to other events, to other horizons, finally to new subjectivations and smoothness. From this klinic, it is possible to derive countless devices, such as the klinic of becoming-woman, becoming-black, becoming-multiple sexes, becoming-nature, becomings-ancestral, becomings-animal, becoming-guerrilla, becoming-witch, etc.

References

Âkerlund, J. (2019). *Lord of chaos* [Film].

Baremblitt, G. (1998). *Introdução à Esquizoanálise*. Instituto Félix Guattari.

Baremblitt, G. (2019). *Esquizodrama: 10 proposições descartáveis*. Instituto Gregorio Baremblitt.

Deleuze, G. (1969). *The logic of sense*. Columbia University Press, 1990.

Deleuze, G. (1981). *Cursos sobre Spinoza* (3rd ed.). EdUECE, 2019.

Deleuze, G. (1993). *Essays - Critical and clinical*. Verso, 1998.

Deleuze, G. (1994). *Gilles Deleuze's alphabet book*. Vídeo.

Deleuze, G., & Guattari, F. (1972). *Anti-Oedipus: Capitalism and schizophrenia*. University of Minnesota Press, 1983.

Deleuze, G., & Guattari, F. (1975). *Kafka: Toward a minor literature*. University of Minnesota Press, 1986.

Deleuze, G., & Guattari, F. (1980). *A thousand plateaus: Capitalism and schizophrenia*. University of Minnesota Press, 1987.

Deleuze, G., & Parnet, C. (1977). *Dialogues*. Columbia University Press, 1987.

Federici, S. (2010). *Caliban y la bruja: mujeres, cuerpo y acumulación originaria*. Tinta limón.

Guattari, F. (1989). *Schizoanalytic cartographies*. Bloomsbury, 2013.

Haraway, D. (1985). Manifesto Ciborgue. In T. T. Silva (Ed.), *Antropologia do ciborgue: vertigens do pós-humano*. Autêntica, 2000.

Kopenawa, D. (2015). *A queda do céu: palavras de um xamã yanomami*. Cia das letras.

Lapassade, G. (1980). *Socioanalisis y potencial humano*. Gedisa.

Lapassade, G., & Luz, M. A. (1972). *O segredo da macumba*. Paz e terra.

Murphy, R., Falchuk, B., & Canals, S. (2018). *Pose*, season 1, episode 2 [Series].

Preciado, P. B. (2008). *Testo Junkie*. n-1, 2018.

Rolnik, S. (1989). *Cartografia sentimental: transformações contemporâneas do desejo*. Estação Liberdade.

Zourabichvili, F. (2012). *Deleuze: A philosophy of the event together with the vocabulary of Deleuze*. Edinburgh University Press.

Chapter 7
The Body Without Organs and Its Clinic

One of the most used, important, and difficult-to-understand concepts in schizoanalysis is the Body without Organs (BwO). As it does not refer to an entity, or thing, it receives different interpretations, some quite mistaken. The BwO should not be understood as an object, but rather apprehended as a movement, an intensive production, which is one of the main purposes of schizodrama.

In this chapter, we investigate the concept of BwO to discuss possible contributions to the theory of the technique in the clinic in schizoanalysis and schizodrama. First, we carry out a theoretical review of the different definitions that the BwO assumes in schizoanalytic work and, second, we elaborate a kind of diagram and typology of the BwO to offer references for the clinic and interventions in a generalized way. We are not restricted to philosophical discussion and we seek to explore the pragmatic dimension of the concept.

BwO: Theoretical Conceptions

The BwO is portrayed in different ways in schizoanalysis. It is first worked on in *The logic of Sense* (Deleuze, 1969), receives development in *Anti-Oedipus* (Deleuze & Guattari, 1972), but assumes its "final form," and most "popularized," in *A Thousand Plateaus* (Deleuze & Guattari, 1980), which is revisited in other works, such as *Francis Bacon—Logic of Sensation* (Deleuze, 1981b).

In Brazil, the BwO is discussed in works from the most varied areas, such as Philosophy, Psychology, Medicine, Education, Literature, Performing Arts, Dance, Architecture, etc. Generally, they deal with deterritorialization and reinvention in their different fields, providing a discussion in which the BwO acts and inspires their reflections and doings.

D. U. Hur, *Schizoanalysis and Schizodrama*,
https://doi.org/10.1007/978-3-031-94657-8_7

The BwO is a concept that is at the interface between art and clinic. In schizoanalysis, there is a custom of working passages of authors from literature, art, theater, as a way to figure and become their reflections. Some of its concepts even receive greater inspiration from art than from science, or even philosophy.

The proposal of the BwO is referenced in the work of the playwright Antonin Artaud, more specifically in the radio broadcast *To be done with the Judgment of God*. Artaud, as in all his work, makes an acidic critique of morality, America, money, God. The French artist usually denounces the large strata that block movements and forces. Flávia Soares (2018) identifies these blocking strata as the consciousness, the soul, and the organism. Strata that cage the body, that diminish the power of life. So, Artaud, with his BwO, does not fight the body, nor the organs, but what blocks it: the organism, the stratified organization of partial objects, of organ-machines, of the body. He undertakes a struggle against the organization and the instituted organism that curtail the powers of life. That's why he calls for a body formed of "blood, fire and bones" (Artaud, 1947), that fights the judgment of God. Circulation, intensities, and structure. Energy and force. Fire that burns and shines, that produces becomings and events.

In *The logic of Sense*, Deleuze apprehends this body without organs, intensive, from the schizo experience. There is a mode of processing that breaks with the surface and that operates by another register, which is not the signifier:

> Triumph may now be reached only through the creation of breath-words (*mots-souffles*) and howl-words (*mots-cris*), in which all literal, syllabic, and phonetic values have been replaced by *values which are exclusively tonic* and not written. To these values a glorious body corresponds, being a new dimension of the schizophrenic body, an organism without parts which operates entirely by insufflation, respiration, evaporation, and fluid transmission (the superior body or body without organs of Antonin Artaud) (1969, 88,[1] italics in original).

Instead of significant, symbolic, phonetic values, we have in this body the tonic values, or even words without articulation, that correspond to the field of intensities and degrees of power (Deleuze, 1968), that is, to the realm of the asignifying. A fluidification and propagation that refer to a drift of movement, at this point, the philosopher names as the rupture of the surface toward a fall into the abyss.

Obviously, without romanticizing the schizo process, Deleuze (1969) understands that there is an ambiguity in it, a paradoxical space, that can distinguish the production of various bodies from this journey: the schizo body does not result only in a glorious body, but it can also result in a sieve body (porous), a shattered body, or even a dissociated body. It should be noted that before his meeting with Guattari, the philosopher already sketched a typology of different bodies that can result from the schizo experience, with one modality assuming a very distinct characterization in relation to the BwO: the shattered body, or the shattered organs, which is situated

[1] In this book, we chose to put the year of the original publication of Deleuze and Guattari's books, but with the pagination of the English language editions (online) found in the references. The quotes that were not found in English were translated by us with the support of Artificial Intelligence.

at the opposite pole to the BwO. There is a double polarity between a pierced body, the body of hatred, and a glorious body, the body of fullness. The organs without a body (Žižek, 2006) are the antithesis of the body without organs.

To develop this concept and discuss its operation, Deleuze (1969) establishes a dialogue with the schizo-paranoid and depressive positions of Melanie Klein's psychoanalysis (1971; Klein et al., 1969). Nevertheless, the philosopher does not allude to one of these two positions, but to a previous one, the schizoid, to deal with the processes and the schizophrenic body. Unlike the Kleinian tradition, he treats the schizo process separately from the paranoid process. He understands that the schizo position, in opposition to the paranoid or depressive, does not refer to the introjection of partial objects, but to "(...) an organism without parts, a body without organs, with neither mouth nor anus (...)" (Deleuze, 1969, 188). There is a body, a space, of indistinction, in which the limits are not precise, which carries a certain liquidity and viscosity: "(...) body without organs and liquid specificity are bound together, in the sense that the liquid principle ensures the soldering of the pieces into one block, even if this were a mass of water" (1969, 351–352). In this sense, the BwO forms blocks of coexistence between different elements, a phenomenon that later gives rise to the concept of plane of consistency, more worked in *A Thousand Plateaus* (Deleuze & Guattari, 1980). Then, BwO performs the schizo position.

In *Anti-Oedipus* (Deleuze & Guattari, 1972), there is a slightly different understanding of the BwO, which can bring some confusion to the reader. The BwO is treated by two different terms: Body without Organs and Full Body without Organs. These terms discriminate different processes, but are sometimes used as synonyms, even by the authors themselves. In different passages, it is asked what is the BwO of a society, as well as it is stated that society has a full body without organs. At the beginning of the work, the authors argue that: "The full body without organs is the unproductive, the sterile, the unengendered, the unconsumable" (Deleuze & Guattari, 1972, 8). Later they affirm that the BwO "reinjects producing into the product" (1972, 72). We note that this concept presents a double valence, a bipolarity, in which on one side, the full body without organs is antiproduction, but on the other, the BwO is production. To oppose these two operations, we call the Full Body without Organs, as the Full Body (FB), as Baremblitt (1998) does.

Thus, when Deleuze and Guattari (1972) question what is the BwO of a certain social formation, we understand that they are asking what is its FB. In the chapter *Savages, Barbarians, Civilized men*, they map out what is the FB of each investigated formation: the primitive territorial machine, the imperial-despotic formation, and the civilized capitalist machine, that is, they reflect on their constituted force maps. Later, the idea of FB is translated by Deleuze (1986a, 1986b) into the notion of diagram, a concept created by Foucault.

In *A Thousand Plateaus*, the BwO is no longer associated with the unproductive, or the antiproduction, but rather as a practice, production. "The body without organs is not a dead body but a living body all the more alive and teeming once it has blown apart the organism and its organization" (Deleuze & Guattari, 1980, 30). The BwO brings a flaming, productive, process, "which is continually dismantling the organism, causing asignifying particles or pure intensities to pass or circulate, and attributing to itself subjects that it leaves with nothing more than a name as the trace of an intensity"(Deleuze & Guattari, 1980, 4).

In the specific plateau about the BwO, Deleuze and Guattari (1980) adopt a somewhat unusual narrative to start a philosophical, academic text. They start from a masochistic program full of whips, seams, needles, in which a contract, an agreement, between two is made visible. There is already a kind of exercise of cruelty, in bringing explicitly something that we glimpse in common sense as a taboo, or a depravity. There is an inversion, a twist, in which the structure of a traditional philosophy text is subverted (Safatle, 2007).

The theme of masochism is not new in Deleuze's work. He previously published a book presenting the work of Leopold von Sacher-Masoch. Due to his narrative style, Sacher-Masoch had his name associated with the clinical entity masochism. Among a series of issues developed in this work, Deleuze (1967) denounces the mistreatment given to masochism, in which it should not be understood as the negative of sadism. It is not its opposite, as masochism has its own singularity. Hence, it is a nonsense to suppose that there is a clinical entity called sadomasochism, as both have quite distinct configurations. Masochism, unlike sadism, instead of having destruction and transgression of the law as its priority, is based on a contract that makes intensities pass. A contract in which the one who even gives the instructions to the pair is the masochist himself and not the dominatrix (Safatle, 2007). It operates by the association of the contract and not by the negation of the law. Therefore, the masochism is not apprehended as a disease, or perversion, as we commonly treat it in common sense. It is a program, device, machine, that will generate something.

Masochism should also not be apprehended as a death drive. The masochistic body should not be treated as a phantom, metaphor, interpreted as a set of significances and subjectivations, but rather as an experimentation program. It does not seek pain, the return to an inorganic state, nor is it a diverted pleasure. It does not aim at suffering and pain in itself. Masochism intends to produce a BwO, which can only be filled with intensities of pain. It is as if suffering were the price to pay in this experiment. Painful waves that behave like packs, flocks, populations and that do not seek pleasure, but to put forces, desire, into circulation. There is a disconnection of the pseudo-link of desire with pleasure (Deleuze & Guattari, 1980). This program consists of two stages similar to the destructive and positive tasks of schizoanalysis (Deleuze & Guattari, 1972):

First, manufacture the BwO, empty it, incite the flows to break the strata and, second, make the intensities circulate, pass, transit in this body.

We cite another example of masochistic assemblage worked on by Deleuze and Guattari (1980), which breaks into two distinct series: the horse and the masochist. In this program, the masochist is tied up, like a horse, in order to fabricate a transmission of energies, a process of involution. There is the contagion of the horse's becoming-animal, of its domesticated innate powers, to the masochist, as a way of working (or domesticate) his own innate powers. From this machine an explosive series ensues, which results in the increase of his power and intensities. It is an experimentation of power production, which should not be reduced to pleasure and neither to sexuality.

We quote a Brazilian example of BwO production, from the method of actor preparation by Fátima Toledo.[2] The actor Stênio Garcia prepared himself to dramatize an indigenous person in the movie *At Play in the Fields of the Lord* (Babenco, 1991). He narrated his experience in four moments. In the first, there was a meditation music and he was instructed to perceive the vibration of the body with the accumulation of energy in the solar plexus. In the second, he observed the circulation of energy in the body as a whole. In the third, he spun with his arms open, like the dervishes of Eurasia. In the fourth, Stênio stated:

> I was getting dizzy and practically lost all my senses and when I woke up I was coiled up like a snake and after some time I began to become aware and realized that I was vomiting, urinating and defecating as if I had emptied everything inside my body and I didn't know right what I was saying. After some time I told Fátima what I felt, because after the spin it was as if I had lost all control of my behavior and then we decided to call it "stake zero", that is, I had deconstructed all my bureaucratic and western knowledge and conditioning of representation (...). After all this work we continued to meet in the tent where the vibration happened, the observation of energy, the construction of forms of animals, objects, plants and elements like fire, water, wind, rain, etc. And then we were working sounds, imitations of animals, in short, we created a very large repertoire of animate and inanimate beings. However, it was only after thirty days that we start to work on the figure of the Indian (quoted by Cardoso, 2014, 66).

In this fragment, the production of a BwO is evidenced with the double movement of deterritorialization and circulation of intensities. First there was the emptying, the demolition of coercive strata, which Stênio understood as the downfall of the bureaucratic and western conditioning of representation. There was a radical scraping. When they reached zero degree, the circulation of flows, of intensities, was fostered, from the inscription of the beings of the forest, of the four elements, of the multiple forces of nature, organic and inorganic. There was an inscription of desiring investments from the full body of earth that allowed a becoming-indigenous to be produced. The experience was so intense that this emptying also occurred on the somatic level. From this method, it was possible for him to constitute a smooth space, his own plane of consistency (Deleuze & Guattari, 1980), for the embodiment of his character. This is a Latin American example of BwO production, with an original method, in which an actor with decades of experience went through something very singular with these new machines (Assis, 2009).

Nonetheless, the BwO production program is not always successful. The failure of this journey is exemplified with a parade of lugubrious bodies, BwO that got tired of their organs and traced a line of self-emptying (Deleuze & Guattari, 1980). Bodies that carried out only the first stage of deterritorialization, but that were not successful in fulfilling the second stage, of making the intensities circulate, which

[2] Fátima Toledo is the most recognized casting coach in the country. Responsible for the preparation of the actors of the most emblematic Brazilian films, such as *Pixote* (Babenco, 1981), *Central Station* (Salles, 1998), *City of God* (Meirelles & Lund, 2002), *Elite Squad* (Padilha, 2007), *Marighella* (Moura, 2019) and dozens of other successes of Brazilian cinema. She created the Fátima Toledo Method (FT Method) of actor preparation which due to its great intensity, we consider to have many convergences with schizodrama (see Hur, 2023).

the populations occupied and migrated through the desert of the BwO. Deleuze and Guattari narrate a whole *Lovecraftian* atmosphere: the hypochondriac body, with its destroyed organs, the paranoid bodies, with their attacked organs, the schizo body, which fought a previous battle with catatonia, the cold body of the drug addict, which is an experimental schizo body, and often sinks into a black hole. All these gloomy bodies are fractured bodies and not full, they emptied without the necessary prudence. Instead of becoming an intensive BwO, they became empty, paranoid, or destructive. They traced a line of escape so intense, that it turned into a self-abolitionist line.

However, in the BwO, only intensities pass and circulate, it produces and distributes them in a continuous zone of intensities, and not extensive. The BwO is not a place, nor representation, it is practice, experimentation and production. It is intense and unformed matter, not stratified, as well as everything that populates it, like "subatomic and submolecular particles, pure intensities, prevital and prephysical free singularities" (Deleuze & Guattari, 1980, 43). It is the intensive zero degree, "full egg before the extension of the organism and the organization of the organs" (Deleuze & Guattari, 1980, 153). The BwO is the desire that produces a plane of consistency only by tracing it, by propagating itself. That's why it is never reached: it is the threshold of intensive variation.

It is a difficult proposition to understand, because BwO is not defined by its extensions, strata and materialities, but by aspects that refer to its intensities, to its degrees of potency, "by axes and vectors, gradients and thresholds, by dynamic tendencies involving energy transformation and kinematic movements involving group displacement, by migrations: all independent of accessory forms" (Deleuze & Guattari, 1980, 153). Therefore, it is defined by intensities and vectors of forces, regardless of the extensions that cover it.

Then, the BwO is the movement in flux, in which the organs lose all constancy. It must be apprehended in the logic of the connection of desires, conjunction of flows, continuum of intensities. "The BwO is the *field of immanence* of desire, the *plane of consistency* specific to desire (with desire defined as a process of production (...))" (Deleuze & Guattari, 1980, 154). It is the magmatic desire that in its propagation produces its own plane of consistency.

The BwO is not an enemy of the body, but of the organism, of what organizes and reduces its forces. The organism, the judgment of God, the FB, is the antagonist of the BwO. It is a "phenomenon of accumulation, coagulation, and sedimentation that, in order to extract useful labor from the BwO, imposes upon it forms, functions" (Deleuze & Guattari, 1980, 159). It is a stratum on the BwO, layers over the intensities and flows. The strata (and the Self) cling to the BwO, slowing down and diminishing its potential of forces. In this sense, there are three major blocking strata: the already alluded organism, signification, and subjectivation (Deleuze & Guattari, 1980). These are three modalities of FB that refer to the formed desiring circuits, with a tendency toward closure and the constitution of a cloister.

Signification produces a reduction of experiences and senses into signifiers and formatted and instituted meanings. It is a mutilation of the experienced multiplicity to just one thing. It is the "That's it!" And often the "That's it!" was a past Oedipal conflict with the father, which obviously is very different from the conflict that one has today with the boss, the society, or life. In this process of sociopolitical Oedipalization, there is the reduction and concealment of all the problems of capitalist domination, to a self-blaming of the Self. For example, "If I am acting like this with my boss, it is not because he is one of the agents of incitement of hyperproduction and oppression of Capital, but rather, because I am updating a problem from my childhood with my father, in his figure."

And subjectivation is also a great danger. Because usual subjectivation is not open to metamodelization, transduction, and expression, but rather in the reproduction of a formatted subjectivity, like the capitalist subjectivity, or the neofascist. So, the psychoanalytic clinic, or the confessional, is not a space for creating a new ethic of living, but rather a stereotyped way of living, which is the formatting of a capitalist-Oedipal subjectivity from a moral regime of guilt and codification.

In this perspective, Deleuze and Guattari (1980) rescue the figure of the priest, worked by Nietzsche (1887) in *On the Genealogy of Morality*, updated in a new persona. Today it is the psychoanalyst who instills morality, resentment, and blockages, he is the one who turns the force against itself. The priest, or the psychoanalyst, carries the triple curse:

First, the negative Law: he affirms that desire is lack. Second, the extrinsic rule: he connects desire to pleasure. But on the contrary, one must disconnect desire from pleasure as extrinsic measures, to deduce the plane of consistency of desire. However, one cannot fail to highlight the innovation of psychoanalysis, that desire does not submit to procreation nor to genitality. Third, the transcendent Ideal: there is a fixation on ideals, which are apprehended in the logic of fantasy. Thereby, everything is fixed in a transcendent, unrealizable logic.

On the other hand, the BwO opposes the organism, signification, and subjectivation to disarticulation, experimentation, and nomadism as procedures. It seeks to undo these strata, the codifications, opening up to connections, compositions, and creations that result from these movements. It aims to establish a plane of consistency that arises from the fissures of the stratification surface. The actualization of the flow of duration, smooth, as opposed to striated chronological time (Deleuze, 1966).

Therefore, the BwO should not be interpreted but experienced. It is a practice and not a metaphor. The BwO should not be thought in the logic of being, nor of representation, but rather in the logic of the becoming block. Instead of parallel evolution between homogenous, a-parallel evolution between heterogeneous = involution. It is not a death drive, the production of a BwO is the propagation of desire itself, in its concomitant creation of a plane of consistency.

Schizoanalytic Schemes

The concept of BwO can directly reference clinical practice and research. A first warning is that one should not simply dichotomize the BwO to the FB, as if the production of the BwO was necessarily a positive program of deterritorialization and the FB was something negative. In this movement, the activity of prudence is fundamental and indispensable (Deleuze & Guattari, 1980). Prudence is the "rations" of territory, a *locus* of provisions and firm land, so that one can investigate the stratum and draw new lines.

Prudence is a territory for the body not to empty and not to lose itself excessively, because the production of a BwO can touch the false, the hallucinatory, the illusory, and psychic death. Accordingly, several examples of territories of prudence are cited in literature with Artaud and even Carlos Castañeda. Finding a place, composing with your allies, letting the flows run, producing the becomings-animal, discovering and dealing with new beings (*tonal* and *nagual*), a whole problem that articulates the FB to the BwO (Deleuze & Guattari, 1980). A cartography must be carried out, an analysis of what produces, circulates, and blocks in this body. What populates it, what passes, what obstructs it? What can a body do? What is the power of a body?

So that our reflection does not become too abstract, in this topic we elaborate schemes to facilitate the visualization of the coordinates of the schizoanalytic interventions. These schemes will reappear in Chaps. 8 and 9 of this book and are figurations that assume a didactic function, not a reduction of phenomena. Because there is always a risk of reducing processes to dichotomies, to just two poles, and that is not what we intend here.

We propose a first axis of analysis, horizontal, which refers to the poles of cognitive/affective production and antiproduction (Fig. 7.1). Like Spinoza (Deleuze, 1981a), we consider that the processes of body empowerment can lead to the development of cognition/affection activities as a whole, because cognition and affection do not form antithetical pairs, or zero-sum relationship, as some classic theories of social psychology believe (Le Bon, 1895). Thereby, the greater the affective potential, or the higher the power to affect, the greater the cognitive achievements can be. Thus, there are cognitive/affective production movements when the body is potentiated from relations of composition with other bodies. And there is the opposite, antiproduction processes, when the body decomposes in relation with other bodies, or with itself. In this sense, cognitive modalities become precarious as they move

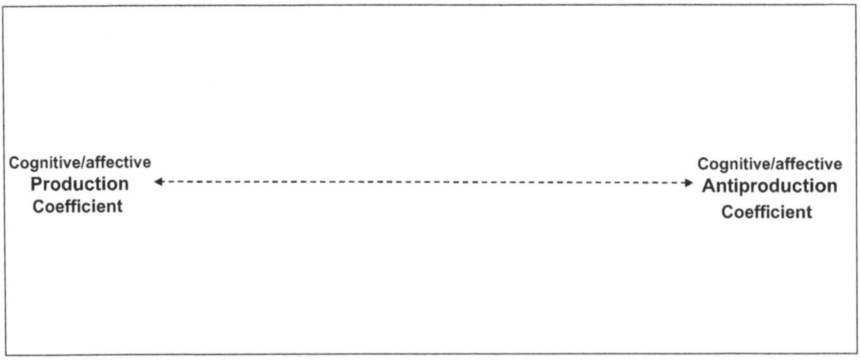

Fig. 7.1 Axis of the coefficient of cognitive/affective production–antiproduction

toward the antiproductive pole, no longer operating from the logic of plurality, but from the logic of dichotomy, in other words, moving from the perspective of multiplicities to the logic of negativity. And the effects of the intervention are located in this space between the poles, not just in one or another, but in dynamic positions between them.

We also propose a second axis of analysis: which contains the poles of deterritorialization and territorialization, which are close to the functioning of the schizo and paranoid poles (Deleuze & Guattari, 1972) (Fig. 7.2).

In *Anti-Oedipus*, two types of investments are stipulated that operate both socially and psychically: the schizo pole and the paranoid pole (Deleuze & Guattari, 1972). As mentioned in Chap. 2, this denomination refers to the type of functioning of the processes and not to a psychopathological typification of the phenomena.

As already discussed in the first topic of this chapter, the schizo pole refers to a moment prior to the schizoparanoid position theorized by Melanie Klein. It refers to the moment of flow, chaotic, where there are processes of indistinction, mixture, and fusion. The magma, a body without organs, which lacks significant definition and organization. However, it is linked to a second position, the paranoid pole, which can be related to Klein's definition of the schizoparanoid position. It is the binary pole, stratified, of primitive and uncontained affects, often voracious and

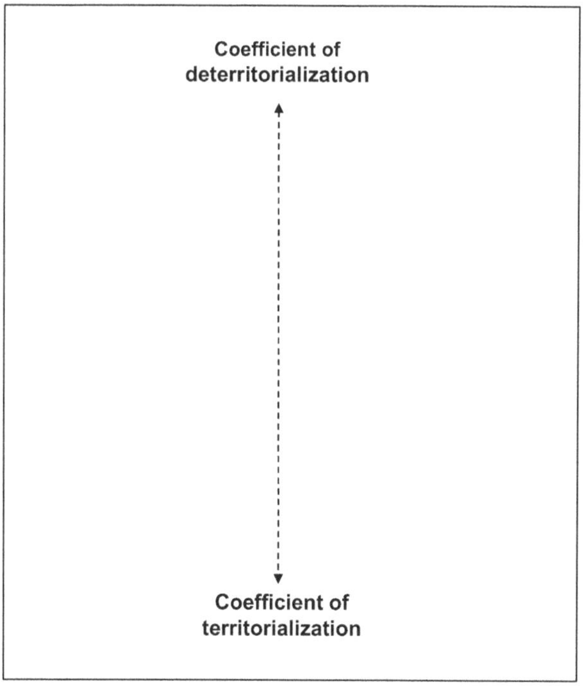

Fig. 7.2 Axis of the coefficient of deterritorialization–territorialization

destructive, which refer to processes of conservation and fixation. The schizo pole is close to what Bleger (1975) calls the glyceric-caric moment, also prior to the schizoparanoid position and which relates to the processes of mixture and fusion. A magma, mixture, oceanic broth, close to a smooth space (Deleuze & Guattari, 1980). We consider that this position should be treated both in its potential for agency and creation, as well as indistinction and indiscrimination. The schizo and paranoid poles refer to processes converging to the coefficients of deterritorialization and territorialization, because the schizo pole is the nomadic, disjunctive, and centrifugal, while the paranoid pole produces segmentations, strata, with eminently centripetal forces. Another possible approximation can also be made with the instituting and instituted moments (Baremblitt, 1992).

We draw a vertical line where at one of the extremes are the processes related to the coefficient of deterritorialization (Deleuze & Guattari, 1975) and the schizo pole, while at the other, the coefficient of territorialization (Guattari, 2013) and the paranoid pole. At one of the poles there are the cutting edges of deterritorialization, the establishment of a smooth space, unbound energy, while at the other, the territorial sides that provide a fixity, as well as the establishment of a striated space (Deleuze & Guattari, 1980).

However, the axis of production and antiproduction is not analogous to the axis of deterritorialization and territorialization. The two axes do not carry convergent processes, but divergent ones, because deterritorialization, the schizo flow, the schiz (Baremblitt, 1998), does not have only characteristics of potentiation of activities but can also generate depotentiation and decomposition (Deleuze & Guattari, 1980). So they are not parallel processes, but perpendicular ones, that's why we cross one axis with the other, where the coefficient of deterritorialization–territorialization is placed in the vertical, while that of (anti)production is horizontal (Fig. 7.3).

In the articulation between the vertical and horizontal axes, it is noted that not every process of deterritorialization is productive and not every movement of territorialization is unproductive. In each quadrant, there is the propagation of a certain type of line. In the deterritorialization/production connection, there is the diffusion of lines of flight; in the territorialization/production intersection, segmentary lines; in the territorialization/antiproduction connection, abolitionist lines; and in the deterritorialization/antiproduction zone, the self-abolitionist line (Fig. 7.4). Then, in the left hemisphere we have the prevalence of individual and collective progression modalities, and in the right, individual and collective precariousness.

Finally, in the four quadrants, derived from the articulation of the processes of deterritorialization–territorialization to those of production–antiproduction, there is the emergence of different bodies and movements (Fig. 7.5). The production of each body refers to the actualization and intensification of the propagation of each line, which can also transmute into its own movement of diffusion. As static as it may seem, this scheme should be seen in its dynamics, in a vibratory movement that transits between the four quadrants, where it accelerates its speed in the upper hemisphere, and decelerates the closer it gets to the pole of territorialization.

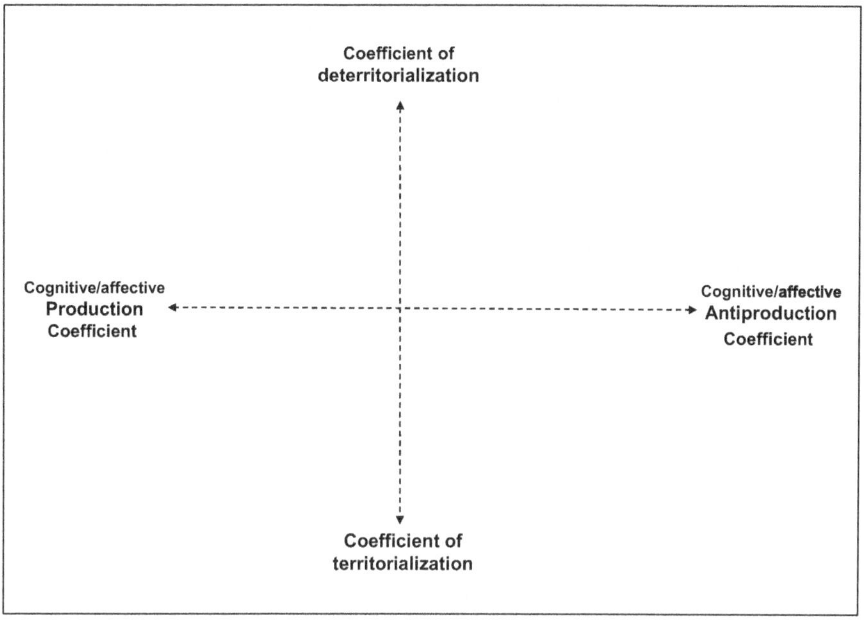

Fig. 7.3 Articulation of the axis of (anti)production with the axis of (de)territorialization

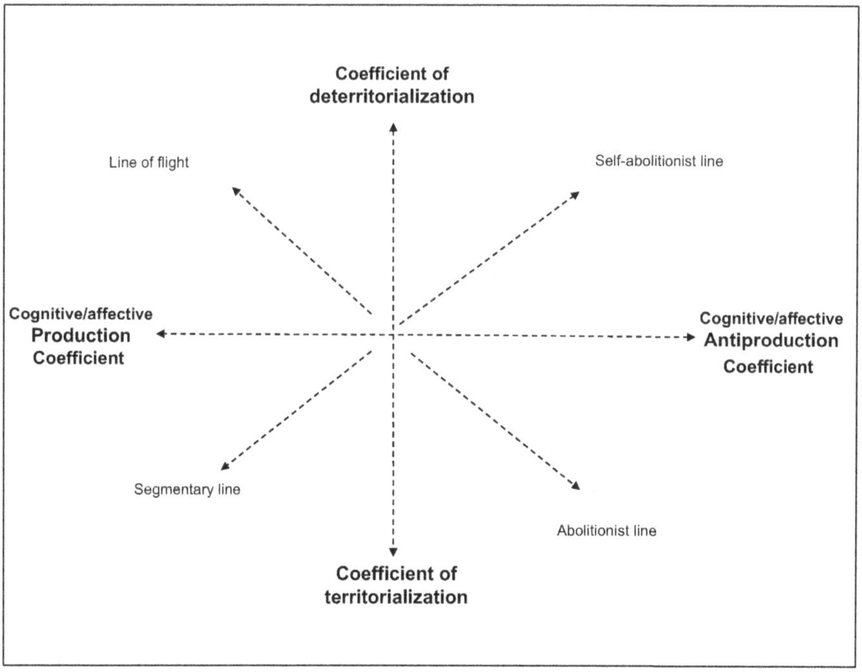

Fig. 7.4 Lines resulting from the articulation of (anti)production-(de)territorialization

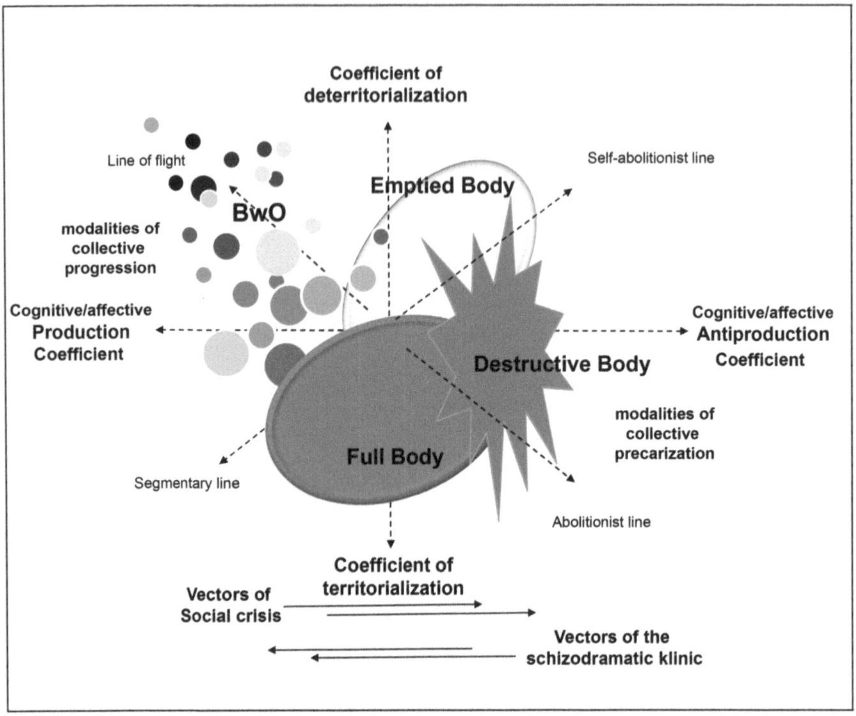

Fig. 7.5 Production of Bodies without Organs (BwO)

The BwO and the Schizoanalytic Clinic

In *A Thousand Plateaus* (Deleuze & Guattari, 1980), there is a new typology among different types of bodies, different from what is worked in *The Logic of Sense* (Deleuze, 1969) and in *Anti-Oedipus* (Deleuze & Guattari, 1972). In *The Logic of Sense* there is the BwO, the porous body, the shattered body, and the dissociated body. In *Anti-Oedipus*, the BwO and the FB. In *A Thousand Plateaus*, not counting the aforementioned lugubrious bodies, there are three types of bodies that antagonize the BwO: the FB, the emptied body, and the cancerous body,[3] which we place in Fig. 7.5.

In the lower quadrants, there is the conformation of the body characteristic of contemporary society, the FB, which constitutes the lines of segmentation and strata. The FB is the one that forms a desiring circuit around itself. The vectors of forces are directed to the body itself, in a centripetal way, that is, directed to a center, in which it can maintain a quantum of production and propagation of segmentary lines, from the logic of the Self (lower left quadrant).

[3] In this book, we chose to rename the "cancerous body" as "destructive body."

With the increase of the territorialization coefficient, there is a tendency that the segmentation becomes more rigid and thick, resulting in a hard segmentarity. With a desiring investment in which everything is vectorized inward, a voracious body is constituted, an even more swollen body. The boundaries of the FB become rigid, they turn into armors, and exchanges with the outside become obstructed, blocked. With the intensification of closure and rigidity, there may be a turn to the lower right quadrant, culminating in antiproduction processes. The FB tends to swell and close more and more, and the forces only circulate inward, going through a process of entropy and suffocating itself in this "internal." There is a hyperterritorialization in segmentary lines, either in its own body, to the Self, in code regimes, religious beliefs, conservative values, and ideology. There is a hardening of the logic of the Self, a reterritorialization in the ego, that is, a process of eroticization of the Self called *egoticization*, that is, the desiring investments directed centripetally to the Self. Egoticization is a socially dangerous process, because with the recentration and stratification of the Self, it can foster processes of rupture of the social bond, entering a regime of paranoia and opposition to other bodies.

Thus, the FB can suffer from retention processes, or even adopt procedures of violent discharge, with little metabolization of the content that is being expelled. In the concrete and updated scope in a person, the FB makes it continuously want to be the target of recognition, legitimized, loved by others, always absorbing, but often giving nothing in return, as the vectors of forces are only centripetal. The "rotund" figures painted and sculpted by Fernando Botero are the pictorial expression of the FB today. They are not fat people, but stiffened, as if everything revolved around their body, and there was nothing to look at in the "external" (Hur, 2018).

If the rigidity and stratification are very intense, the FB can calcify and shatter, producing shattered bodies in social space. As examples we see the intensification of social isolation, the practices of individualism, the *standby* phenomenon, social apathy, insensitivity to the Other, and at its limit, hatred of the other. And often traditional clinical practice, such as *coaching,* performs this excessive strengthening of the Self, the egoticization, especially in times of psychosocial crisis, ignoring the pitfalls that this can cause.

On the other hand, if the FB is not very stratified, if its territorialization coefficient is reduced, it can produce lines of flexibility and perhaps even deterritorialization, reaching a potential for cognitive/affective production, positioning itself above the segmentary line in the lower left quadrant.

The schizoanalytic clinic must be committed to the unblocking of these forces and the production of a BwO, in a movement that leads to the upper left quadrant of the scheme. It must create devices that can transmute full bodies, depotentiated, on the path to a BwO, intensive, Dionysian and orgiastic. Bodies that are occupied by active life forces. Potentiated and not self-intoxicated or enclosed. Because:

> The task of schizoanalysis is that of tirelessly taking apart egos and their presuppositions; liberating the prepersonal singularities they enclose and repress; mobilizing the flows they would be capable of transmitting, receiving, or intercepting; establishing always further and more sharply the schizzes and the breaks well below conditions of identity; and assembling the desiring-machines that countersect everyone and group everyone with others (Deleuze & Guattari, 1972, 362).

The BwO is produced by lines of flight that fracture blockages and armors, that allow the propagation of flows, the irruption of deterritorialization processes. Nevertheless, for its realization, scraping is not a sufficient condition, there must be a second movement of composition of a new desiring circuit, with the occupation and circulation of forces and populations in this body. Connections must be established, which are a way "that provides the means of eliminating the empty and cancerous bodies that rival the body without organs, of rejecting the homogeneous surfaces that overlay smooth space, and neutralizing the lines of death and destruction that divert the line of flight" (Deleuze & Guattari, 1980, 508).

To maintain its production coefficient, the cultivation of the BwO is located in a paradoxical space between deterritorialization and reterritorialization, between comings and goings, in a zigzag, relationship between line of flight and segmentary line. But this segmentarity must be transitory, the organs are seen as transients, because the BwO is not defined by the absence of organs, but "by the *temporary and provisional presence* of determinate organs" (Deleuze, 1981b, 48, italics in the original). The organs are seen as intensities, through which the body can "escape," as portrayed in the paintings of Francis Bacon. In a connection and transmutation between stratum and flows, where the machine is always machine of the machine (Deleuze & Guattari, 1975).

If this paradoxical zone is not constituted, there is a risk that the production of the BwO will revert to antiproduction. Insofar as it draws the line of flight very intensely, if the deterritorialized body is not filled with intensities, this line can turn into a self-abolitionist line that empties the body, leading to a process of radical deintensification. There is an attempt to create a BwO, but it remained only in its first stage: of deterritorialization and emptying. The vector of forces leaves the upper left quadrant and quickly moves to the upper right quadrant, constituting the emptied body (Fig. 7.5).

In this case, prudence was lacking, the body was not filled, the forces of circulation and propagation, attraction and repulsion, did not come into play in the creation of a miraculous machine. A program of rejection of everything that is external was manufactured, with maximum porosity for centrifugal forces and maximum blockage for centripetal forces. From an orgiastic BwO, the emptied body ensues and can gradually fade away.

A holey body is constituted that aims for a radical emptying of intensities, as well as a cloister that prevents the entry of any external force. A policy of refusal to what can shake its body. An arid and uninhabitable desert is built, with a self-abolitionist, self-destructive line of flight. Degree of emptying affection that gradually leads to the exhaustion of life. Such functioning can be seen, for example, in anorexic, bulimic, porous, or drugged bodies. The anorexic body is not a "disease" produced by a kind of alienation, distortion, in relation to self-image, but is a positioning of the affirmation of a policy of closure, of the production of a desert. In the case of the drugged body, there is the risk that, instead of producing an intensive BwO, it erects "a vitrified or emptied body, or a cancerous one: the causal line, creative line, or line of flight immediately turns into a line of death and abolition" (Deleuze & Guattari, 1980, 285).

The intensification of the abolitionist and self-abolitionist lines, which respectively produce the FB and the emptied body, results in the grinding of these bodies, in which there is a transit to the lower right quadrant. Such precariousness gives rise to another type of body: the destructive body. This bodily modality can result from both intense processes of deterritorialization, as well as hyperterritorialization. Both can lead to the pulverization of these bodies, either by a suicidal line, or an extremely destructive one: the destructive body is the apex of the deterioration resulting from either the FB or the emptied body. In the intensification of the swelling and enclosure process of the FB, or the self-abolitionism of an emptied body, "a cell becomes cancerous, mad, proliferates and loses its configuration, takes over everything" (Deleuze & Guattari, 1980, 163). This cell, in conjunction with others, promotes the blockage of the circulation of flows, or even a self-asphyxiation of the body itself, an attack on the other cells and molecules. Bodies and organs that close or open excessively, attacking other organs, or even themselves.

In *A Thousand Plateaus*, there is not an extensive theorization of what the destructive body (called cancerous) is, just some features. But a relationship is stipulated between this quantum of blockage and destructiveness with fascism, which is a war machine that takes war itself as its final task and draws a self-abolitionist line of flight, constituting a suicidal State and life.

We conjecture that the destructive body actualizes the reactive and resentful forces, characteristic of nihilism. Bad conscience, will to nothingness, and abolition of life, at its limit self-abolition (Deleuze, 1962). Reactive functioning that is updated in destructive and self-immolation behaviors today, hatred and extermination of difference, will to abolish oneself. Consequently, modes of collective precariousness arise, in the attack and depreciation of the other, as can be clearly seen in this period of political extremism. We understand neofascisms and microfascisms as the symptom of the malaise of contemporary society, which from high emptiness, or swelling, produces destructive bodies that mortify the social collective body, and even the planetary-environmental. Therefore, the vectors of social crisis incite the processes to move to the right of the scheme, adopting a coefficient of antiproduction; they encourage the increase in the proliferation of the antiproductive FB, of the emptied body and of the destructive body, fostering a generalized necropolitics.

FB, emptied body, and destructive body are three bodily modalities that can impoverish and depower people and collectives. Thus, the schizoanalytic and schizodramatic clinic must operate in such a way that its intervention vectors foster a movement to the left of the scheme, toward the production of an intensive BwO, and escape from the black hole of the antiproductive FB, from the depowering of the emptied body, or from the (self)annihilation of the destructive body. To do this, it must track the constituted desiring circuits, the functioning of the different machines and flows, with the aim of establishing lines of flight and processes of potentiation and creation. It should behave like a vibrational machine that seeks to scrape off the coercive strata, to foster the circulation of the intensities, and finally raise the degrees of body power and social valence. These scraping actions, circulation and vibration of intensities elicit lines of flight, disruption, and deterritorialization, as well as movements of reinvention and new desiring circuits. Therefore, we must prevent the elicited processes from remaining in the quadrants to the right and our purpose is to trigger a movement that intensifies the coefficient of cognitive/affective production, through the processes of deterritorialization and reinvention.

In the schizoanalytic clinic, we must seek, invent, and handle clinical–political machines and intervention devices in several spaces, such as the private office, the studio, and in the institutional, community, and public policy field, to manufacture the BwO, because "abstract machines or bodies without organs, this is desire"(Deleuze & Parnet, 1977, 105). And schizodrama is the set of many BwO creation machines, with various levels, or plateaus, of intensities and vibration. However, it is necessary to understand the risks of the effects of radical deterritorialization, which can become too violent, as well as intensive hyperterritorializations, the proliferation of strata. It is important that in the propagation of desiring flows we can map what refers to the constitution of a plane of consistency, with its processes of deterritorialization and reterritorialization, because there are various types of movements that are elicited in this journey.

In Fig. 7.5, we have drawn directional vectors that can contribute as a map of forces for clinical and interventional practice, such as in the choice, operationalization, and conduct of intervention devices. It is emphasized that this scheme should not be viewed as stagnant and static points but in the dynamics of its vibration plateaus. Because we are always in zones of vibration, of agitation, in continuous variation. The body is a field of intensities and the rhythm, the vibration, is a vector of sensation, "it is what makes the sensation pass from one level to another" (Deleuze, 1981b, 72). Often the body may be obstructed by its stratifications, by its organism, at another moment in the vibration of an orgiastic BwO, but soon vibrate centripetally as a FB. We must grasp the vibrations of the molecules, the circulations of forces and desiring investments, because they modulate the entire journey and can take us to other plateaus of intensity, to new processes of social and aesthetic reinvention.

References

Artaud, A. (1947). Para acabar com o juízo de Deus. In C. Willer (Ed.). *Escritos de Antonin Artaud*. Porto Alegre: L&PM, 1983.

Assis, W. (2009). *Stênio Garcia: força da natureza*. Imprensa oficial do Estado de São Paulo.

Babenco, H. (1981). *Pixote* [Film].

Babenco, H. (1991). *At play in the fields of the Lord* [Film].

Baremblitt, G. (1992). *Compêndio de Análise Institucional*. Rosa dos Tempos.

Baremblitt, G. (1998). *Introdução à Esquizoanálise*. Instituto Félix Guattari.

Bleger, J. (1975). *Simbiosis y Ambigüedad*. Paidós.

Cardoso, M. (2014). *Fátima Toledo—Interpretar a vida, viver o cinema*. LiberArs.

Deleuze, G. (1962). *Nietzsche and philosophy*. New York: Columbia University Press, 2006.

Deleuze, G. (1966). *Bergsonism*. New York: Zone Books, 1988.

Deleuze, G. (1967). *Masochism: Coldness and cruelty*. New York: Zone Books, 1991.

Deleuze, G. (1968). *Difference and repetition*. New York: Columbia University Press, 1994.

Deleuze, G. (1969). *The logic of sense*. New York: Columbia University Press, 1990.

Deleuze, G. (1981a). *Spinoza: Practical philosophy*. San Francisco: City Lights Books, 1988.
Deleuze, G. (1981b). *Francis Bacon: The logic of sensation*. New York: Continuum, 2003.
Deleuze, G. (1986a). *Foucault*. Minneapolis: University of Minnesota Press, 1988.
Deleuze, G. (1986b). *El poder: curso sobre Foucault (Tomo 2)*. Buenos Aires: Cactus editorial, 2014.
Deleuze, G., & Guattari, F. (1972). *Anti-Oedipus: Capitalism and Schizophrenia*. Minneapolis: University of Minnesota Press, 1983.
Deleuze, G., & Guattari, F. (1975). *Kafka: Toward a minor literature*. Minneapolis: University of Minnesota Press, 1986.
Deleuze, G., & Guattari, F. (1980). *A thousand plateaus: Capitalism and Schizophrenia*. Minneapolis: University of Minnesota Press, 1987.
Deleuze, G., & Parnet, C. (1977). *Dialogues*. New York: Columbia University Press, 1987.
Guattari, F. (2013). *¿Qué es la Ecosofía?: Textos presentados y agenciados por Stéphane Nadaud*. Buenos Aires: Cactus editorial, 2015.
Hur, D. U. (2018). *Psicologia, política e Esquizoanálise*. Alínea.
Hur, D. U. (2023). Esquizodrama e dramatização: contribuições do método de preparação de atores de Fátima Toledo. *Mnemosine, 19*(1), 163–185.
Klein, M. (1971). *O Sentimento de Solidão, Nosso Mundo Adulto e Outros Ensaios*. Imago.
Klein, M., Heinmann, P., Isaacs, S., & Riviere, J. (1969). *Progressos da Psicanálise*. Zahar.
Le Bon, G. (1895). *Psicología de las masas*. Madrid: Morata, 2005.
Meirelles, F., & Lund, K. (2002). *City of god* [Film].
Moura, W. (2019). *Marighella* [Film].
Nietzsche, F. (1887). *On the genealogy of morality*. New York: Cambridge University Press, 1994.
Padilha, J. (2007). *Elite squad* [Film].
Safatle, V. (2007). Curso *Introdução à experiência intelectual de Gilles Deleuze* - (mimeo.), Filosofia - USP.
Salles, W. (1998). *Central station* [Film].
Soares, F. A. (2018). O corpo anárquico na obra de Antonin Artaud: [des]encarceramento e crueldade na sociedade contemporânea. Master's dissertation in Psychology. Federal University of Goiás.
Žižek, S. (2006). *Órganos sin cuerpo: Sobre Deleuze y consecuencias*. Pre-textos.

Chapter 8
"Altered States" of Consciousness

A common situation in the clinic and in social intervention is the fixation of the collective-client on their ordinary modeling of daily life, or even the creation of rigid cognitive defense mechanisms. This situation of anchoring, or armoring, can block the flow of new content and associations. With rigid conscious and discursive defenses, the clinical-political intervention can take an excessively long time, or even present low efficacy, since there is intense resistance to change (Pichon-Rivière, 1983), in other words, a psychic work to not transform (Kaës, 1997; Fernandes, 2005).

The schizoanalytic and schizodramatic clinic seeks to scrape the rigid, coercive strata that block the flow of desiring forces and investments. From devices that promote movements of deterritorialization and reinvention, it aims to make bodies stir, reach higher vibrational intensities, molecularization of processes, so that they can reach new plateaus of intensity (Baremblitt, 1998, 2019) and other subjectivations and singularization. They provoke lines of flight, ruptures, and cuts in the established desiring circuits, for the production of new desire machines (Baremblitt et al., 2020). It is noteworthy that currently desire is not repressed, it always runs, circulates, even in systems that seem to desire repression and oppression. For example, the State and even fascism are also desiring assemblages (Deleuze & Guattari, 1975) (see Chap. 5).

The promotion of other "consciential states" is one of the strategies of schizodrama to incite movements of deterritorialization. It is emphasized that schizoanalysis does not oppose a state of normality to madness, or to psychosis. This theory apprehends the psychopolitical processes within the scope of fractalities, in the logic of multiplicities. It "approaches all modalities of subjectivation in light of the mode of being in the world of psychosis" (Guattari, 1992a, 63[1]). Thus, in this chap-

[1] In this book, we chose to put the year of the original publication of Deleuze and Guattari's books, but with the pagination of the English language editions (online) found in the references. The quotes that were not found in English were translated by us with the support of Artificial Intelligence.

D. U. Hur, *Schizoanalysis and Schizodrama*,
https://doi.org/10.1007/978-3-031-94657-8_8

ter, we discuss the so-called altered states of consciousness as a possible device for the production of deterritorialization and singularization in the field of schizoanalytic clinic.

Our working method starts from a theoretical discussion about consciousness in schizoanalysis. We seek to understand how consciousness is apprehended, making an articulation with our clinical experience and personal experiments of altering consciousness,[2] to discuss its functioning and its modes of "transition." We also make a connection with the studies on holotropic breathing in the transpersonal psychology of Stanislav and Christina Grof (2011), privileging and managing the schizoanalytic conceptions. We divide this chapter into three parts: first, a general discussion about consciousness; second, the proposition of the cartography of the distinct consciential positions; and, to finish, a reflection on the transitions between the different consciential modes.

Consciousness

What is consciousness? Is it a thing, a state, a spark, light, epiphenomenon of matter? In schizoanalysis, the discussion articulated to consciousness permeates the entire extent of its work and appears in various forms, whether with the debate conscious and unconscious in psychoanalysis, consciousness in Marxism (Deleuze & Guattari, 1972), bad conscience in Nietzsche (Deleuze, 1962), moral consciousness (Deleuze, 1967), etc. Due to the breadth of definitions and treatments on this issue, we have selected only some passages that refer to the mode of operation of consciousness.[3]

Unlike common sense, in schizoanalysis, consciousness is not reduced to perception, knowledge, morality, or the person. It is not what is circumscribed to the imaginary, nor what is restricted to the psychic, bodily envelope, as if images resided "in consciousness and movements in space" (Deleuze, 1983, 56). An articulation is operated not only between the inside and the outside, but also between the bodies themselves, their images, and movements. The data and the body relate directly as image-movements, fissuring the limits and boundaries instituted by common sense.

This operation of extrapolation of the limits between consciousness and the field is also carried out by phenomenology, when Edmund Husserl decided to replace the noetic mode of apprehension for the noematic, from *noesys* to *noema*. At some point of his work, the founder of phenomenology chose to modify the operation of conscious apprehension of data, which ceases to be restricted to the internality of a consciousness, and moves to the field (Husserl, 1931). Although this conception has

[2] Experiences that are not addressed in this book, but that were mentioned for having been fundamental to the elaboration of the reflection of this chapter.

[3] Evidently, the discussion about consciousness in the work of Deleuze and Guattari deserves a long analysis, in a dimension of a new book. However, as we prioritize "altered states," we discuss only some schizoanalysis issues about consciousness.

in a certain way influenced the notion of transcendental field (Deleuze, 1969), and later plane of consistency (Deleuze & Guattari, 1980), there are crucial differences in which Deleuze presents himself as an unusual mix of a Bergsonian (Deleuze, 1966, 1983) empiricist (Deleuze, 1953) and operates an inversion in relation to the Cartesian cogito.

In his first book, Deleuze (1953) criticizes this foundation of modern philosophy when dealing with the constitution of knowledge. He takes an opposite position to that of "Cogito, ergo sum," of "I think, therefore I am," because he considers that this notion of the priority of a being, of a consciousness, which thinks about the given and the world, is a mistake (Hur, 2018).

Knowledge does not derive from the attitude of a subject who apprehends the given to constitute it. It is not the Self that constitutes the object and existence, by thinking and cogitating them, but the reverse. There is a primacy of the given, of data, of flows, in which the affections of the territory on the being constitute the possibilities of knowledge production and the subject itself.

The given is considered to be the flows, forces, and movements of the territory, which is prior to the subject of knowledge, although it is always marked, striated, by it in this co-construction (Zourabichvili, 2012). Matter and data are taken as lines or figures of light (Deleuze, 1983).

Consequently, it is not consciousness that first attributes meaning to the data of the world, but the opposite. The transcendental field presents itself as an "a-subjective" consciousness, pre-reflexive, impersonal (Deleuze, 1969), in which the subject and a consciousness with Self (Deleuze, 1993) are produced by the forces of the outside. In this sense, it is not the Self that thinks the world, but it is the field, the territory, that "thinks" and produces the Self. There is a shift from a Philosophy of cogito, to a Philosophy of affections (Deleuze, 1953), which is totally convergent with the discussion of the haptic dimension (see Chap. 3).

Unlike phenomenological intentionality, that consciousness is consciousness *of* something, "it is indistinguishable from the thing, that is from the image of light. (...) In short, it is not consciousness which is light, it is the set of images, or the light, which is consciousness, immanent to matter" (Deleuze, 1983, 60–61). Consciousness appears more like a black screen, a center of indetermination. Hence, it is not consciousness that "illuminates" the data, in the vectorial sense from the subject to the object, there is a reverse sense, it is the luminosity of the objects themselves that affects it and gives it light and phosphorescence (Deleuze, 1969): this luminosity forms and *populates* consciousness.

Thus, instead of a process of internalization of things in consciousness (*noesys*), or externalization of consciousness to the field of things (*noema*), it operates in a transcendental field, in a plane of immanence that is established by a machinic assemblage of images-movements and its processes of affections.

The articulation of this collection of flows produces synthetic mechanisms of action, which are schemas and habits (Deleuze, 1953), for example, the habit of saying I (Deleuze, 2003). Consciousness becomes a kind of network of indetermination, a centerless system that articulates a collection of images-movement (Deleuze, 1983) through various action schemes, mediated by affections (Deleuze, 1953).

In brief, the Deleuzian proposition is singular, because, first, it removes consciousness from a supposed bodily internality and, second, it assumes that it is not filled only by images of thought, but has a dynamism, in which it even articulates the images to movements (Deleuze, 1983). Here it is worth mentioning some modifications that Deleuze's own definitions undergo throughout his work. In *Difference and repetition*, Deleuze (1968) makes a critique of the static character of the image of thought, arguing that thinking is the opposite of its image, it is disaggregation and movement (see Chap. 5). However, in his studies on cinema, he begins to articulate the image to movement (Deleuze, 1983), to a certain "liquidity," so that in his last book with Félix (Deleuze & Guattari, 1991), the image of thought also begins to have a dynamism, in face of the staticity that was once criticized.

Thus, consciousness, unlike a thing, person, or place, is a kind of machine, an arrangement of processes. Due to this machinic and operative function present in the schizoanalytic repertoire, we propose that consciousness is a circuit of operation, articulation, between different elements and images-movement. More than a "being," it is singularized by its "functioning." Consciousness acts as a variable and heterogeneous assemblage that operates with different degrees of contraction and distension with porous and fluid "borders." It selects various aspects of the field with a unique way of operation. It does not function only with a collection of images–movement, but also with their concatenation and processing. Therefore, consciousness is not a thing, something restricted to interiority, or synthesis of images. It is a machination that brings together at the same time two different movements: (a) selection, apprehension and (b) mode of operationalization. In movement (a) it selects, covers, a series of aspects, images–movement, on a more reduced or expanded scale; in movement (b) it operationalizes them in various ways, either just from the functional point of view, of cause and effect, or from a more ethical perspective, of a collective well-being, of a broader connection with nature, the cosmos, the ancestries. So, consciousness always operates through the heterogeneity of a double and concomitant operation: (a) articulation of different elements, images–movement, with (b) different processings and frequencies. This operation can occur with an apprehension of a greater or lesser degree of field data, and with different modes of operationalization.

In this proposition, consciousness is always movement, a multiple flow of duration (Deleuze, 1966), even though in the established realm of common sense it seems to operate more through stratified images of thought. By starting from the field, it can be taken as a mode of deterritorialization in relation to it, because "(...) consciousness is also a passage into a new dimension, a raising to the power two (which can be achieved through 'a series of enlarging close-ups', but which may equally make use of other techniques)" (Deleuze, 1983, 35). Finally, with the (a) selection and (b) operation of the distinct elements and movement-images linked to the body, it is possible to access new indices of luminosities and produce new perceptions, reflections, affections, actions, and realities. In short, consciousness is an assemblage.

Due to the heterogeneity of the assembled and articulated elements, consciousness operates as a threshold of differential relations (Deleuze, 1988). Consciential thresholds that are distinguished by various and different degrees, such as fractalities. Bergson alludes to a succession of multiple "planes of consciousness," which operate from "a division, a development, an expansion" (Deleuze, 1966, 66), that is, a multiplicity of planes in virtual coexistence. Hence, consciousness expresses itself much more by a logic of multiplicities, with its vibrational plateaus, translation movements, emission of ripples and jumps, than something stabilized, totalized, and concluded. Then, it should not be taken as a state, it is by no means static. Consciousness is something that works, operates, and produces an articulation, rotation, of processes with different frequencies. So, instead of a "state," which can refer to static phases, it is more correct to say that it is constituted by "positions," or better, frequency plateaus in translation, because they are dynamic positions, not phases, in which the machinery of consciousness transits and operates. From this understanding we abandon the notion of altered states of consciousness, replacing from now on "states" by "plateaus," "positions," or consciential "modes."

We also abandon the notion of "altered," because this proposition maintains the logic of negativity, discipline, in which there supposedly must be a "norm" of consciousness, and its deviations, which are the "altered states"; or a "state of wakefulness," considered normal, and another, of delirium, which is seen as abnormal. Even the idea of conscious and unconscious reproduces this dichotomization in the logic of negativity. We understand that the disciplinary assumption between norm and alteration presents some misconceptions, or at least a reductionism that restricts the positions of consciousness to only two poles.

So there is no "normal mode" of consciousness. If there is a mode considered "normal" by common sense, it is the one that is domesticated by the civilizing process, which is overcoded and axiomatized by work, such as the imperative of the "capitalist consciential mode." On the contrary, we argue that there is a great variation and coexistence of several consciential modes, in which at any moment one can transit from one conscious degree to another.

Due to the variability of consciential degrees, we propose another treatment to consciousness, different from the one elaborated by Spinoza. In Deleuze's work (1981a) on the Dutch philosopher, it is noticed that there is a certain negativation of consciousness in opposition to the body, in which consciousness captures and reduces its power. In order not to fall into the logic of negativity, we choose to leave the model of opposition of consciousness to the body and complexify its own phenomenon, expanding it, because consciousness is not a thing, nor a "state." In this case, we hypothesize that the target of the Dutch philosopher's criticism would not be consciousness in general but some specific consciential modalities: those related to judgment, to the attainment of power, to dominion, to governmentality, such as the *sovereignty consciential mode*, and nowadays the *capitalist consciential mode*. In the next topic, we specify the different positions or consciential modes, discussing their functions and configurations.

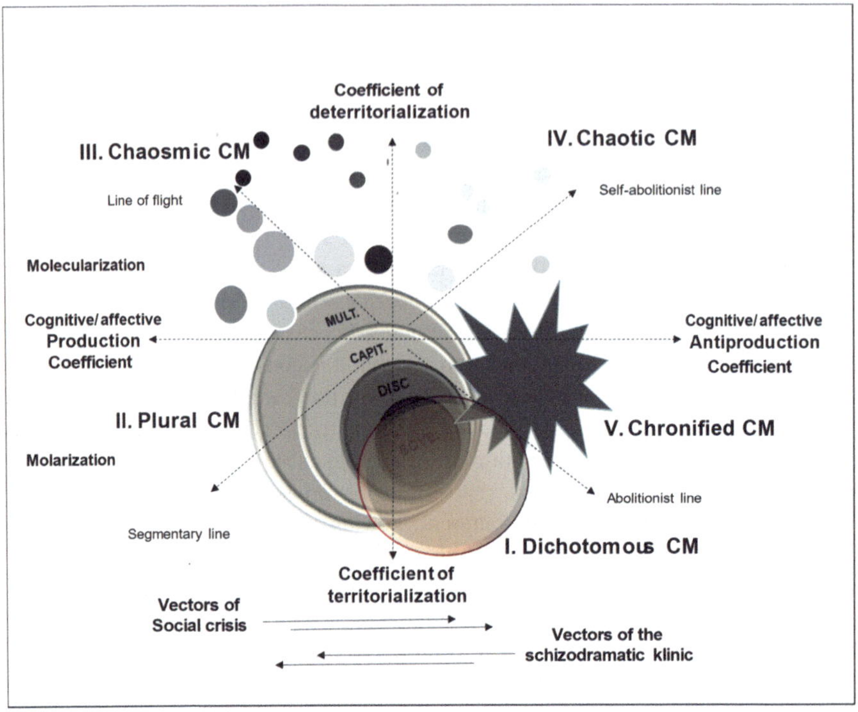

Fig. 8.1 Cartography of the different consciential modes (CM)

Consciential Modes (CM)

In this topic, we articulate the proposition of consciousness as a machinic assemblage of movement-images and different aspects of the field to the schizoanalytic scheme of (anti)production and (de)territorialization[4] (see Fig. 7.5 of Chap. 7). From this connection, we elaborate a new model of consciousness that is not restricted to the logic of negativity, to two poles, but unfolds into five positions: the Consciential Modes (CM) I. Dichotomous, II. Plural, III. Chaosmic, IV. Chaotic and V. Chronified. It is noteworthy that the "II. Plural CM" presents four subtypes: (a) sovereignty, (b) disciplinary, (c) capitalist/performance and (d) multiplicity/ecosophic (Fig. 8.1).

[4]As presented in Chap. 7, the horizontal axis refers to the coefficient of cognitive/affective production and antiproduction. On the left are the processes with a production coefficient, and on the right those of antiproduction coefficient. The vertical axis refers to the deterritorialization and territorialization coefficients. In the upper hemisphere, there are the cutting edges of deterritorialization, the production of lines of flight, the processes of molecularization, while in the lower hemisphere, the territorial sides, the processes of segmentation and stratification (Deleuze & Guattari, 1980).

The five proposed CM are situated in the dispersion between the two axes, positioning themselves at the intersections between the different quadrants. They are different consciential positions that act by continuous variation and express the phenomenon of dispersion of consciousness. We emphasize that this model results from our own singular elaboration, referenced in the schizoanalysis of Deleuze and Guattari, in the schizodrama of Baremblitt and from clinical and personal experience with different CM. Therefore, it is a model that is not found in this form in the pioneering work of schizoanalysis, and that should still be the object of criticism and discussion for future re-elaborations.

The variation between CM occurs due to the fact that consciousness operates in different ways in relation to the collection of movement–images. Depending on the context and the constellation of forces at stake, consciousness "subtracts from the thing whatever does not interest it" (Deleuze, 1983, 63), providing a mode of selection and operation that is a reduction of the real, which Guattari (1989a) refers to as "sieves" or "existential sieves." Subjectivity is subtractive and offers partial prehensions in the perception of things, instead of the idealization of supposed "total prehensions." It is in this context that the perceptual process always carries in its operationalization attributes of the giver of sense over the given, its own lights cast on the luminosity of things, in an articulation between perception and projection. That is why authors of phenomenology, like Maurice Merleau-Ponty (1996), affirm that in the perceptual process itself there is already a kind of hallucinatory *quantum*.

In the so-called waking states, the consciential machine operates predominantly by a coexisting double system: the I-Dichotomous CM and the II-Plural CM.

The I. *Dichotomous consciential mode* is the most operative mode of functioning, such as the initial cognitive processing of the child in his early years of life. It operates by dichotomies and binarisms, that is, by the logic of negativity (Deleuze, 1962, 1968), in which it divides the world into two poles, or two halves, for example, between positive and negative, good and bad, beautiful and ugly, black and white, etc. It is a less sophisticated way of processing the data of the world and movement-images, in which its complexity and multiplicity are reduced to dichotomized series. It is the most territorialized and stratified CM, so it is located in the lower hemisphere of Fig. 8.1.

We approximate this form of functioning to what Melanie Klein (1971) called the schizo-paranoid position, in which there are binary operations and primitive and intense affects. It predominantly presents a coefficient of antiproduction, but depending on the context, also of production.

The II. *Plural consciential mode* is an expansion of the dichotomized apprehension mode, to more complex models and systems. There is a more sophisticated cognitive processing that dispenses with the binary organization and assumes different arrangements, either in a hierarchical and arborescent logic, or in a multiplicitous model of difference. It acts in the different processes of mold, model, and modulation. That is why the Plural CM is located, to varying degrees, in the four quadrants of Fig. 8.1 and expresses different ways of processing the real.

To reflect on this diversity of consciential processing modes, we rely on Guattari's assertion that consciousness and social functioning are intertwined. "Consciential subjectivation is essentially linked to a certain kind of organisation of society, a system of law and of signification" (Guattari, 2011, 124), that is, consciousness is directly modulated by different social assemblages. Hence, considering that society is always in motion and is formed by different diagrams of social forces (Deleuze, 1979), we articulate the different configurations of forces presented in Chap. 5 with the II. Plural CM.[5] Such articulation resulted in the proposition of some distinct consciential submodes. In short, they present a form of operationalization of the plane of immanence according to the vectors of each selected force diagram: of sovereignty, disciplinary, capitalist, and multiplicity. These submodes operate by different gears and do not present an "evolutionary *quantum*" among themselves.

The *II.a. Sovereign consciential mode* ("SOVE." in Fig. 8.1) refers to the processing of the world from the hierarchical logic of the sovereignty diagram, in which the *one*, such as the father or the boss, has power over the management of life and the desire of others. From this logic of the authoritarian despot, it conforms the world and objects in a steep, vertical hierarchy, in which social domination is legitimized and there is a fixity that resembles the processes of molding. Just as in the despotic imperial formation, desire is overcoded by the body of the despot (Deleuze & Guattari, 1972), so it is more territorialized and antiproductive, primarily located in the lower right quadrant. It is noted that it is a mode of operation close to the I. Dichotomous CM, but it is more sophisticated. It does not only act in the pairing between the elements, in which the one is taken as positive, and the other as negative, but arranges them in a hierarchical and arborescent pyramid with different social posts. Generally, it is the CM that legitimizes autocratic discourses and practices, the conservatism and the patriarchy.

The II.b. *Disciplinary consciential mode* ("DISC." in Fig. 8.1) is the one that operationalizes the world and things no longer from the hierarchical logic of sovereignty, of the State, but rather from what Michel Foucault (1975) calls the disciplines resulting from *psy* knowledge and practices, that is, from the norms that result from scientific discourse. Instead of the fixity of the mold, it operates by transmitting a model. It is noted that it is another desiring gear in operation, which does not process the world only by the logic of the vertical imperatives of the Law and the State, but with the *norms* resulting from experiments and reflections from *psy* disciplines and practices. Here science occupies a central place of governmentality, having a quantum of normativity of life, of creation, in the sense attributed by Georges Canguilhem (1966). On the other hand, the norm becomes the new "despotic signifier," even being captured by the State logic, or by established semantics, such as positivism, psychoanalysis, Marxism, etc. Thereby, it still presents a great character of territorialization and fixation to established rules, being located in the lower hemisphere, but with a greater potential for production, if compared to the previous CM. Due to the primacy of a normative CM, it can also couple with the

[5] However, we separate the coding machine into two submodes (sovereign and disciplinary) and the neofascist machine refers to the chronified consciential mode.

functioning of the I. Dichotomous CM, which fits the norm that the equal is positive and everything that deviates from it is negative.

The II.c. *Capitalist consciential mode* ("CAPIT." in Fig. 8.1), or performance, refers to the modality of processing reality from the functioning of the hegemonic diagram of social forces: the axiomatic of capital (Deleuze & Guattari, 1972). The capitalist machine modulates consciousness in an accelerated way for more work and more production, but not for creative leisure, or a dive into chaos. The distinct elements of the field are apprehended to articulate them aiming at greater productivity and efficiency. Consequently, the current conscious processing refers to the acceleration of the productivity of any object (Deleuze, 1979). It uses both scientific operation and sovereign logic as means of incessant increase in productivity and profits, always managing a certain quantum of deterritorialization and reterritorialization, so it can be located both in the upper and lower hemisphere of Fig. 8.1. It accelerates the rotation of flows in an incessant productive hypertrophy, without end, in a kind of addiction, which cannot be stopped, combining the coefficient of production and antiproduction. It is often questioned why the acceleration of productivity continues, even when the desired answers and gains are not obtained, and production turns into antiproduction. The fatigue and exhaustion resulting from the axiomatic of capital lead people to anxious situations that direct the conscious operation to the dichotomous mode. The I. binary CM couples with the capitalist consciential submode and results in the search for increased yield, even greater work efficiency. In this case, consciential positions that differ from the "wakefulness frequency for production" are taken as undesirable and are pathologized: productivity is positive and leisure is negative. Then a hypertrophy of production is sought with a high degree of automation and alienation. That is why it cannot be said that the Capitalist CM is an "evolution" in relation to disciplinary consciousness, as such a configuration of automation and exhaustion can culminate in the depotentiation of life and in the Chronified CM (V).

This CM produces the so-called capitalist subjectivity, as if only it existed, or was legitimized, while the others are seen as dysfunctional, archaic or a waste of time. And what is subjectivity, if not this machine of consciential apprehension that articulates distinct elements (in greater or lesser degree and quantity) and processes them in a specific, particular way?

Even being hegemonic and with universalist tendencies, isn't it the Capitalist CM that is the deviant, instead of the "normal"? A CM that is exhausting life and the planet, generating global warming, increasing the domination and extermination of animal, plant, mineral, and even human populations. Indigenous thinker Ailton Krenak (2019) states that the white man exploits and destroys nature, because he does not identify with it. In a way similar to the Cartesian operation of the split between subject and object, he separated himself from nature itself, fictionalizing himself as an independent, autonomous, "superior" being. The Self became the subject, the protagonist, while the world, the flows, became the object. He mutilated reality, objectified the flows, the beings of nature, no longer comes into contact with them, does not engage with the mountains, does not understand their signs. A hierarchy is established in the relations of forces, in a primacy of the Self, with a serious split between "subject" and world. As a result, there is an unspeakable fracture with the milieu, in which the person is dissociated from its ecology, from nature, apprehending himself as an independent being; moving from an *ecosophy*, to an *egosophy*, eminently narcissistic. There is a shift from an apprehension of the contour, the outside, to a perception by the primacy of the "inside."

Beings cease to be taken for their potential for agency, to be grasped only by the exploitation of their potential for use. In this modality, there is no ecosophic apprehension, a *religare* with *Pacha Mama*, *Mother Earth*, but rather operations on how to extract the largest amount of profit, regardless of their costs. On the one hand, we have Krenak, who talks to his mountains, and Kopenawa, who apprehends the forces of nature and dances with the xapiris, on the other hand, we have the Capitalist CM that develops means and technologies to dominate and profit more from the exploitation of nature. The human becomes the man of the commodity, as Kopenawa (2015) calls it, reducing everything to its utility. With this logic of transcendence, which updates the capitalist exploitation machine, he destroys nature, carries out genocide via neoliberalism, which attacks and compromises all populations. See the destruction that mining causes in the environment of indigenous reserves, contaminating the waters, devastating the forest, spreading diseases and ending lives. From an ecosophic point of view, the Capitalist CM is the alienated, the destructive, the "abnormal," the unethical, not being linked to the production of life, nor of health, only to numerous types of surplus-value.

The *II.d. Multiplicity consciential mode* ("MULT." in Fig. 8.1), or ecosophical, is the one that can better articulate the differences and take them as multiple positivities. The world, the real, and the elements cease to be apprehended and operationalized only by the sovereign, disciplinary, or capitalist consciential logic, and begin to be selected and articulated by the logic of complexity. They are not taken as elements that enter into a logic of mutual negation, or normative, nor of yield. It does not operate in poles, but rather as a dispersion in a gradient of intensities. There is the development of an ecosophical consciousness that does not only focus on psychic, consciential and subjective aspects, but also focuses on social relations and the environment in which it is inserted (Guattari, 1989b, 2013). So, it is a mode of cosmic consciousness that expands to the ecological and machinic dimension in a relationship of amplification and feedback with the chaotic dimensions. It is the CM that updates what schizoanalysis calls the ethical-aesthetic-political paradigm, as it is conducive to *poietic* processes, of creation, in the production of relations of sympathy and solidarity among the different people who occupy a certain *ethos*, as well as an agency of forces that can transform power into potency. That's why it is located more in the quadrants referred to the coefficient of production, also having a certain quantum of deterritorialization.

These first two CM, I. dichotomous and II. plural, are coexistent. It does not only oscillate from one to another, as interchangeable positions, but one can operate from both at the same time, as a coexistent double machinery, as mentioned above. Obviously there is a prevalence of mode I or mode II in different situations. In day-to-day life, people handle with established schemes of consciousness, *ready-made* recipes (Schutz, 1979), sometimes very precarious, but which are functional for the exercise of daily activities. For example, in moments of danger, in situations of attack, or of high degree anxiety, the I. Dichotomous CM becomes the most operationalized, offering more agile conducts of vigilance, of self-preservation, etc.: one can escape, fight, make a decision, with greater speed. In these cases, the I. Dichotomous CM can be more effective for life than the II.d. Plural CM of multiplicity. Already in less anxious contexts, where there are no threats, or exacerbated fears, there is a tendency for mode II to be more predominant, allowing more sophisticated cognitive achievements that result in aesthetic and artistic production, in reflections, actions, and more careful and creative work. Evidently there is also a transition between the subtypes of plural CM. Therefore, more elaborate activities and reflections work with greater potency with a more expanded CM, be it the plural with the subtype of multiplicity, and not the merely binary.[6]

These first two CM I and II refer to the positions of consciential cosmos, to the surfaces of registration. Here the cosmos relates to the known, structured, and schematized. There are many consciential cosmos, some more limiting, others more expanded, as discussed above.

Nevertheless, very intensive and deterritorializing experiences also can lead us to the production of a III. *Chaosmic consciential mode*. This position intersects with the II.d. Plural CM and is located in the upper hemisphere of Fig. 8.1. It is a transitional, intermediate position, which is the result of the comings and goings to the IV. Chaotic CM for the II. Plural CM. Different from the territorialization of the cosmic CM, it implies a diagrammatic opening. Thus, there is a zigzag between eruptions of chaos, rapture by intensities, with the creation of new territories, other settlements, new flows and senses. It results in the construction of other universes of references, new cosmos and of another being, possibly still in a larval position. The production of a body without organs is a possible way to the fomentation of these chaotic positions. But there should always be a deterritorialization with prudence, in which Castañeda argues that *nagual* does not destroy *tonal* (Deleuze & Guattari, 1980), in a sowing of new lands, other possibilities. In the last topic of this chapter the issue of deterritorialization is better discussed.

The IV. *Chaotic consciential mode* is the one that refers to the forces of the outside, to the free and unconnected energies: the space–time of infinite speeds and accelerations. Chaos is not taken as in common sense, in the negative sense. It is a pre-existing condition, movement of infinite speed and continuous variation, vertigo, and destabilization. It expresses a magmatic logic, of irruption of the whirlwind of intensities and the risk of vertiginous fall into the abyss: there is the maximum coefficient of deterritorialization. It is an instantaneous, intensive outlet, liminal, borderline position, in which we vibrate with it, achieving processes of radical molecularization of the body and that does not last for a long time. Depending on the conjuncture of forces, it can foster a creative, revolutionary, and

[6] For the elaboration of this double and coexisting machinery, we also drew inspiration from the model of Affective Intelligence of Political Psychology by Marcus et al. (2000). In it, a double coexisting scheme of intelligence is stipulated, called the surveillance system and the dispositional system, which operate similarly to the I. Dichotomous CM and the II. Plural CM, respectively.

transformative CM. "Chaos, instead of being a factor of absolute dissolution of complexity, becomes the virtual bearer of an infinite complexification" (Guattari, 1992a, 1992b, 78). After reaching this peak, there may be a process that makes us reterritorialize in the III. Chaosmotic CM, in which, in possession of particles of chaos, we can fabricate new movements, lines, increasing the potential of agency, forces, mobilization, and transformation. From the production and territorialization results the cosmos, just as the strata derive from the reduction in speed and energy power of the lava. On the other hand, if the experience is too dizzying and emptying, it turns into antiproduction, tracing a self-abolitionist line that touches on psychic death (Deleuze & Guattari, 1980), or that can make us hyperterritorialize in an urgent and depowered way in the V. Chronified consciential mode.

The V. *Chronified consciential mode* is the apex of depowering and can result from both a 1. chaotic experience, as from a 2. continuous and totalizing stratification, characteristic of cosmic CM (I and II.a., b., c.).

1. When there is no exercise of prudence in the "trip" and the anchoring territories were not taken on the journey to chaos, there is a risk of getting lost in extremely deterritorializing experiences and tracing a self-abolitionist escape line, that is, a suicidal line of flight (Deleuze & Guattari, 1980). Excessive deterritorialization can lead to acute processes of depowering and positions of emptiness. In these specific cases, conditions of vulnerability and helplessness that cry out, as a way of containing discomfort, for emergency reterritorializations (Guattari, 2011). Early recoding and limping that triggers processes of chronicity and freezing.
2. Rigid and continuous stratification in the same CM, like the submodes of sovereignty, discipline, and capitalist, generates a closure of the body to the forces of the outside, in which there is a high degree of energy loss and depowering. It results in a full stratified body, where energies do not run or circulate in exchange with the milieu (Deleuze & Guattari, 1980). Both this condition, as the imbalances and instabilities arising from the IV. Chaotic CM, make us anchor ourselves in just one conscious position of life, or only in an identity version, which is often managed by what Deleuze and Guattari (1972) call the paranoid pole. Thus, "pulverizing-pulverized consciousnesses only have as a resource to abandon themselves to *individualization of* despair, to a personal implosion of value universes" (Negri & Guattari, 1999, 9). Here is a phrase from the classic *The man without qualities* by Robert Musil: "the sane person is full of countless insanities and the insane person is possessed only by one" (quoted by Guattari, 1989a, 206). In our consciential cartography, we can translate it as: the "healthy" person moves through a multiplicity of consciential positions, the chronic is fixed in just one. And by trafficking only in one version of things, produces coded modes of life that lead to situations of blockage of the flow of forces, psychic suffering, rupture of social ties, and generalized depowering.

The V. Chronified CM, in the collective scope, can also be the way of functioning of political extremists. They start to be dogmatized by their set of beliefs, values, and ideologies, whether from right or even left politics and do not accept discourse different from yours, even if they are objectively wrong (Hur & Sabucedo, 2020).

They assume a position of monopoly on the truth (Dono et al., 2018), overcoding the real from it. They often adopt belligerent and intolerant stance toward difference. For example, right-wing extremists assume a position of combat and hostility toward social minorities, such as ethnic-racial minorities, of sex/gender, of social class, etc. (see Chap. 5). It is a chronic way of being that ends up suppurating the social bond, acting in an abolitionist and destructive way of life. It is eminently territorialized and unproductive, so it is located only in the lower right quadrant of Fig. 8.1. This is the CM that can generate the microfascist behavior and that for ethical-political reasons must be fought, as it is a type of conduct that mortifies the whole-body social.

Due to these different consciential positions, terminologically it is not very accurate to say that there is a holotropic consciousness, as transpersonal psychology names it. There is no consciential position toward the whole (*holos*), because consciousness itself is the articulation of heterogeneities, fragments, differences, with their operating variations. Thus, if there is a "whole," it is always a whole fragmentary, disjointed, that operates by disjunctive syntheses (Zourabichvili, 2012). And even if we can get close to this conscious expansion, the conjunctural conditions can always lead to other CM, such as the dichotomized and the chronified. On the other hand, apart from this highlight, the idealized model by Grof and Grof (2011) is closer to what we call the III. chaotic CM.

Transition Between Consciential Modes: Klinic of Chaos–Chaosmos–Disorder

The cartography of the different consciential positions aims to expand the conception about the model of consciousness. There is not only the displacement from a "normal" consciousness "mode" to another, "abnormal" but the transition from one consciential position to others, which are configured as fractalities, like a crystal image, with multiple and heterogeneous faces (Deleuze, 1985), which do not have delimited and rigid borders. It is highlighted that there is a regime of virtual coexistence and not of exclusion between the different positions, which operate by different gears.

So, how to create healthier consciential modes, of life, in the face of the destructiveness and extremism of a V. Chronified CM? How to get out of the automated movement of the II.c. Capitalist plural CM, of its fatigue and indebtedness? How to overcome the I. Dichotomous CM and access other degrees of intensity of life, and not just binarisms and polarizations? How to reach other consciential positions, aiming for experiences of empowerment?

There are several ways and devices for promoting the transition between CM that aim to potentiate life. The ethical-aesthetic-political purpose of schizoanalysis and schizodrama is the fight against chronified, paranoid, resentful, and de-potentiated positions of life.

For example, Jean Oury, the founder of the historic La Borde clinic, states that when there is a management of ambience, alteration of people's relationships with the milieu (as happened there), travel, territorial, or even affective and organizational displacement, there can be an expansion of consciential processes. In these cases, a person can move from a V. Chronified CM, to, for example, a II. Plural CM. As a result, he stops operating in the paranoid pole, which sometimes causes panic attacks, catatonia, and manages to enjoy the experience of being in a new place, to the point that he even comes to dispense with the medications he uses.

However, there are many cases that when returning from this "trip" to the psychiatric institution where they reside, there is a return to the same conditions prior to displacement (Oury, 2009). In this return to the instituted, there was something like the return to the symptom, a "shrinking" of consciousness. In these cases, we can see the influence that the ambience has on consciential processes, and the management that must be done so that the person does not become frozen in chronified and dichotomous consciential strata.

One way to produce other CM is the promotion and management of deterritorialization processes, whether in individual and/or group therapy. "The schizo fracture is the royal road of access to the emergent fractality of the Unconscious" (Guattari, 1992a, 64). With the deterritorialization we seek to make the passage (give the pass), circulate the processes, work the submergence (Oury, 2009), establish spaces of heterogenesis.

Baremblitt operates these movements with the *klinic of chaos-chaosmos-cosmos*. He seeks to actualize the immanent forces of the virtual, of chaos, of real, of *realterity*. In the relationship chaos–chaosmos–cosmos there is a composition of intertwining chaotic and cosmic forces, of the indiscernible and the structured, of free energy and bound energy, of the larval subject and the identified and organized full body. There is an interrelation, in which "ontology is the dice throw, the chaosmos from which the cosmos emerges" (Deleuze, 1968, 199). And not mere succession, or derivation, but the coexistence and self-production of a chaosmosis (Guattari, 1992a).

Social machines often try to turn the rhizome into tree, but paradoxically, at any moment, rhizomatic shoots erupt from their stems, or even where it might seem impossible, like, for example, weeds that sprout from the cracks in the concrete. There is the actualization of a double coexisting force, paradoxical and with opposite vectors. Coexistence and mixture between centrifugal and centripetal forces. Flow and propagation that try to be dammed and channeled into ducts of significance. But ducts that crack, that let escape lines of flight. Everything always leaks, no matter how much there is a great effort of containment.

It is sought through several devices, body intervention, dance, sounds, modulation of breathing, etc., trigger, elicit, a whirlwind of flows, waves of affections and intensities that can actualize the forces of chaos. To experience the real that implicates us, and not the codes that explain us. To shuffle the codes, the meanings. To scrape the *clichés* and establish the dimension of the untimely, of the catastrophe, a field of diffuse forces in movement: a removal zone. A whirlwind that skins the configured, the forms, with the purpose of producing an intensive and deterritorializing body without organs in the full, emptied, or destructive body, of the instituted diagram of forces. To make the dormant and underground lava erupt to the tectonic plates. To put people and collectives in a germinal state, convulsive and open to the forces of the outside. To problematize, affect and destabilize, and not clarify and rely on presupposed answers. To follow the chaos-germ formula, or catastrophic-larval (Deleuze, 1981b). Obviously, it is not excessive to reaffirm that the exercise of any deterritorializing device must be permeated with care and prudence, both in relation to its handling, as well as the preparation of the participants.

Among the several practices used, one that stands out are the breathing exercises. The different breathing practices, such as hyperventilation, and the so-called holotropic breathing (Grof & Grof, 2011), are important tools for the production of new vibratory modes. Evidently, they are not the only ones. Baremblitt used the breathing exercises as a possible deterritorialization device in about five decades of clinical work.[7]

We do not perform here a mere transposition of part of the repertoire of Grof's transpersonal psychology to schizodramatic practice. We find some similarities, approximations, convergences, yet some theoretical and technical distinctions remain. It can be said that there was an "a-parallel evolution" between schizodrama and transpersonal psychology.

With the intensification of breathing process, we seek to provoke a scraping of stratified consciential modes, to crack the one to multiplicities, manufacture a molecularization that "accelerates" the consciential processes. To incite the emission of lines of flight, of fractures in the CM of wakefulness, so that new plateaus of intensities can be reached. And with this, generate a liberation of forces that leads to a variation between the various consciential positions, reaching for example the IV. Chaotic CM.

As a result, forces that are inscribed in the body, once paralyzed, blocked and indiscriminate, emerge and begin to circulate and flow. Both, the forces that erupt in an open and free flow, and those that refer to short-circuited systems, in other words, their disempowering symptoms. Or even bodies with enclosed and armored forces, bodies emptied, porous, that let their forces leak, without being filled again. Pressured, tired, exhausted bodies, in different conditions, but equally depowered.

Thus, a fundamental mode of operation of the device is the intensification of the emerging processes and elements, shared management by both Baremblitt and the Grof couple. To foster their experimentation and circulation, not only from the discursive logic and of the signifier but in the logic of intensities and the exchange of consciential modes.

> The work of analysis consists in changing the enunciative coordinates and not in giving the explanatory keys. It is not only about elucidating, of making discernible already existing components, but also of producing components that are not yet present, and that will become "always already present at the moment they are engendered", due to the very logic of these multiplicities, whose molecular arrangement works at an infinite speed below space, time and ontological orders (Guattari, 1992a, 1992b, 82).

[7] Baremblitt (2021) also mentions the use of psychedelics as a means of achieving other conscious modes, procedure that he used at the beginning of the invention of schizodrama, in the 1970s. This controversial debate is also not addressed in this book.

This mode of intervention makes that the forces not only expand the different elements grasped in the conscious process, but also cause a kind of disarray in the established CM, be it dichotomous, plural, or chronified. It can result in a "collapse," an energy flow that causes the fluxes' overflow into other configurations, producing new components. Free and intensive flows that disperse and shape themselves into different reference universes (Guattari, 1989a). Erupting lines of flight, intensive, delirious, and magmatic production.

The intensification of the processes, the acceleration and deceleration of the consciential frequency, can lead to other vibrational modes, fostering the jump from one plateau of intensities to another. The *ritornelization* (Guattari, 1989a), which produces the displacement between conscious plateaus, overflows into new desiring circuits.

In this journey of fractalization, one is no longer on the plane of totalized objects, but of movements, vectors, forces, and intensive flows. The becomings are more prominent than the being, as well as the packs and hordes of forces than the isolated individual. Deliriums and imagetic and affective flows, instead of the old established certainty about everything.

However, it is not only the acceleration of the rotation frequency that leads from one consciential mode to another. It is a necessary condition, but not sufficient, as one can accelerate or decelerate the frequency of pulsation without leaving the same consciential mode. With the intensification of movements, the handling of an *existential shifter* (Guattari, 1989a) is sought. We exemplify, in a reductionist way, the functioning of this *shifter*, the transition between CM, with the change of the mechanical gear of an automotive vehicle. In the handling of the gears, there is concomitantly the alteration of the rotation gear with the (de)acceleration of speed, that is, there is not just a change in the pulsation frequency, there is a change in the vibrational logic itself, its ellipse of translation, which makes possible to reach other movements and territories.

The emerging affects, the intensive flows, and the experience produce other routes and new paths. One can reach a conscious expansion in which the individual manages to perceive their ramifications with the *machinic phylum*, such as the character Neo, when awakening from Matrix (Wachowski & Wachowski, 1999). But in this case, one is not subjected, alienated, by the phylum, but rather agencied and formed. Because the simple naked eye, the ordinary functionalist consciential modes, can hardly map the diagram of forces and the intertwining of multiple materialities and incorporeal universes.

In the IV. Chaotic CM, the intensive quantum of consciential ripples can even cause a kind of "channel" change, to modes that are called *trance*. It is emphasized that there is also a gradient of variation in trance, be it more intense trances, and others softer, in which one has "consciousness" of what is happening. In these situations, the schizodrama functions as a device for the production and experimentation of "clinical-laboratory trances."

The trance is so multifaceted that it becomes a kind of con-fusional disposition for those who live it, in which the person has an imagetic, affective, intensive, "free," and boiling flow. Images, affects, forces, and becomings of all kinds pass through their body. The tranceunic mode is a dimension between, *medium*. In this plateau, one feels the world in different ways, he accesses the others in a more intense way. The *medium* produces his senses from the field between, with the other, with the set. He is not a mere receiver, he is a producer, the *medium* is not an unveiler but a cartographer. He manufactures senses from the block of intensities of the common energy field, using his own repertoire and the forces of the outside to access the other. An energy transmission, or daydreams in the cartography about the body or its affective state. It can result in experiences considered parapsychological (Baremblitt, 2014), such as the sensation of thought transmission, which is not entering the other's head. But composing the same field, sharing the same plateau, a common becoming, the same energy vibration.

Trance can also be the moment to perform delusions. A certain narrative is dramatized with intensity, which may seem to have nothing to do with this life. A past life, archetypal, the dramatization of some primal force of nature. The force of gestation and childbirth. The force of fire and *Xangô*. To make the body catch more fire, feel the burning of power. To produce a body without organs in the strictest sense. The delirium goes beyond the Oedipal triangle, delirious about races, ancestries, migrations, the drift of continents, and between continents. The passage and movement. The pain and the crying. The joy and the will to live.

The emerging flows are so strong that they often need a depository, that gives them containment. Because in this mode there are very intense discharges of energy. Unnameable, bizarre and strange sensations make people seek to name, code, and categorize them, being materialized in various ways. The attempt is made to understand the becoming experienced through the logic of being, which is so intense and unnameable that it is considered a transcendental, paranormal, spiritual experience. "I incorporated a spirit," "I left the body," "I traveled far away," "my third eye opened" are some of the possible representations for the experience. This anchoring, or deposition, ends up being offered by the person's own interpretive repertoires, resulting from his reference universes. They offer a set of material beliefs, experiential, religious, spiritual, mystical, transcendental, which serve as a basis to mold and contain the free and loose flows. They provide the deceleration of the process, its anchoring and psychic regulation.

In the common sense, people try to embody the experience into familiar images of thoughts, causal past places, or even seemingly meaningless daydreams. This is clearly seen in the function of myths in ancient times. Participants may often attribute a transcendent meaning to the constitution of their existential territory, or anchor themselves in very distant recesses of their history. There are cases where the person even speaks in practically unknown languages, which he does not handle and had little contact with.

The forces, in the form of delirium, can travel "light years" to problems not yet known, not yet faced, but they can also be incorporated into traumas experienced at any time in the biography, such as in childhood, adolescence, in relation to one of the parents, or friends. The intensive affect can even incarnate in the imaginary of intrauterine episodes, the perinatal period, or even in the dream production of other lives and characters, which was hastily named as regression to past lives.

We consider that these experiences do not refer to regressive aspects, to memory in the fetal period, a life lived, or idealized, in a centuries-old, millennial past, but rather to the fabulation of new possibilities, even if they are picturized in ancient times. This apparently transcendental experience refers to a stratum of symbolization of the forces elicited by the transition of consciential modes: it is a figuration and actualization of the emerging forces of the flow of present duration. Therefore, the narratives produced refer more to *masks*, shells, paints, and forms that cover the becoming and the event: portions of cosmos. It is not a factual *magic*, but rather a virtual *magic*, of the virtual coexistence between the multiple planes of temporality.

The deterritorializing experience coming from the IV. Chaotic CM makes the intensities gush in the present in a dissymmetric flow, altering the experience of a supposed linearity and continuity of time. The diachronic and disjunctive temporal flux follows the Bergsonian duration flow (Deleuze, 1966), in which there is an inversion in the causality between past and present. Instead of the past overcoding the present, past is modulated and orchestrated by the present. When "reliving" the past, the affect of the present is repeated in it. Because the present is the sieve, the filter, the lens, that produces the senses about the past, as well as selects, and even figure-distorts the fragments of the past. Deleuze resorts to the work of Marcel Proust to figure this twist of temporality, in an interesting inversion: "by loving his mother the hero of In Search of Lost Time repeats Swann's love for Odette" (1968, 105–106). In this quote, it is seen that it is not the love for the mother (past temporality) that is transferred to Odette (present temporality), but the opposite. The love of the past refers to the repetition of the love of the present. It is the present that repeats itself in the past, and not the opposite, as is glimpsed in common sense. A virtual past is produced from the free flows that are elicited by the process of deterritorialization in the present; the event and the becomings are covered by an imagery, disparate signs and codes. So, it is not the past that is first, but the becomings, the affective lines, which are incited by deterritorialization and are updated in the fractalities of the multiple coexisting temporal planes (Deleuze, 1966).

Nevertheless, we must be careful not to absolutize the fables produced, the narratives, the images and the adventures erected, placing them in a supposedly original past. They should not be totalized as a truth, but as a *version* in the process of actualization the experienced affections. It is a symbolic production related to forces and symptoms, which is more prospective than regressive. A trace, clue, index, actualized and materialized but not necessarily referring to lived facts as they were in the past. It is an update and incarnation of the virtual forces at stake; a deceleration of the infinite speeds of chaos.

One misconception that some therapists have is to believe in these reports as a reconstruction of past facts, as if a drawer, a file, were opened and the "truth" emerged, just as it was in the past. The mistake in analysis is to establish the cause–effect relationship of the past on the present, when there is another movement: the arrow of time gushes in the coexistence of the present with the past (Deleuze, 1966). If we stick to the regressive narrative as a truth, we fall into the same logic of cause and effect of a mythical past that supposedly determines all subsequent processes.

And it is at this point that we distance ourselves most from the analysis of the Grof and Grof (2011) of transpersonal psychology. Even though it has surpassed Freudian psychoanalysis and Jungian analytical psychology, it still maintains a strong inheritance from them. For didactic reasons, we briefly differentiate the method of analysis of transpersonal psychology and schizoanalytic and schizodramatic clinic.

The method of analysis of transpersonal psychology still reproduces two "habits" of psychoanalysis, which we should avoid. First, to maintain a primacy in regressive analysis, in which it still sustains a cause-and-effect relationship between past traumatic experience and its effect in the present, and second, to maintain the analysis in the logic of negativity between conscious and what is not conscious, that is, there is still a strong anchorage in the proposition of psychoanalytic unconscious, even though it acquires a distinct conformation.

Regarding causality in the temporality of analysis, transpersonal psychology tends to code people's manifestations to past experiences. In their analyses, it still remains very focused on the biographical aspect. However, it does not only focus on the first years of the individual's history to grasp the genesis of his main personality traits, it adds two more stages: the perinatal period and the transpersonal dimension. By proposing the perinatal period as a fundamental stage for the constitution of the being, it somehow performs an even more regressive analysis, more directed to the past, in which it apprehends the different stages of intrauterine life and of the birth period, understanding that there are four Basic Perinatal Matrices (BPM I to IV). On the other hand, the opening to the transpersonal dimension, articulated to the idea of Jungian collective unconscious, the work with mandalas (Grof & Grof, 2011), which can be understood as circular cartographies, make way to a prospective analysis, open and directed to the future. There is a rupture with the logic of causality and effect, in which the causes supposedly reside in a lived past, for the creation of possibilities. Therefore, this prospective methodology presents a clear convergence with the method of experimentation and production in schizodrama.

On the other hand, even if it has ascended to the transhuman dimension, going beyond materiality to the plane of the incorporeal reference universes, it continues to operate with the proposition of the unconscious, now collective. Even having expanded the notion of "altered states of consciousness" to "uncommon," or "non-ordinary" states of consciousness, it continues to refer to this "bottomless pit" called unconscious.

We consider that Guattari's proposition (1989a) of incorporeal reference universes and existential territories are broader conceptions than that of collective unconscious. Because there is not only the stasis of archetypes, but movements, flows, an energy–space–time constellation, which dispense these formations, models, and patterns. Thus, conscientíal positions do not operate with the dual model conscious/unconscious, as they all carry their gradient of discernibility-indiscernibility, structuring themselves as fractalities.

The clinical experimentation, after reaching the peak of deterritorialization, the IV. Chaotic CM, seeks the production of a III. Chaosmic CM, in a deceleration of intensities and its actualization in processes of creation, expressive and aesthetic.

Because the schizodramatic clinic does not perpetuate itself in a vertigo without end, in an unprecedented boiling and deterritorialization. Amid the processes of rapture, it is also open to movements of restratification and reterritorialization, with softness and lightness. "A composition is always a set, a structure, but that unbalances, disaggregates" (Deleuze, 1981b, 23) and that can reinvent itself. At this moment, aesthetic and expression processes are used as aid to operate the processes of precipitation of forces. Trafficking the lines of chaos to the frontiers of aesthetic production and enunciations, so that there is a gradual and procedural reterritorialization, in which the objective is for the actant to carry out an autocartography of his desiring circuits, his short-circuits, becomings, from different resources of semiotization of affections: discursive, pictorial, musical, bodily, dramatic, meditative production, etc. Strata and territories that function as temporary fixation plateaus, base of anchorage for new journeys. Portion of firm land where pupae, nymphs, and other organisms can form. Meta-stable state that can provide further progressions, deterritorialization, and reterritorialization: *metamodelization*.

The purpose of the experience is for people to leave feeling more empowered and in touch with their affections, with the configuration of their bodily flows and blockages, in order to carry out transformative actions in their desiring, relational, working, and sociopolitical lives. From the chaotic and chaosmotic experience, it is expected that the actant can position himself in the II.d. Plural CM of multiplicity, ecosophic, resulting in the creation of new existential machines, a more potentiated, creative life, a body with greater potential for affection and desire. An open cosmos to the forces of the outside, permeable to the intensities of chaos, in a productive feedback that produces possibilities.

It should be emphasized that each consciential mode does not only create a Self, but also constitutes singular ways of relating to others, the beings, as well as a specific mode of composition of the reality. Consciential positions manufacture different types of real. Thus, there is not a single and transcendent real to all, a universal real common, a uniform whole. But rather a *realterity* that is shaped and moves at every moment, acquiring different attributes and modes in its composition. Therefore, due to the different movements and affections actualized, we articulate ourselves in different assemblages, in which we assume different subjective configurations, producing several and multiple compositions of real.

References

Baremblitt, G. (1998). *Introdução à Esquizoanálise*. Instituto Félix Guattari.

Baremblitt, G. (2014). Dilemas de los aprendices de hechiceros (dudas en la pragmática autoinventiva de los jóvenes esquizoanalistas y esquizodramatistas). *Teoría y crítica de la Psicología, 4*, 24–50.

Baremblitt, G. (2019). *Esquizodrama: 10 proposições descartáveis*. Instituto Gregorio Baremblitt.

Baremblitt, G. (2021). Posfácio. In A. Rossi (Ed.), *Formação em esquizoanálise: pistas para uma formação transinstitucional* (pp. 151–164). Appris.

Baremblitt, G., Amorim, M. A., & Hur, D. U. (2020). Esquizodrama: teoria, método e técnica – klínicas. Ed. IGB.
Canguilhem, G. (1966). *O normal e o patológico*. Rio de Janeiro: Forense Universitária, 2002.
Deleuze, G. (1953). *Empiricism and subjectivity: An essay on Hume's theory of human nature*. New York: Columbia University Press, 1991.
Deleuze, G. (1962). *Nietzsche and philosophy*. New York: Columbia University Press, 2006.
Deleuze, G. (1966). *Bergsonism*. New York: Zone Books, 1988.
Deleuze, G. (1967). *Masochism: Coldness and cruelty*. New York: Zone Books, 1991.
Deleuze, G. (1968). *Difference and repetition*. New York: Columbia University Press, 1994.
Deleuze, G. (1969). *The logic of sense*. New York: Columbia University Press, 1990.
Deleuze, G. (1979). *Derrames II: Aparatos de Estado y axiomática capitalista*. Buenos Aires: Cactus editorial, 2017.
Deleuze, G. (1981a). *Spinoza: Practical philosophy*. San Francisco: City Lights Books, 1988.
Deleuze, G. (1981b). *Pintura: el concepto de diagrama*. Buenos Aires: Cactus, 2007.
Deleuze, G. (1983). *Cinema 1: The movement-image*. Minneapolis: University of Minnesota Press, 1986.
Deleuze, G. (1985). *Cinema II: The time-image*. Minneapolis: University of Minnesota Press, 1989.
Deleuze, G. (1988). *The fold: Leibniz and the baroque*. Minneapolis: University of Minnesota Press, 1993.
Deleuze, G. (1993). *Essays—critical and clinical*. London: Verso, 1998.
Deleuze, G. (2003). *Two regimes of madness: Texts and interviews—1975-1995*. Los Angeles: Semiotext(e), 2006.
Deleuze, G., & Guattari, F. (1972). *Anti-Oedipus: Capitalism and Schizophrenia*. Minneapolis: University of Minnesota Press, 1983.
Deleuze, G., & Guattari, F. (1975). *Kafka: Toward a minor literature*. Minneapolis: University of Minnesota Press, 1986.
Deleuze, G., & Guattari, F. (1980). *A thousand Plateaus: Capitalism and Schizophrenia*. Minneapolis: University of Minnesota Press, 1987.
Deleuze, G., & Guattari, F. (1991). *What is philosophy?* New York: Columbia University Press, 1994.
Dono, M., Alzate, M., Seoane, G., & Sabucedo, J. M. (2018). Development and validation of the monopoly on truth scale. A measure of political extremism. *Psicothema, 30*(3), 330–336.
Fernandes, M. I. A. (2005). *Negatividade e vínculo: A mestiçagem como ideologia*. Casa do Psicólogo.
Foucault, M. (1975). *Vigiar e Punir*. Petrópolis: Vozes, 1984.
Grof, S., & Grof, C. (2011). *Respiração holotrópica: uma nova abordagem de autoexploração e terapia*. Capivara.
Guattari, F. (1989a). *Schizoanalytic cartographies*. New York: Bloomsbury, 2013.
Guattari, F. (1989b). *The three ecologies*; London, New Brunswick, NJ: Athlone Press, 2000.
Guattari, F. (1992a). *Chaosmosis*. Indianapolis: Indiana University Press, 1995.
Guattari, F. (1992b). *Caosmose* (p. 34).
Guattari, F. (2011). *Lines of flight. For another world of possibilities*. New York: Bloomsbury, 2016.
Guattari, F. (2013). *¿Qué es la Ecosofía?: Textos presentados y agenciados por Stéphane Nadaud*. Buenos Aires: Cactus editorial, 2015.
Hur, D. U. (2018). *Psicologia, política e Esquizoanálise*. Alínea.
Hur, D. U., & Sabucedo, J. M. (2020). *Psicologia dos extremismos políticos*. Vozes.
Husserl, E. (1931). *Meditações cartesianas: introdução à Fenomenologia*. Porto: Rés, 1983.
Kaës, R. (1997). *O grupo e o sujeito do grupo: elementos para uma teoria psicanalítica de grupo*. Casa do psicólogo.
Klein, M. (1971). *O Sentimento de Solidão, Nosso Mundo Adulto e Outros Ensaios*. Imago.
Kopenawa, D. (2015). *A queda do céu: palavras de um xamã yanomami*. Cia das letras.
Krenak, A. (2019). *Ideias para adiar o fim do mundo*. Cia das Letras.

Marcus, G., Neuman, R., & MacKuen, M. (2000). *Affective intelligence and political judgment*. University of Chicago.
Merleau-Ponty, M. (1996). *Fenomenologia da percepção*. Martins Fontes.
Negri, A., & Guattari, F. (1999). *Las verdades nómadas & general intellect, poder constituyente, comunismo*. Akal.
Oury, J. (2009). *O coletivo*. Hucitec.
Pichon-Rivière, E. (1983). *O processo grupal*. Martins Fontes.
Schutz, A. (1979). *Fenomenologia e relações sociais*. Zahar.
Wachowski, L., & Wachowski, L. (1999). *The matrix* [Film].
Zourabichvili, F. (2012). *Deleuze: A philosophy of the event together with the vocabulary of Deleuze*. Edinburgh University Press.

Chapter 9
Groups and Schizoanalysis

The group is seen as a crucial device for carrying out processes of transformation in the different collectives that are intervened, whether with psychotherapeutic techniques, theater, dance, etc. However, its theorization by the creators of schizoanalysis is scarce. Guattari (1972) operates with a perspective on the group divided into two moments, the subject-group and the subjected-group, but does not enunciate in a more detailed way how to intervene, within the theory of the technique, for the transition from the subjected-group to the subject-group. Deleuze (1972) briefly addressed the dangers of group psychotherapy, in which it can become: an Oedipalized formation, a perverse group, or a catatonic formation.

Among the publications on schizoanalysis and groups in Brazil, we highlight the book by Regina Benevides de Barros (2009), which provides us with an excellent theoretical discussion and conceptual clues about the device, postulating its rhizomatic character, of multiplicity and openness. Baremblitt (1998, 2019) also provides us with fundamental guidelines, in which he understands that in schizodramatic devices coercive and blocking processes should be scraped off, and the circulation of flows and production in the group space should be encouraged: the incitement of lines of flight. However, his work emphasizes more what schizodrama is, new concepts, experimentations and interventions that go beyond discursive management. Accordingly, he did not publish a more detailed analysis of the different moments of group functioning, such as, for example, its blockages.

In psychology with a schizoanalytic reference, the group device is carried out in three main forms: *group cartography*, *workshop*, and *schizodrama*.[1] Group cartography brings together a series of heterogeneous practices that aim to map and track group and institutional events. It intensifies the method of research-intervention, in which it becomes impossible to think of one of the dimensions without the other. The workshop device refers to a practice that emphasizes creative and aesthetic

[1] The schizodrama was presented and discussed in Chap. 2.

D. U. Hur, *Schizoanalysis and Schizodrama*,
https://doi.org/10.1007/978-3-031-94657-8_9

procedures, using machines of artistic, musical, bodily expression, which incite processes that go beyond the symbolic register. Both modalities, as well as schizodrama, use schizoanalysis as a theoretical tool to analyze and discuss the emerging processes from collectives (Hur & Viana, 2016). However, some unanswered questions remain: how can schizoanalysis provide a singular analysis of group processes? How does the schizoanalytic perspective differ, for example, from the psychoanalytic approach? If we think about the different effects in the group, in its assemblages, what is the configuration assumed?

In this chapter, we reflect on the conceptions of the group that can derive from the knowledge of schizoanalysis, for the elaboration of a schizoanalytic group scheme. Is there a unique model, distinct from the teachings of Pichon-Rivière or Bion?

For our reflection, we discuss some considerations of schizoanalysis about the group; we conduct a debate with group psychoanalytic theories, mainly with the perspectives of Pichon-Rivière and Bion, with which we have also worked for more than two decades; we conjecture the different movements of the group from the quadrants of schizoanalytic schemes; and we conclude with a critique of Freud's mass psychology and a debate on the power of minorities.

Group as Assemblage

In schizoanalysis, the group is not taken merely as an aggregate of people. It is grasped by its movements, connections, and compositions among its participants. It is sought to be understood by its forces in interaction, desiring investments and strata formed. The propagation of flows forms systems, distinct desiring circuits, which function in heterogeneous ways. Desire always forms assemblages, machines (see Chap. 5). So, the group is an assemblage that articulates the several flows at stake, resulting and being resultant of a collective desiring circuit.

In the group, people should be apprehended as links in different circuits. Actants that enter into processes of composition, as well as repulsion, obstruction, antiproduction (Deleuze & Guattari, 1972). In this sense, there is at least a double place of the actant in the set, something also affirmed by psychoanalysis (Freud, 1914; Kaës, 1997): the person as a constituted part, as well as constituent, of the collective. He can be taken as a line, or branch of lines that, linked to others, forms a large arrangement, tangle, or even, knots: a large network of actants.

The group, as a machine, is resultant from the agency processes between people, who connect and are modulated by this assemblage. The links form a mesh, network, texture, and vibrate according to the forces and tension of the plane (Rolnik, 1997). The fabric folds, vibrates, with the different frequencies of the rotation of resonance. The ripples and propagation of forces occur through processes of molding, modeling, modulation (Deleuze, 1981d), as well as through lines of flight. And it is up to the schizoanalyst to map the different forces and movements at stake.

In the group assemblage, there is a resonance of the forces and desiring flows that go through processes of channeling and stratification, either in the scope of its flow, and even of its repression. The desiring channeling can be figured as a river affluent, a bay, dam, in which not necessarily all flow follows the same direction. There are lateral undulations, whirlpools, splashes to the outside. Strokes that produce new routes. Thus, the group in schizoanalysis is taken as a desiring machine, in which there is a joint co-functioning that transversalizes the different actants, constituting a dynamic of interindividual links. If each person is already a degree of power in variation (Deleuze, 1981b), his articulation with others produces a cauldron, a polyphony of voices and affects. Therefore, the group-machine behaves in countless ways, depending on the resonances of forces, affects, and their modulation processes.

A Double Functioning?

Guattari (1972), at the beginning of his career as an institutional analyst, conceived a typology of groups called (a) subjected-group and (b) subject-group. The subjected-group is the one that has a more instituted configuration, being yoked to the relations of force, being alienated in front of the rules, laws, and shared values (Baremblitt, 1992). The subject-group, on the other hand, expresses instituting powers, being the protagonist of its actions and history. Later, Félix came to criticize this dichotomous conception, stating that he would not work with it anymore (Guattari & Rolnik, 1986). He preferred not to talk about the subject-group, but about processes of subjectivation and semiotization, as they involve elements that go beyond the person and the group, like infrapersonal, organic, perceptual, ideal, machinic processes. On the other hand, even with this criticism, the term subject-group returned in his last works, such as in *The Three ecologies* (Guattari, 1989).

This double machination of groups is seen in a convergent way in the main theories of institutional analysis and group psychoanalysis. In these theories, there are generally two moments of the group: a more primitive one and another more sophisticated, or of "regression" and "progression" group, in which both positions are mobile, and the collective can momentarily situate itself in each polarity. These two moments can be seen in Bion (1975) with the (a) basic assumption groups and the (b) work group, in Pichon-Rivière (1983) with the moment of (a) pre-task and the (b) task, in Kaës (1997) with the moment (a) ideological and the (b) mythopoetic, and even with what Sartre (1966) calls (a) seriality and (b) group in fusion. It is noteworthy that this is just an approximation, as these different authors describe singular mechanisms at each moment and do not necessarily focus their analysis only on these two.

Most of these authors articulate the functioning of the group with the inseparability between cognition and affect, such as Pichon-Rivière (1983), who proposes a direct relationship between the functioning of the conscientical machine and the action produced in the environment. From the schizoanalytic perspective, we understand that cognition, affect, action, and group configuration co-function together. They are heterogeneous instances, irreducible, but inseparable. So, the greater the cognitive–affective sophistication, there is a tendency for more productive group achievements, and the more primitive the cognitive-affective functioning, the more regressed the group behaviors may be.

A schematic figuration of these group positions results in the model of group progression and regression of Fig. 9.1. It is a scheme with two poles, one of (a) group regression, whether it is the basic assumptions in Bion, or the pre-task in Pichon-Rivière, and another of (b) group progression, like Bion's work group, or Pichon's task group. The pole of the primitive group is situated in the half to the right, while in the half to the left is the work group. Moving toward the extreme of the left pole, there is a gradual increase in cognitive/affective productive potential. Similarly, its antiproductive potential continuously increases, as it follows the direction of the extreme to the right.

In this scheme, the effects of the social context on the group are also noted. Crisis situations can lead to a precariousness of processes that increase antiproduction. On the other hand, the goal of the schizoanalytic and schizodramatic intervention is to make a fold so that the vector assumes the opposite direction, toward the coefficient of production. In a synthetic way, from the different theoretical perspectives, the two types of group functioning can be systematized according to Table 9.1:

This model divided into group progression and regression may seem a bit Manichean, as it remains in a two-pole scheme. Nevertheless, it is one of the hegemonic forms of analysis in the perspectives of group psychotherapy, and it ends up being more advanced than the conceptions of Le Bon (1895) and Freud (1921), who only theorize the regressed character of the group. We also highlight that the term

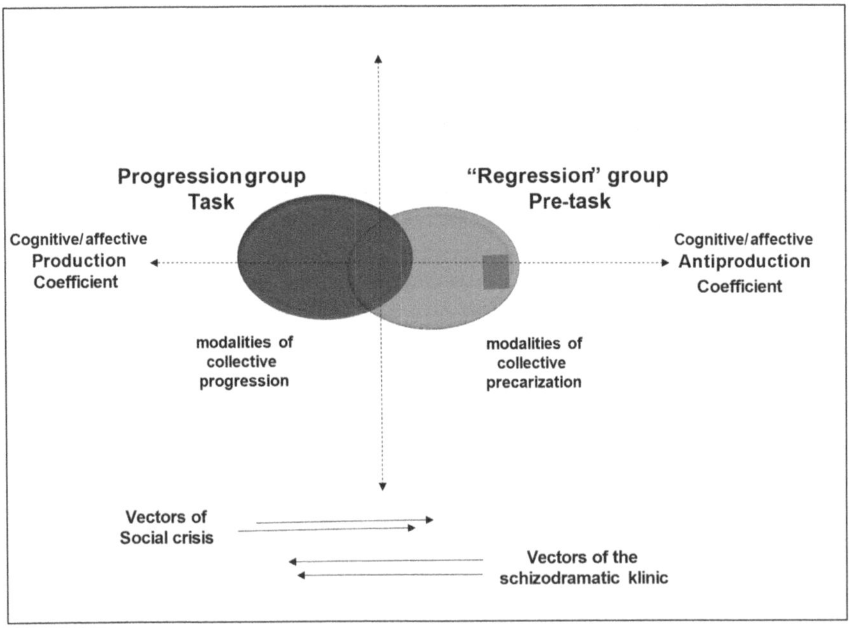

Fig. 9.1 Model of group progression and regression

Table 9.1 Group characteristics at two moments

"Regression" group	Progression group
Anxiety, fear of attack and loss	Reflection and elaboration
Schizo-paranoid position	Depressive position
More primitive affects	More elaborated affects
Pre-task: resistance to change	Task and project: change
Repetition of the same	Production of difference
Paralysis, stereotypy	Creation, singularization, potentiation
Indiscrimination, massification	Discrimination, differentiation
Rivalry, hostility	Sympathy, solidarity
Competition, rigidity	Cooperation, flexibility

regression is not very precise, as it refers to a certain linearity, a return to a past configuration, even though Klein, as well as Bion, or Pichon-Rivière, already spoke of mobile positions, not phases.

We consider that a group scheme with only two modes of operation can bring some misunderstandings to the analysis, or at best, a reduction. We noticed in our work with Pichon-Rivière's operative group that there is a risk of interpretation leading to a certain conformism, or a "pathologization of criticism." There may be a tendency to understand conflicts, or attacks, as a process of expiation, or pre-task (even if not always). However, the attack does not necessarily refer to the pre-task. The attack can be (d)enunciative, constructive, part of the associative process, and not just expiation of guilt. But sometimes it seems that there is a tendency to positivize dialogue that is in harmony, in a relationship of "affective stability," with the absence of criticisms. Diversity is defended, but with the absence of conflicts, in a utopia where differences are expressed, but there is no criticism, or attack on anyone. Because there is a bias to analyze the attack being associated with the schizo-paranoid position and persecutoriness.

We understand that the problem is not Pichon-Rivière's method of analysis, but rather the reproduction of the binary logic between two moments, even though there is the assumption of a third moment, called the project. Even with its existence, we consider that the appropriation of this type of analysis gives priority to the comings and goings between pre-task and task. We raise the following questions: Can the functioning of groups be seen in a different way from the bipolar model, in which it does not follow one direction or another, but rather a more multiple and complex configuration? How can we move away from dichotomies and complexify the perspective of analyzing group practices?

Schizoanalytic Group Model

We argue that the theorization of schizoanalysis can provide a more complex perspective of analysis, which does not operate only in the dichotomy between Guattari's subjected-group and subject-group, or in the two poles of regression and progression group. Thus, we do not work only with the axis of cognitive/affective production coefficient. We propose to articulate it, as in the schizoanalytic schemes, to the axis of the coefficients of deterritorialization/territorialization, of the schizo/paranoid poles (Deleuze & Guattari, 1972), resulting in another configuration of group moments.

We consider that the coefficient of deterritorialization/territorialization operates convergently to the schizo/paranoid poles. The upper hemisphere refers to the schizo flows; the closer it gets to its extreme, the greater the process of deterritorialization and discharge of intensive vectors. In the lower hemisphere is the paranoid pole; the closer it gets to its extreme, the greater the process of territorialization, stratification and fixation, as can be seen in Fig. 9.2.

If the group is arranged by the coefficient of territorialization, the processes of conservation, stratification, and paralysis prevail. And if it is equipped by the coefficient of deterritorialization, processes of elaboration and creation can occur, as well as resulting in symbiosis and fusion. This moment that promotes mixing and indistinction can be seen as a hinge, the *intermezzo* space between the schizo and paranoid pole. As a result, there may be a hyperterritorialization of urgency, anchored in the paranoid pole, as an attempt to contain the fear of losing the limits of the boundaries of the body and psyche, constituting a full body. This results, for

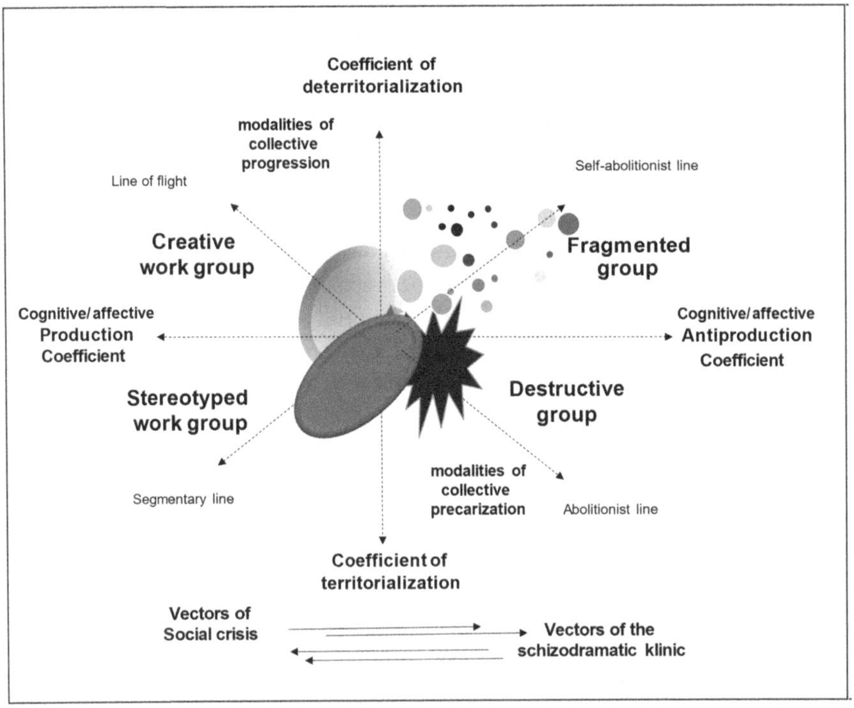

Fig. 9.2 The quadrants of group functioning

example, in the stratification of a stereotyped identity as a defensive mechanism against the fear of acceleration and falling into the abyss of chaos.

Our proposal for the analysis of the functioning of groups is to maintain the horizontal axis of the coefficient of cognitive-affective production/antiproduction (see Figs. 7.5 and 8.1), crossing it with the vertical axis of the coefficients of deterritorialization/territorialization. In the articulation between the two axes, horizontal and vertical, a new schematization of the functioning of groups results. It results not only in two but at least four modes. The dichotomies between regression and progression, or pre-task and task, are no longer established. Four main moments, or modes of operation, of the group are derived, which we call: stereotyped work group, creative work group, fragmented group, and destructive group. We try to map the quality and vector of the forces to identify the moment the group is in, how it functions and to plan the types of intervention and modes of conduction. We reinforce that this proposition of group analysis is not found in schizoanalysis, but rather the theoretical bases that allowed this elaboration.

In Fig. 9.2, the different modes of group operation are not stagnant moments, or phases, they refer to plateaus of intensity, to vibration zones and continuous variation (Deleuze & Guattari, 1980). Even if its figuration seems static, we must apprehend it in motion, in variation. The group is movement and not structure, in which there is a continuous dynamic of interpersonal links that result in different modes of operation, such as: stereotyping, production, transformation, fragmentation, and destruction. Thus, we no longer operate with the two moments of pre-task and task, which appear as two distinct plateaus in Fig. 9.1.

In the four valences, the group is always in action, even if it is a repetition, a work for resistance against change, apathy, etc. So, depending on the processes of connection and composition, the vectors of forces make the group move to each of the quadrants of the plane, to locate itself at the intersections, or to get closer to one of the extremes, always in variation. We describe these modes of operation following the clockwise direction of Fig. 9.2.

The first mode of operation is located in the lower left quadrant: (I) *the Stereotyped workgroup*. There is a functioning oriented toward (re)production, but which follows a repetitive model, often dichotomous, or which reproduces a certain scheme of action.

There is the drawing of a segmentary line with a centripetal directional vector that seeks to produce strata and new segments. The repetition of the same is what expresses the group conduct of this valence. Action schemes, identities, and the logic of being are repeated through a "contracting contemplation" (Deleuze, 1968) of the world. Schemes are repeated because of their effectiveness, or the legitimacy that is attributed by others. Thus, it can remain stagnant in stereotyping, in its practico-inert field, being a practice, but that remains in reproduction. Stereotyped roles, crystallized ideas, and channeled affections are therefore common.

In the concrete scope, the group is on task, because it is producing something, or at least reproducing an action. But in Pichonian terms, no; it is in the pre-task, due to its reproductive and stereotyped logic. We consider that a limitation of Pichon-Rivière's conception of task is that there must always be an associative process, of creation, production. From this perspective, few work teams in organizations, companies, and even educational ones would be on task.

In the political sphere, this modality is usually expressed by groups that tend to adopt one of the sides of social polarization. But it can also refer to the functioning of capitalist subjectivity (Guattari, 1977; Hur, 2018), which remains in an incessant productive repetition, in an eternal "doing."

If it is located below the segmentary line, it will act primarily in a binary logic, of negativity, creating antithetical pairs. Often the production of segments is related to a regulation mechanism, of homeostasis, or even of defense and anchoring, that refers to the discomfort experienced in the destructive group, or in the fragmented group. Then it seeks to fix itself in images of thought, established models, and belief systems for its operations. It behaves similarly to what Kaës (1980) calls an ideological position. It can result in a greater movement of contraction of the group body, which makes it less porous to the forces of the outside, constituting a full body group with a high coefficient of territorialization, as well as narcissistic, thus the boundaries of the group become very rigid. Soon, the forces stop circulating between inside and outside, resulting in a decrease in its potential for affectation. The group creates a cloister, an imaginary bubble, a machine that wants to be self-sufficient, becoming a closed full group, with a high entropic degree. There is a stratification that results in the intensification of reactive forces and the risk of moving to the quadrant on the right, to the valence of the destructive group. On the other hand, if the group remains above the segmentary line, keeping its porous boundaries that allow exchanges with the outside, it results in an operating mode that, from its repetition, may be capable of producing difference, such as a refrain, a *ritornello* (Deleuze & Guattari, 1980). Hence, it constitutes itself as an intermediate repetition group that can move to the upper left quadrant, to the creator group.

In the (II) *Creative workgroup*, it is noted that the forces are in transit in the collective and in the body. There are exchanges between the actants, between the group and the outside, which carry a process of circulation of forces and affects. There is the production of a common group body that pulses desiring flows, in a continuous system of propagation of intensities. Affection, production, circulation, and transmission of forces.

The movement makes it always reach other plateaus of intensity. There is no affective "stability," as the affects are never static; they are always in a dynamic, in variation. Possibly, the notion of the stabilization of affects is linked to a proposition of normalization, formatting, and social harmonization. It is a formulation resulting from the disciplinary diagram, in which life is governed by norms (Foucault, 1975). People would have to have regulated and stabilized affects in order to be able to work and produce as much as possible, without interruptions to the order and configuration of established forces. That is, having stabilized affects is not breaking the normalized desiring circuit, the established power relations, the conditioned trainings. We consider that the norm of the stabilization of affects is related to a governmentality of populations, in which people with regulated affects are more obedient and seek to transform their restlessness into adaptations to power relations.

The circulation of forces in the collective is directed toward its connection and composition, in which the intensities and affects enhance its production. The affects of composition refer to active forces, which can result in the creation and transformation. There is the production of a desiring circuit, of a machine, an assemblage, which has the following characteristics: forces of connection, addition, and composition (Deleuze, 1981a) that result in forces of sympathy, altruism, associativism, and gregarious-collectivism. Relationship of association (institution) and not of negation, or interdiction (Law) (Deleuze, 1953). It is this circulation of desire and the power to be affected that provides the greatest affective, cognitive, and intensive achievements of the collective body.

In this desiring circuit, there is the constitution of a plateau of intensities and forces in continuous variation. A mode of relationship is configured that refers to an acceptance and appreciation for differences. As much as there are anxieties and anguish, the group operates in an associative chain, producing new processes that enable the composition of a *common*. The production of the common is the connection of heterogeneities, of differences in the same realization and creation, in a similar perspective to what Pichon-Rivière advocates about the task. The common is a line, integral curve, a block, between. The group space always refers to paradoxical formations, to heterogeneities connected to a link, sometimes fragile and in perpetual recomposition. In the creative group, the common is always the fabrication of difference, which is also in motion and self-alteration. Therefore, the common produced by the group is continuously mutating, like a permanent revolution, or rather, a composition of becoming-revolutionary (Deleuze, 2003). A process similar to the production of a body without organs (Deleuze & Guattari, 1980), of an orgiastic group.

The circulation of forces allows the group to better deal with tension and conflicts, learn from crisis situations and fractures. As the plateau is in motion, circulation, conflicts are not so drastic, as they refer to another type of vectorial movement that can be re-agency. And the conflicts themselves can drive the group to produce other solutions, activate and agency new desiring circuits. Thus, the group in flux has a greater potential for reorganization, but runs the risk of stabilizing-consolidating its operation when it moves down, to the stereotyped group, staying in the zigzag between deterritorialization and reterritorialization, between intensive line of flight and segmentary line. On the other hand, when it is above the intensive line of flight, it can undergo processes of fragmentation and dispersion, the "fall into the abyss," moving to the upper right quadrant, which refers to the third valence.

In the (III) *Fragmented group*, there is an emptying, dissociation between the elements, which makes the collective lose its cohesion and linkage, either between the members themselves or between the group and the outside. In this desiring circuit, the forces stop circulating, or close in on themselves. They do not settle in the group, and their circulation refers to a diffusion without return. The group becomes emptied, as if it were an empty shell, with a very intense porosity, which is updated in the lack of linkage between the actants. A group that dries up and pulverizes with the absence of intensive circulation in itself, with the "lack of irrigation" of new intensive flows: a *celibate machine*. Desire begins to be modulated by the will of nothingness. Nihilism that results in a certain positioning of seriality and even apathy. The molecules become independent and stop conjugating. The desiring flows flee, do not compose, only decompose. A self-abolitionist line of escape is drawn.

We propose that there are two modalities of fragmented groups. First, *the porous emptied group*, closer to the schizo pole, and second, *the closed emptied group*, which is below the self-abolitionist line. In the first type, the group behaves like a sieve, a funnel, all holey and pierced, that lets the flows pass and leave. There is no constancy, only emptying of desire, or the desire for emptiness. The members lose the linkage between themselves and one can fall into a laissez-faire activity. The escape line of denial of the real can produce it, as well as the drug experience, in which transcendence, or change, will always be considered better than what one lives. In the second type, there is an intense emptying, yet with the borders no longer porous, but rigid, like a cloister. The members of the group do not lose the linkage between themselves, but between the group and the forces of the outside. The closed emptied group behaves in a similar way to the bodies of anorexia and bulimia. A dome is constituted around itself, in which everything is rejected, in the constitution of a repulsion machine. Nothing should enter, everything should leave. This modality of group is closer to the pole of antiproduction, in which a suicidal escape line is drawn. Perhaps this second type is even more dangerous and deadly. Why is there an emptying of desire? It is not that there is no more desire, but the flows flee to other fields, fix themselves to the transcendence of ideals, in other spheres, which often one knows to be unrealizable. In Pichonian terms, this operation would be a second modality of pre-task. If a great antagonism to the outside is produced, there is a transit to the paranoid pole, migrating to the quadrant below.

The fourth valence is located in the lower right quadrant: (IV) *the Destructive group*. It is the moment when a plateau of intensities is reached in which the forces are eminently reactive. The encounter with others mobilizes persecutory anxieties that produce more mismatches. A decomposition of relationships, subtraction of the power of each link in the chain. The cognitive-affective activity of people and the collective is becoming increasingly precarious. There are processes of repulsion and attack, whether within the group, or between groups. It is a moment of group precariousness and situations of *acting-out*.

It is the valence that most closely approximates the paranoid pole, updating resentment, bad conscience, hatred of the other and of life. The forces of repulsion and rejection are so great that the different elements begin to destroy and self-destruct. The group behaves as if it were filled with elements that gnaw at each other, self-consume. Destructive cores that decompose the whole, which have a similar conduct to an autoimmune disease. Its operation is the same as the chronified consciential mode (see Chap. 8) and the destructive body (see Chap. 7).

This type of functioning can be understood as a third modality of pre-task in Pichon-Rivière, but a toxic-destructive-decomposer pre-task, in which the group only ruminates on its problems, with complaints, criticisms, entering into conflict with itself or with the external social reality. The group gets stuck, does not produce, attacks the external, or attacks itself, members isolate themselves, or are isolated. Thereby, it actualizes the destructive action of the mass described by Le Bon (1895), or the group basic assumption of fight–flight,[2] theorized by Bion (1975). In both examples, the collective, even if it is formed by people with sophisticated cognitive abilities, assumes a precarious and primitive position, where the motto is the attack and destruction of the other, who is conceived as the enemy. And that is why, often, after leaving the conflicting situation of the mass, or the basic assumption, the person can function in another more sophisticated consciential mode, not the chronified one, but perhaps even the plural (see Chap. 8). Thus, we consider that the supposed irrationalism of the masses does not come from the simple fact of being in a group or crowd, as Le Bon (1895) affirms and Freud (1921) perpetuates, but rather to the types of forces, affects, and conscious degrees that are shared in collective spaces. Because it is concretely possible to access sophisticated functioning and consciential modes in collectives and large groups, reaching great achievements.

Nevertheless, in the destructive group, there is a vector of corrosion forces, which updates all the power of subtraction and decomposition. Reactive forces, persecutory feelings, which draw an abolitionist line, combating composition and potentiation between elements, and perhaps even seeking to abolish life and its productive processes. Its action is based on attacking the other, external or internal, and persecutoriness is its fuel. Fear and hatred drive their attack and decomposition action. Anger can also perpetuate this corrosive behavior, when it turns into a greater elevation of hatred. On the other hand, the affect of anger itself can also undergo a fold, a twist, when indignation, the feeling of injustice, instead of maintaining its quantum of destruction, operates a qualitative change in its force vector. Often anger turns into energy for the group to configure a new composition of forces, transmuting reactive forces into active ones. In this case, anger triggers a process of invention and collective construction. Thus, the destructive group can abandon relations of antagonism, directing itself to a productive operation, which makes it move from quadrants, elaborating a new task, assuming another configuration.

The mapping of power relations is very important at this time, when reactive desire and resentment are predominant. As the anxieties experienced can be intense, it is common for the group to fixate on some ideology, belief, in a rigid and fundamentalist mode, either in its emptying modalities or even in the stereotyped group. The further the group goes to the right and below, the more intensely the destructive line is drawn. There is a tendency that when it is located below the abolitionist line there are more intra-group conflicts, as there is a greater fragmentation between the elements, in a climate of a "war of all against all," where persecutory anxieties are more intense. And when situated above this line, the tendency is for more intergroup conflicts, in an "us against them." Politically, it actualizes in extreme right-wing and neofascist groups, where the goal is to eliminate and eradicate the other, considered as an enemy.

[2] But only in its combat pole, and not in the escape one, since this second polarity refers to the operation of an emptied group.

Anxiety, Mass (Freud vs Lenin), and Minority Movements

In this chapter, we propose a model of group functioning from the perspective of schizoanalysis. By crossing the axis of the coefficient of cognitive/affective production with the axis of the coefficients of deterritorialization/territorialization, we have as a result four distinct group modalities: the stereotyped work group, the creative work group, the emptied-fragmented group, and the destructive group. In each quadrant, depending on whether it is below or above its singular line, there are two types of functioning, which can result in eight group operation modalities. They are inter-individual links that collectives act from different dynamic positions. We understand that this model configures itself as a kind of navigation map for group coordinators.

With this model we intend to transcend binary analyses, such as the model of subjected-group and subject-group of Guattari (1972). It also differs from Bion's (1975) basic group assumptions, either by its theoretical genesis, or by its functioning, which cannot be linked to the assumptions of dependence, fight–flight, and pairing.

From this model, another treatment of anxiety emerges. In Pichon-Rivière's analysis, anxiety is seen as something paralyzing, with the fear of attack or the fear of loss, which can lead to stereotyping or regression. However, it cannot only be considered a negative characteristic, due to the decomposing action of the task, as it can also lead to group action and mobilization (Marcus et al., 2000). We thus propose a dual vector to anxiety. The first modality, paralyzing, refers to the vector directed at an affective overflow that generates behaviors of armoring, decomposition, self-consumption, reactive forces, and resentment. In this case, it is articulated with the quadrants III, IV, and partially, I. On the other hand, anxiety can generate a twist that does not just feed resentment, but becomes the ignition for action and change. Forces can erupt that lead to the production of a fold in the line of force, the transmutation of reactive forces. From anxiety experienced as a catastrophe, new vectors of forces can germinate, and soon the creation of traits that refer to other possibilities. This affective modality can lead to quadrant II, of creation and production. Therefore, anxiety can be paralyzing, directing to processes of fragmentation, stereotyping, destruction, as well as being mobilizing, leading to processes of composition and construction.

From this model we also criticize Le Bon's (1895) assumption, recovered by Freud (1921), of the irrationality of the masses. We consider that Le Bon only read the crowds in terms of the paranoid pole and the coefficient of antiproduction. His description of the masses is positioned in the lower right quadrant, of the destructive group. He ignored the other modalities of group functioning, failing to see that they are mobile, variable positions, and that the processes of irrationality are situational. Thus, he only pathologized the behaviors in group formations, social movements, revealing his bias and social class commitment. And Freud (1921) reproduced this same statement in the classic work *Group Psychology and the Analysis of the Ego*, developing more the statements about suggestion and group contagion, which are based on the coupling between the ego ideal and the mass leader. He even hypothesizes the potential production of the small group, but what was perpetuated from his work was the Le Bonian focus, of the regressed masses, still exalted by psychoanalysts today. We consider that his reading is one-sided and biased, because depending on which quadrant is located, the group can enable great achievements. On the other hand, if Le Bon and Freud pathologized the achievements of the mass, Lenin exalted them. The crowds can, on the one hand, cause destruction, but on the other, produce political awareness, participation, and Revolution, as well as numerous other achievements. The masses don't just operate antiproduction, they also produce the movements and becomings of the world. That's why society is much more "intelligent" than the isolated individual, be it bees, or humans.[3] Societies have highly complex mechanisms, while most isolated people continue to act in very simple ways. Therefore, it is not society that turns the "good savage" into a "competitive wolf." People and collectives always oscillate in the gradient between the quadrants, depending on how much they feel threatened, calm, safe, etc. There is no antithesis between person and society; this is just another discourse with the purpose of governmentality to negate the social bond and increase isolation and collective demobilization.

We understand that this model contributes to a reading of the social movements and collectives, which also move between the different quadrants, depending on the lived contexts and the faced challenges. Obviously, a social movement is not only situated in the polarity of creative group, moving to other types of functioning. And this is the focus that the schizoanalyst, the activist, must have: the displacements that provide a greater potentialization to the social collective. Let's take the example of identity social movements. It is not because they are organized by identity traits, whether sex-gender, racial, class, etc., that they are in themselves a stereotyped group, a mere full body. This is a criticism that comes from a mistaken analysis, or nourished by a strong class bias. Everywhere we have full bodies, microfascisms, but social elites always prefer to point-deposit "authoritarianisms" in the political left and social minorities. Identity movements should be apprehended as the word itself says: "movements," in all their expression and power: movements of minorities, or better, the minorities that move (Krenak, 2015). For their constitution, they had to do the opposite of a full body. First, they had to create escape lines with a movement of scraping and deterritorialization, in which the primacy of the majority being, the white-cis-hetero-civilized-urban-capitalist man, is decoded, letting minority insurgent becomings overflow to assume the power of difference and dissidence. Guilt, or debt, for not being the same or reproducing the model of the majority norm, is abandoned. Second, there is an assemblage of dispersed singularities in a collective, in a coordination, in a movement, in which they are connected from their identity affirmation of being a minority, in the power of becoming-minorities, in the production of a common that is in itself difference. Thus, an identity movement is not synonymous with stereotyped, hard line, but is agency of the common of a dissidence: its creation in itself is a revolution. To subtract oneself from the power of the majority, or from the impotence of one's state, to *minorize oneself*, in the power of their becomings-minority (Bene & Deleuze, 1979). It is the constitution of solidarity

[3] For example, Lazzarato (2006) reminds us that a software is a collective production of many people.

within differences (Krenak, 2015). In this perspective, the praxis of schizoanalysis, of schizodrama and of identity minorities is in extreme convergence: it is always decolonizing and dissident. We must be attentive to the displacements and transitions of collectives so that they do not freeze into certain forms, such as the stereotyped group, and even less into the destructive group. Do not fall in love with the power, nor to fixate on the established identity, on ideological issues, as if they were a single and dogmatized truth; we have to escape from fundamentalisms. Possibly one way is to apprehend identity movements as plateaus, as thresholds, in continuous variation, for action and transformation. Identities that are a territory constituted for the expression of these becomings-insurgent, perhaps, nomadic social movements (Hur, 2018) in a permanent self-transformation? To take identities as "transient organs" (Deleuze, 1981c), in the sense of what makes escape?

It is known that often a majority-being emerges within a minority movement; but this should not be an argument to depreciate it in itself. The collective often produces a full body, a stereotyped group, to achieve its permanence, its perpetuation. Or it positions itself as a fragmented group, in the production of its dissidences in opposition to some despotic imperative. Or even, it constitutes itself as a destructive group to fight against an enemy that threatens its existence, or like the indigenous guerrilla machines of Pierre Clastres (1988) that fought to prevent the constitution of a State. Hence, there are not necessarily "bad" types of group functioning and others "good." Its "value" is always situational. Because, on many occasions, identity minorities have to "harden" to fight, create their guerrilla tactics, especially when they are being exterminated. It is not always possible to combat the rifle with flowers. In these cases, the destructive group can be an index of life and power, contrary to what was mentioned in this chapter. Obviously, taking care that it does not become chronified and perpetuated in the absence of threats and conflicts.

To conclude, we synthesize in Table 9.2 the main features of operation of this model of groups. It is noteworthy that we also included the two modalities of emptied-fragmented group, for presenting more differences than the divisions of the other three quadrants. We have put in this table five group operations, instead of the possible eight. Obviously, it is a model that also needs to be better discussed, criticized, to be developed.

Table 9.2 Functioning of the schizoanalytic group model

	Stereotyped work group	Creative work group	Porous emptied group	Closed emptied group	Destructive group
Vector of forces	Centripetal	Circulation	Centrifugal	Centrifugal, repulsion	Destruction
Operation	Filling	Exchanges	Emptying	Emptying, cloister	Attack
Process	Repetition	Potentiation	Fragmentation	Isolation	Rejection
Affect	Anxiety	Joy	Insecurity	Apathy	Hatred
Valence	Ambivalent	Positive	Ambivalent	Negative	Very negative
Social organization	Polarization	Self-management	Laissez-faire	*Standby*	Extremism

References

Baremblitt, G. (1992). *Compêndio de Análise Institucional*. Rosa dos Tempos.

Baremblitt, G. (1998). *Introdução à Esquizoanálise*. Instituto Félix Guattari.

Baremblitt, G. (2019). *Esquizodrama: 10 proposições descartáveis*. Instituto Gregorio Baremblitt.

Barros, R. B. (2009). *Grupo: A afirmação de um simulacro*. Sulina.

Bene, C., & Deleuze, G. (1979). *Superposiciones*. Artes del Sur.

Bion, W. (1975). *Experiências com grupos*. Imago.

Clastres, P. (1988). *A sociedade contra o Estado*. Francisco Alves.

Deleuze, G. (1953). *Empiricism and subjectivity: An essay on Hume's theory of human nature*. New York: Columbia University Press, 1991.

Deleuze, G. (1968). *Difference and repetition*. New York: Columbia University Press, 1994.

Deleuze, G. (1972). *Derrames: Entre el capitalismo y la esquizofrenia*. Buenos Aires: Cactus editorial, 2005.

Deleuze, G. (1981a). *Spinoza: Practical philosophy*. San Francisco: City Lights Books, 1988.

Deleuze, G. (1981b). *Cursos sobre Spinoza*. (3rd ed.) Fortaleza: EdUECE, 2019

Deleuze, G. (1981c). *Francis Bacon: The logic of sensation*. New York: Continuum, 2003.

Deleuze, G. (1981d). *Pintura: el concepto de diagrama*. Buenos Aires: Cactus, 2007.

Deleuze, G. (2003). *Two regimes of madness: Texts and interviews—1975-1995*. Los Angeles: Semiotext(e), 2006.

Deleuze, G., & Guattari, F. (1972). *Anti-Oedipus: Capitalism and Schizophrenia*. Minneapolis: University of Minnesota Press, 1983.

Deleuze, G., & Guattari, F. (1980). *A thousand Plateaus: Capitalism and Schizophrenia*. Minneapolis: University of Minnesota Press, 1987.

Foucault, M. (1975). *Vigiar e Punir*. Petrópolis: Vozes, 1984.

Freud, S. (1914). Sobre o narcisismo: uma introdução. In *Edição standard brasileira das obras completas de Sigmund Freud* (Vol. XIV, pp. 75–109). Imago. 1996.

Freud, S. (1921). Psicologia de Grupo e análise de Ego. In *Edição standard brasileira das obras completas de Sigmund Freud* (Vol. XVIII, pp. 87–179). Imago. 1976.

Guattari, F. (1972). *Psychanalyse et transversalité: Essais d'analyse institutionnelle*. Maspero.

Guattari, F. (1977). *Molecular revolution: Psychiatry and politics*. Harmondsworth, middlesex; New York: Penguin, 1984.

Guattari, F. (1989). *The three ecologies*. London, New Brunswick, NJ: Athlone Press, 2000.

Guattari, F., & Rolnik, S. (1986). *Micropolítica: Cartografias do desejo*. Vozes.

Hur, D. U. (2018). *Psicologia, política e Esquizoanálise*. Alínea.

Hur, D. U., & Viana, D. (2016). Práticas grupais na esquizoanálise: cartografia, oficina e esquizodrama. *Arquivos Brasileiros de Psicologia, 68*(1), 1–15.

Kaës, R. (1980). *L'ideologie: etudes psychanalytiques*. Dunod.

Kaës, R. (1997). *O grupo e o sujeito do grupo: elementos para uma teoria psicanalítica de grupo*. Casa do psicólogo.

Krenak, A. (2015). *Encontros*. Azougue.

Lazzarato, M. (2006). *Políticas del acontecimiento*. Tinta Limón.

Le Bon, G. (1895). *Psicología de las masas*. Madrid: Morata, 2005.

Marcus, G., Neuman, R., & MacKuen, M. (2000). *Affective intelligence and political judgment*. University of Chicago.

Pichon-Rivière, E. (1983). *O processo grupal*. Martins Fontes.

Rolnik, S. (1997). *Psicologia: subjetividade, ética e cultura* (Saúdeloucura, 6: Subjetividade). Hucitec.

Sartre, J. P. (1966). *Crítica de la Razón dialéctica*. Losada.

Chapter 10
Questions of Method for Producing Life in Times of Death

The coronavirus pandemic, the extermination of the black population, the peripheral population and the indigenous peoples, the prejudice against immigrants, and the practices of extreme right-wing governments are the expression of the spirit of the times, the *zeitgeist*. The politics and practices of death are exercised, total and generalized necropolitics, propagated not only by sovereign power (Mbembe, 2018), but predominantly produced by the axiomatic of capital (Deleuze & Guattari, 1972[1]). Families who suddenly lose a loved one, indigenous people who are expelled from the smooth space of their territories centuries ago, the young black boy who walks cautiously down his street on his way home from work, fearing a stray bullet. We are all living with death lurking, in which the social body itself mortifies society. Thanatopolitics. We live in a wasteland, not deterritorialized. We are dispossessed, we have been subtracted, and they subtract our territory, our lives, constantly and strongly. And we lament and resent it.

In this scenario of vilification and destruction of the planet, either by neoliberal diagram, or with microfascisms and extremisms, we reiterate a question from Guattari (1989a): what movements will be able to scrape off exacerbated exploitation, exclusionary authoritarianisms, and reinvent the world in a revolution of intelligence, affectivity, and creation?

This question inspires us to seek alternatives. We must produce other proposals, devices, new guerrilla machines, whether clinical, political, aesthetic. In Latin America, we are recreating our experiences with the framework of new incorporeal universes of reference to manufacture other subjectivations and existential territories, such as ancestries, autochthonous collectives, black feminisms, becomings-trans, the

[1] In this book, we chose to put the year of the original publication of Deleuze and Guattari's books, but with the pagination of the English language editions (online) found in the references. The quotes that were not found in English were translated by us with the support of Artificial Intelligence.

D. U. Hur, *Schizoanalysis and Schizodrama*,
https://doi.org/10.1007/978-3-031-94657-8_10

anti-racist, anti-capitalist, and anti-colonial struggle. In the search for new enunciations, the worldview of indigenous thinkers like Ailton Krenak and Davi Kopenawa, who have been fighting for decades to guarantee the lives of their peoples and the planet, has gained a lot of visibility. Both express a whole ecosophical cosmology. In the work of the Yanomami shaman it is explicit the constitution of a plane of immanence, with his relationship with the forest and their beings, nature, and spirits. We must use these references, not as a new product, nor as something to be consumed, but as inspiration for new actions, devices and for an empowerment of life.

This chapter aims to discuss clues for the production of life in current times of propagation of death, both individually and collectively, that schizoanalysis and schizodrama can inspire us. We conclude *Psychology, Politics and Schizoanalysis* (Hur, 2018) with a more political, forceful chapter, dealing with the different facets of nomadic social movements, with their insurgent subjectivities, lines of struggle, and nomadic politics. Here we seek to trace softer movements to escape from the reactive forces, from resentment, to the production of new possibilities, both in the clinical field, as in immediate life, from a personal perspective, as well as collective. To present some more methodological questions and movements for opening trails that escape the politics of death.

We carry out our reflection in an unusual way. In the first topic, instead of personally "distancing" ourselves from the investigated theme, we implicate ourselves to the maximum, insofar as we start from our own singular, individual experience, and articulate it with the *zeitgeist* of death. We read the present from a vibrating gaze (Rolnik, 1997), a haptic dimension (Deleuze, 1981c), in which the researcher's gaze is affected by the forces that surround him in a modality of a "tactile gaze." Evidently, in the first topic, in constructing a narrative from a "me," one seeks to articulate to a "we," in an affective resonance between singular and collective experience. Next, we develop the clues in five movements that can contribute to the creation of possibilities, of lines of flight that escape this diagram of death, and we conclude with an interlude on becoming-revolutionary, systematizing methodological questions for a schizoanalytic life.

Zeitgeist of Death

My personal experience accompanies the same diagram of death updated in the social field, but for other reasons. I do not suffer the ethno-racial and economic-social mishaps, even though I occupy the paradoxical place of possessing a "yellow flesh," nor have I been hit by the viral infection of COVID-19. But due to a chromosomal translocation, a molecular transmutation, there was a genetic alteration and my partner's bone marrow started producing blastic cells that "attack" the organism itself, causing the decline of platelets, leukocytes, and red blood cells. Acute lymphoblastic leukemia, Philadelphia positive. An auto-implosive reaction in which the organism mortifies its own body, and which is not located only in one organ, tissue, or stratum, but circulates throughout the whole body, navigating through its blood streams. It is not possible to tackle them in a specific territoriality, enclosing the pathogenic cells within the "walls of an establishment," as the disciplinary logic of biopower operates (Foucault, 1975), because the cancer cells are propagated in the open field of the whole body. It is not possible to extirpate a part of the tissue, or to isolate it. It is in the hematopoietic system itself that the deadly cells are produced. One can draw the parallel between what occurs in this body with fascism, for it is the cellular agents themselves, endowed with reactive and destructive forces, that cause the social body to become mortified (Deleuze, 1986).

The discovery of leukemia left us banished. We have been swept away by the flood of death. The chances of survival are 30–40% in the next 5 years. We were hit by the fall from the sky that Davi Kopenawa (2015) tells us about. We glimpse the end of the world, the end of our worlds, as Ailton Krenak (2019) and countless other indigenous sages warn us. Death and the razed earth were presented to us in an a-parallel fashion. Different origins of the causes of death, different forces, but the same affection (Deleuze, 1981a), actualized in the personal and collective spheres, takes place. The result is an affection of sadness, of impotence, which subtracts the power of the individual and social body (Deleuze, 1981b), and can lead to a situation of fatalism.

And the treatment of leukemia manages to be even more deadly than the disease itself. The chemotherapy is so strong that it burns all the tissues. To eliminate the cancer cells, it also extinguishes the "healthy" blood cells: red blood cells, white blood cells, platelets, neutrophils; everything is destroyed. The "security mechanisms," "biopolitics" (Foucault, 1976), of combating the infectious agent use the scorched-earth tactic. As warfare occurs in every open field of bodily space to eliminate the blasts, what remains of the "healthy" body must also undergo this purification and abolition. An immune paradigm ensues (Deleuze, 1986), in which there is almost total destruction to ensure the life of the body, leaving it open to bacterial and viral infection.

However, even with the scorched-earth strategy, there is no cure by medication, by any chemotherapy. Being Philadelphia positive, the "cure" is achieved only by transduction of the hematopoietic system from an external being: bone marrow transplantation. That is, there must be the migration of a creation system of new cells, molecules, other people's, that inhabit this body, the newly razed land, the desert, producing a new world, another desiring system and circuit. A new occupation by populations of creating cells that germinate another body and a new living.

But what lives to produce? In our case, we will not be able to follow mainstream models of lifestyles, either in their disciplinary or capitalist type. We will not update the traditional and "normative" model of an arborescent family with children, due to the sterility caused by chemotherapy, nor the neoliberal modulation of performing ever more intense physical and sporting feats. Even if we wanted to, due to the reduction of the body's motor power, it would not be possible to follow the neoliberal imperative, of the axiomatic of capital and body-capital (Hur, 2015), to always accelerate the productivity of any object, in which the body-machine must hypertrophy and operate at the highest possible frequency.

Finally, with death and the fall looming, what to do? Deny reality and curse? Accept fatality and cry? Hate and deplore the other and the difference? We are banished, with the shadow of death, and no presupposed models to follow. There are no transcendent ideals to anchor, no hope of State power to take, but the forest of immanence to navigate. As Krenak (2019) teaches us, to slow down the fall, we must open parachutes, as colorful as possible, to produce deviations and other possibilities. There is no teleology, or ready-made recipe, but in this fall we can create new trajectories, differential relations, deviations: clinamen (Deleuze, 1969; Baremblitt, 2019). Possibly Krenak's thought is closer to schizoanalysis than we imagined, even if both had a very distant conceptual-geographical genesis. And as the indigenous thinker Casé Angatu also inspires us, we have taken five centuries of beatings, but we keep fighting, laughing, "whipping the enemy." Active forces must break out of all the reactivity and nihilism we live in, no matter how much we die. We will all die. But here it is not an action toward death, of having a finite and limited time, such as a Heideggerian perspective. Rather, it is an action for life, for the production of other lives, intensive and infinite, even with the boundaries of their limitations.

We must create our own lines, believe in our own power, and insist and re-exist in life (Fumiato & Santa Cruz, 2005). Even with the wasteland, we have a body, which we should map as much as possible, feel it, experience it, even if in many cases we are still unaware of its power (Deleuze, 1981a).

Movements for the Production of Pathways

To create lines of flight from the politics and practices of death, we seek to adopt some clues for the opening of new pathways. From the fountain of concepts, conceptions and devices that schizoanalysis provides us, we derived some movements. Clues, which, in this case, are not disposable, but indispensable for the production of new configurations of forces and another way of living in times marked by death. Through our historically geographically situated cartography, mediated by our haptic gaze (see Chap. 3), we follow these tributaries as means to think about the creation of other modalities of life, subjectivations, and not reproduce the political hegemonic forces that disseminate resentment and generalized nihilism. They are: working on the power of the *occursus*; valuing the infinitely small; to foster affection, the becomings, as passage; the multiplicitation and the transduction. These clues are not presented from an evolutionist point of view, in which one step would lead to another. There is no order to follow, one can work on any of them, start with any movement, go through them at the same time, without a determinant order.

They are clues inspired and based on the knowledge and practices of Deleuze, Guattari, and Baremblitt, in which we seek the power of their conceptions to deal with the challenges we face nowadays. It is a text-rhizome that tries to migrate its philosophical power as a combat-weapon to pursue and produce a life unmarred by resentment and reactive forces. These movements can be adopted in schizoanalytic and schizodramatic clinics, in institutional interventions, by activists in social movements, as well as by people and collectives interested in cultivating of another living, alternative to the *zeitgeist* of death.

Power of the Occursus of Bodies

A fundamental movement to overcome the current state of affairs is to believe in the power of what Spinoza calls the *occursus*, that is, of the encounter (Deleuze, 1981b), be it in the clinic, in social movements, in life. Encounters always bring the variation of power, the transition of affections. In the encounters we seek the relations of composition of forces that form and result from concrete assemblages and machines. How to create assemblages and compositions with others? How to capture the irruption and potentiation of forces in encounters?

Spinoza discusses what a body can do, the power of a body, from its movements and compositions. He provides us with the fundamentals to apprehend the forces related to affections, as well as an entire analytic of the composition between bodies. To do so, he performs a first inversion, in which he aims to leave the primacy of consciousness to prioritize the relations of affections between bodies. The body ceases to be subjected by segmented consciential modes (see Chap. 8), to be understood as the field of forces, in which one of the many consequences is consciousness. Therefore, we seek to understand the bodily processes, the desiring flows, their forces, affections and compositions, and to dispense the analyses of common sense that focus only on discourse, the signifier, what is symbolized and represented. It is essential to remember that language itself is already a reduction, a trace of the real and of desiring flows.

In these compositions there are relations of affecting and being affected by the other body(ies), in which the different combinations can increase or decrease their degrees of power. If there is a combination between the forces and affections of different bodies, a compositional process takes place that leads to a potentiation of both bodies, resulting in a *good encounter*. On the contrary, if the relation with a body poison mine, subtracting it from its own forces, there is a decomposition characteristic of a *bad encounter* (Deleuze, 1981a). Thus, in the regimes of composition, affections of production of life are associated, such as joy and fruition, while in the relations of decomposition, affections of subtraction of its power, such as sadness and resentment.

In this way, the affections result from relational processes and encounters between bodies, but not only between humans, but also between human and inhuman. There is a composition of (de)potentialization between bodies of heterogeneous materialities that produce events and affective modes (Hur, 2018).

In the cartography of the body, of the connections, it is necessary to find strengths where we think there is only weakness. Compose and not decompose relations. To add and not subtract. To take the forces and produce life in its various faces. To jump the blockages of the "white wall." Escape the centripetal forces of the "black hole." To generate and sow new worlds. Because the connections and the assemblages that we carry out with other bodies amplify our power.

In the composition of the relations of forces, we form new desiring circuits, more powerful, capable of the most unusual realizations. Therefore, in this outcast world, in order to achieve the maintenance of life, we must increase the connection, encounters, and fusion with other bodies. In the example of leukemia treatment, one way to guarantee life is the trans-fusion of red blood cells and platelets. A connection is produced of blood flows with a population of anonymous, mixed flows, in a diagram distinct from the current ones. Instead of a disciplinary diagram (Foucault, 1975), of control (Deleuze, 1990), or of an extremist capitalism, which configures the *Bolsonarist necroliberalism* (Hur, 2021), the production of life is supported by a kind of diagram of care and solidarity, or better, an ecosophy diagram (Guattari, 1989b, 2013). A cell migration occurs between bodies, in a therapy that is based on deterritorialization and circulation, in an authentic production of a body without organs, with all its cruelty and forcefulness. In hemotherapy, scraping and demolition are accomplished by chemotherapy, while the circulation of new flows is provided by trans-fusion and the future creative activity of the hematopoietic system in reconstitution. It is curious that we can say that hemotherapy is schizoanalysis in action, and we risk saying that, unlike psychiatry, it is the most schizoanalytic medical discipline.[2]

It aims to operate in the *occursus* a trans-fusion, not only of blood, but of dreams, affects, intensities, projects, realizations, that take our bodies to previously unimagined dimensions. The isolated body tends to a reactivity, but the body in composition tends to unusual activities, to an assemblage of a desiring guerrilla machine that turns the possible into reality. The production of new desiring outflows that aspire not to the constitution of norms, the arborescent bourgeois nuclear family, the reproduction of the fallacious model of the entrepreneur actualized by the axiomatic of capital, or of all the ideals of transcendence. The power of the *occursus* enables us to escape from these *fictions* to create *affections*, other symbolic productions and affects. Escape from the constituted planes, diagrams, and beliefs to live constituting affections. And what is a great challenge: the encounter must be able to produce potencies (*puissance*) and not only power (*pouvoir*). Potency generates horizontal bonds, solidarity, and collective participation, while power often generates subjugation, domination, and impotence. And what is power if not the domestication of forces (Massumi, 1992), or, according to Baremblitt, the rotten, dead potency?

[2] Another important debate is to reflect on the different diagrams of forces updated by the medical institution and its agents. Evidently, there is a very intense updating of a disciplinary diagram, sometimes even the sovereign, feudal, but also, in some agents, minorities, the diagram of ecosophy or a care, alluded to.

Appreciation of the Infinitely Small

We should not only apprehend the macropolitical transformation, the final result of the action, but also value the infinitely small (Deleuze, 1968, 1981b). Abandon the movement of transcendence, the habit of pursuing unattainable ideals and utopias, such as macropolitical changes that go far beyond our potential for action. For example, if in Brazil the far-right government of Jair Bolsonaro (2019–2022) saddened, upset us, and produce the spread of hate speeches and the amplification of death policies, we should not feel depressed if in our political action we failed to remove it and produce another government. Because the Brazilian State is a concrete machine that refers to a population of about 212 million people, in a macropolitical dimension that far exceeds our scope of action.[3]

It is necessary to abandon the ideal of transcendence, the instituted images of thought, in order to travel in the logic of immanence, valuing the transformations of the infinitely small. The infinitely small is not what has little value, but what refers to differential relations and the variation of degrees of power (Deleuze, 1968, 1981b). We have to focus on the forces, the intensities, which are only apprehended in the relations and differences they produce. Investigate the vectors, the speeds, and slownesses at stake. There must be an attention to the molecularity in which connections and vibrations are produced, changing the apprehension from equality and stability to difference and continuous variation. And to see ourselves no longer as static points, but as becoming in movement. To recognize that we are degrees of power in continuous variation, that create differences at every moment. Each expression of active forces, of desirous fluxes, is already a victory, in a moment when governmentality preached the opposite: sadness, fear, and impotence.

So we should not blame ourselves if our political action, or action in the world, did not succeed in saving women from the Taliban coup d'état in Afghanistan. But rather value what we have altered in the sex-gender power relations in our immediate sphere, in our community. How we deconstruct and scrape away the everyday sexism we reproduce, whether in our small social circle as well as in ourselves. Scraping away the Taliban of the couple, of the circle of friends, maybe even of the neighborhood, as well as demolishing the internal Taliban. To deconstruct our own microfascisms, resulting in small transformations, in lines of flight, that conform clearings for a new softness, another world, without being fixed in the duty with the Revolution. Each day in itself is already a combat and an infinity, regardless of whether we will die tomorrow or 50 years from now. We do not live because 1 day we will die, but for the experience and production of possibles, infinities, all moments, install the Active Utopia of the parturients of Kabul.[4]

---

[3] Unless we are at the head of a large financial conglomerate, a significant sector of the armed forces, an important media group, or a religious Institution with millions of followers.

[4] The Argentine writer Osvaldo Bayer in the article "Las parturientas de Kabul" from the newspaper *Página 12*, Buenos Aires, 29/09/2001, narrates a story of an emotional meeting he attended in Germany, with anti-war activists: "Until a young woman proposed that a global collection be

To do so, it is not enough to live in a social movement, or to call ourselves socialists, or schizoanalysts: we have to produce movements, or rather, passages, trails, clearings, that refer not only to the overcoming of a certain social problem faced, as well as a crossing of oneself. In tips of deterritorialization that sprout from the surface itself, even if small, but that are perceptible by the differential relations that they establish. Affirming ourselves as minorities, dissenters, expressing our intensive powers.

Affect as Passage

In schizoanalysis, there is a double temporality expressed by Chronos and Aion. Thus, in its clinical *setting*, there is the actualization of a singular metric and temporality. Its score is not written in defined bars (simple, binary, tertiary, quaternary), nor determined by the chronological duration of 50 or 30 min of a standard psychological consultation. Its duration is not extensive, chronological, but intensive, *aionic*. This is why Chronos loses his determinacy, opening to the whirlwind, or even to the abyss of chaos. So there is the primacy of temporality that Bergson calls *duration* (Deleuze, 1966).

In *Bergsonism*, duration is seen as the temporality that produces a block of intensities and coexistence between the different temporal planes (Deleuze, 1966). But it is also the phenomenon of connection between two states, two affections. It is the lived transition, at the same time cut and connection, that is, the pure affect: the passage from one affection to another (Deleuze, 1981b). In this sense, the movement of duration implies the affection itself, which produces the passage, a path to another state. It is the affect that passes, that produces bifurcations and lines. It is the affect that provokes the movement, the crossing, making the connection between two states of things (Deleuze, 1981b). In its actualization, which refers to the passage of forces, the flow of desire, it results in an intermediate instance, *between*.

In this way, affect as a passage does not imply only a temporal succession between states of the same body, nor is it internal to a being. Far from being restricted to an internality, or to the logic of the private, it is what is most shared in a relationship between-two, in a group, or in a wider collectivity. Its irruption is related to the actualization of becoming, a flow between, which provokes a gap in the being for other configurations, promoting a connection between different bodies.

Affect works as a "wave" that tunes different bodies to the same frequency. It is the constitution of a block of intensities, which creates a regime of resonance in common and passage between the actants. It is in the link between internality and externality, individuality and collectivity.

---

started to rebuild Afghanistan. And that in this reconstruction of Kabul, they thought about expanding the terraces where the childbearing women could shed the black rags that the religious ones covered them with, and thus take the sun on their skin, a sun that reaches their future children. These will be *the children of eternal peace*, concluded the young woman, with tears in her eyes" (quoted by Fernández, 2007, 231).

This place it occupies, of tuning and resonance between different bodies, can generate the aforementioned processes of composition and decomposition of relations. Every passage, every movement, implies an elevation or decrease of power. Affect thus occupies a fundamental role for the management of life, and one that the State and Mafia Capitalism (Hur, 2018) use explicitly to generate relations of domination and subjugation; but in our case, we pursue as the passage to the production of life and autonomy.

The management of affect as passage can result in the production of distinct affections, as regimes of forces. So, in the clinical realm, an interpretation that tries to make the passage, but breaks down the person, will produce sadness. In the same way, an authoritarian experience in a social movement also carries this depotentialization and resulting the affect of subtraction.

On the other hand, in times of extremism we are closed to affections as passage; they are experienced in the individual sphere, we close ourselves to differences. In order not to access difference, one can close oneself off, or even come to hate the other. To try to avoid contact with otherness, there is the production of "a quantity of immobilized power" (Deleuze, 1981b, 177). In an attempt to prevent what could break him down, he "armors" himself. However, this rigid defense hinders the passages, manufactures a cloister that closes himself to the forces outside and to molecularity, and, consequently, the body's power diminishes. This enclosure generates hatred as a consequence, for "to hate is to want to destroy that which threatens to destroy us" (Deleuze, 1981b, 174). Hate becomes an expression of an attempt at conservation, resistance to change. Therefore, depotentialization and sadness are at the basis of hatred. This is why there are also the joys of hatred, a deploration of the other, which act as a kind of compensatory joy, which follows the same reactive forces and an enclosure to changes and passages.

The schizoanalytic clinic, the schizodrama, or the social movement, should not only deterritorialize, demolish, the processes. For the production of life, it is necessary to grasp how this dimension *between* happens, what occupies it, what produces the crossings. It is necessary to make passages that can be traversed and not throw people recklessly into the abyss; otherwise they close themselves off and armor themselves, because each one has a singular existential territory and creates unique paths. We must produce the affect as a passage, as a transition, to new affects, vibrations, to the variation of the intensive degree, understanding them as the result of the flow of desire, of forces. In short, to operate in this singular temporality that propagates itself in the passages of duration and its resulting regimes of forces, constituting new connections and compositions, for the creation of new commonalities.

Multiplicitation

If life is formatted, coded, modulated by neoliberalism for predominant modes of subjectivity, Baremblitt teaches us another movement that can free the forces of stagnant desiring circuits: multiplicitation. It is the operation of converting the one, the identity, to multiplicities: the event of *multiplicitying*. It seeks to make identity and dichotomized logics transition and open up to the forces and continuous variation of multiplicities, aiming for a person that pluralizes in his various machines and traits, that ceases to be only coded by the State machine, or accelerated by the capitalist machine, or instigated to hate and hostilize by the neofascist machine.

It is necessary to make movements that provoke the transition from the identical, the same, to multiplicities. But not to any type of multiplicity. It does not seek to multiply the identical into identities, into good copies, something that can result in a structural constellation. In the rotation of multiplicitation, there is a dissolution of the Self and of identity, which takes it to another plane, no longer of the model, or of the good copy. Its desiring forces are incited to propagate according to the multiple flow of duration (Deleuze, 1966), which refers to a continuity and plurality of coexistence of temporal and existential planes: a fractal, crystal of time. No longer the successive line of Chronos, but the transtemporal plane of Aion. "Aion is the locus of incorporeal events, and of attributes which are distinct from qualities. (...) is unlimited, the way that future and past are unlimited, and finite like the instant" (Deleuze, 1969, 165).

An intervention plan is established that is not restricted to words, to the remembered, but to percepts, affects, asignifying processes, sensations of numerous natures. Cartography does not focus on the interpretable associative chain, but on the constellation of multiple asignifying flows experienced, on the collective assemblages of enunciations, which in turn, are analyzers of the processes themselves. It focuses on the "assemblages that promote the concatenation of sense and pragmatic effects" (Guattari, 1989a, 19) in an exercise of rapture that brings intensities to the surface of the skin, which multiply the experience of people and collectives. It results in the multiplication of potency and infinity, or as Baremblitt affirms, in an inventive dramatic proliferation. It is to make the tree, rhizome; of being, becoming. Thereby, we are faced not only with Rimbaud's maxim that the "*I is another*," but that the I is a pack of other humans and non-humans, organic and inorganic, material and immaterial, actual and virtual. Or as Walt Whitman says: "Very well then I contradict myself,/(I am large, I contain multitudes)." And it is the task of schizodrama to circulate, populate, connect, express these multitudes, bands, heterogeneous machines that constitute, but often are trapped by the fiction of a unique and identitary Self. That's why Baremblitt created one of the most used devices in schizodrama: the Dramatic Multiplicitation.[5]

Transduction

The being is explained much more as a composition of coexistence of elements, than by a linear, causal temporality. Thus, we should not attribute the primacy of present things to what is at the starting point, in the initial past. There is a succession of aspects that generate different compositions throughout the duration of being. So

[5]It is noteworthy that it is a practice quite distinct from the Dramatic Multiplication of Hernán Kesselman and Eduardo Pavlovsky (1991). We wrote with the psychologist Julia Minossi Munhoz a chapter on the "Dramatic Multiplicitation," which will be present in a work with colleagues from the IGB on "The 5 klinics of schizodrama."

not necessarily a traumatic event from the past is what determines the compound of forces and bodies that we maintain in the present. Obviously, it influences, but it is not the key, or foundation of the problem, it can even figure as a fatalistic and perpetual justification to the mishaps of the present. The question should be posed in another fashion: how to create powerful ways of life from the current composition of forces? Sometimes going back and remembering the past can potentiate the future path for the production of life, but in other times not. Remembering it can mean sticking to it, being vilified every moment we remember it. Sometimes the traumatic scene has such a centripetal, gravitational force, that it becomes an imaginary and affective block for new realizations. In these cases, forgetting is a good method (Deleuze & Guattari, 1980). However, in schizodrama, better than forgetting is its transformation. Instead of analyzing the data, we seek its dramatization; putting the data into play, into movement and simulation. That's why our method is not interpretive-regressive, but cartographic-experimental-progressive, for the production of paths and clearings that are committed to the creation of possibilities of life and its potentiation. Therefore, more than interpretation, we seek experimentation, enjoyment, which incites Dionysian forces, immeasurable, unstable, and not the presupposed models. Instead of normalizing and standardizing, the objective is to deviate, create lines of escape, other exits and alternatives.[6]

Baremblitt operates these transformational processes from the method of *transduction*. This procedure can be seen in the passage of flows between different strata, in the transcoding between one medium and another (Deleuze & Guattari, 1980), in which a regime of signs transforms, becomes something else. The passage between strata does not only make semiotics mixed, but mainly incites that also arise "(...) how new semiotics are detached and produced, and how abstract machines are themselves capable of mutations, inspiring new assemblages" (Deleuze & Parnet, 1977, 114). Thus, in the passage between media, there is a mix, a "shuffle," of various semiotic registers, which foster new aesthetic productions, elaborations, and transformations: a qualitative alteration of movement and the actualization of forces.

Accordingly, it does not seek to perpetuate the repetition of the same trauma, its unlikely extirpation, nor its mere forgetting, but rather its transformation by the device of repetition. Not a repetition in the same context, but crossing the borders to other fields. It seeks to diffract it and take it to other horizons, to other epithelial layers. To create new regimes of enunciations and sensitivities we have to work with a transduction of the sensible. To take what is perceived in one perceptual register to another, for example, the discursive report of an event to its dramatization in the bodily realm. In the journey of transduction from one field to another, there is a transformation of movement and matter, in which transduction is never mere translation.

In the exercise of a drift between the different perceptual registers, the various senses, it operates with a migration and nomadism of moods in which there must be a synesthetic handling. To cross, shuffle, and transversalize the borders of the

[6] For a greater discussion on interpretation and experimentation, see Baremblitt et al. (2020).

perceptual. To produce a block of becoming between perceptions, such as a coupling between touch and smell, or the color of sound. In a work that involves and transits between kinetic expression, the paralinguistic and verbal language (Bateson, 1972). To operate in bodily iconic expressions, in the tonic values of enunciations, as well as in the enunciated semantics. For example, the migration of a tactile pain to its sound in a melody, refrain, vocal. Hence, the sensation, the vibration, the intensive degree, are covered by various garments, materialities. The aim is to make the body vibrate differently on different surfaces, whether in movement, in babbling, in oral discourse. Or in the opposite sense, to make a single significant discourse can be updated in different vibrations, rhythms, or in bodily expression. In serenity, in anger, in lament. Routes that aim for an affect to expand to other possibilities and experimentations. A refrain that opens a line of deterritorialization to new territories. To express the refrain, to mark the contours of the territory, to ride the abstract line of becoming, to reach new territories and a production of the unusual. Because here repetition will always be the repetition of difference.

The shuffling and transduction can be elicited with experiments in the production of becomings, of machines of production–reproduction–antiproduction, with several klinics of schizodrama. It is about fostering processes of deterritorialization and diffusion of flows that reach new configurations of desiring circuits, in a molecularization of the processes that elaborate new gears and machines. Metamorphosis, transmutation, fold of force, and desire. It is noteworthy that on many occasions they may be accompanied by experiences of crisis. For the crossing, the journey, are always processes, or formations, of border, interzone, hinterland. Transition zones from one field to another. Departures from the known to arrivals in the unknown. It is the tracing of lines of flight that actualize intensive blocks in various and other fields, which receive new coverings, other appearances, new figurations. Ephemeral strata that pave territories of anchorage for an intermittent crossing to the production of what we call life.

Thus, transduction is a schizodramatic, Baremblittian method, which does not seek the organization, translation, reduction, tracing, or totalization of the experienced phenomenon, but its disarticulation in disjunctive syntheses and production of other movements and matters. We do not "model" what will be the transformation, the production of the new, but we operate from a *metamodelization* (Guattari, 1989a, 2013), a co-construction and joint invention between schizoanalyst and actants, in which each participant is gestated with their distinct flows, manufacturing their intensities and senses, following their singular space–time dynamics. In the cartography, in the constructivist method, there is no instituted model, an ideal or transcendent image to reach. We follow the tracing of new lines, which refer to desire as potency and affirmation and not as lack and absence. In the concatenation of machines and desiring circuits, a singular process is triggered, which cannot be reduced to a standard, norm, or axiomatic. "Sense is never a principle or an origin, but that it is produced" (Deleuze, 1969, 72). It does not pre-exist but is created from the vectors of forces of events and the ethical-aesthetic-political work of the schizodramatic person–collective. It is always an open and mutant construction, with its eternal processes of self-alteration, *metastable* states, *metamodels*. In the crossing of flows, there is a differentiation, an *othering*, for life is a permanent revolution, obviously, if we open ourselves to the chaosmos and the multiplicity of the real.

In this way, the schizodrama participant is not seen as a mere patient, but as an actant, as someone who agencies, connects, forms a network with the whole process, whether with the schizodramatist, with their social spaces, the desire, the body, and the people around them. An actant who in his intervention process cannot be stuck to his identity, to his Self, as some psychotherapies operate. In the process of deterritorialization and metamodelization, instead of spinning in the centripetal forces of the "I," centrifugal forces of openness and contact with the other/s are fostered, crossing the different thresholds. Therefore, it aims at a reduction of the territorialization coefficient and an expansion of the agency potential of each body. It is worth noting that the actants are not grasped as total objects, but as partial, fragmentary, multifaceted objects, which form various types of assemblages, networks, circuits, from their different parts. Thus, the intervention produces a movement from identities to multiplicities, that is, from the norm to the anomaly, from the cosmos to chaos, from strata to flows, from full, emptied, destructive bodies, to the body without organs, to the plural ecosophic consciential mode, as well as to the collectives of creation.

Becomings-Revolutionary

Throughout this book, we have developed various movements that can arm us in the struggle for the production of life in times of death. If currently there is a diagram that updates death and resentment in different spaces, our concern is anchored in the active utopia of daring to produce life in such hard times. As a way of conclusion, we have selected 15 clues, and not ideals, which differentiate the method of schizoanalysis and schizodrama from traditional *psy* practices. These are movements that effect a methodological turn in relation to common sense, carry another stylistics of existence and can be actualized both on the personal, collective, clinical, political, artistic plane. Clues for a potent and desiring life, for the invention of a schizoanalytic life (Table 10.1).

For the production of life in times of death, we must establish a plane, manage processes, not with the colonizing logic, foreignisms, and international elitism, but above all recognize, merge, depart from, and *construct one's own territory*. Manufacture it with the affirmation of our potency, but with the restlessness of always populating the margins. Move away from disciplinary norms, from the visible, and reach the molecularity of being in order to provoke a torsion of the forces, its folding. The purpose is to expel its reactivity and have it return imbued only with its affirmative characteristics; to finally accomplish a *transmutation of forces*, in which the cartography, scraping, and production triad is the privileged procedure. We must act through differential relations, abandoning the logic of transcendence, idealizations, and travel on the plane of immanence, considering ourselves as degrees of power in continuous variation, that is, map and value *the infinitely small*,

Table 10.1 Methodological clues for the production of a schizoanalytic life

Traditional practices	Schizoanalytic method
Colonization, foreignisms	Asserting one's own territory
Disciplinary method	Cartography-scraping-production
Transcendence	Immanence
Idealization	Infinitely small, differential relation
Future of the revolution	Becoming-revolutionary
Consciousness	Logic of composition between bodies
Primacy of language	Asignifying "flows"
Logic of frequency	Logic of intensities
Interpretation	Experimentation
Dimension of sight and hearing	Haptic dimension
Fictions	Affections
Individualized affect	Affect as passage
Coding, identification	Multiplicitation
Translation	Transduction
Power	Potency

propagate becoming-revolutionary and not only be anguished by the future of the Revolution. To grasp and accompany the flow of desire, of forces, of asignifying flows, the logic of composition between bodies and not just stick to consciousness and language. To do this, move from the logic of frequency, interpretation and sight to grasp intensities, in an experimentation of the haptic dimension. To leave the majorities and assert ourselves as minorities, always restless and maladjusted. To abandon the anesthesia of fictions and elicit becomings, understanding the *affect* not as something individual, but *as passage*, as a transition between affections, or even as a connection, an intensive block between two or more bodies, that produces compositions and a new commonality. To operate with multitudes, with a *multiplicitation* of identities and the Self and not with codifications. In a process of creation and migration of desire, which operates with the *transduction* of the sensible.

This is why schizoanalysis and schizodrama operate as a social movement, in their action to deconstruct capitalist or neo-fascist subjectivity toward other sensibilities. Scraping away individuality on the way to the common, the multitude. Stop falling in love with power, for the power of creating. Expelling anger, resentment, provoking a twisting so that the affection of joy is produced and the potentialization in the constitution of a connection between differences: a heterogeneous community. Common and appropriate ideas for a new way of living, for another world. The flow of desire produces affective states and, on a broader level, corporealities and associations.

Thereby, the clinics in schizoanalysis and schizodrama are apprehended as the art of producing encounters, differences and deviations, as the "art of declension" (Deleuze & Parnet, 1977, 120), which incite haecceities, events. Not a clinic of sight, nor of hearing, but a clinic of forces, or rather, a clinic of intensities. Not analysis and reproduction, but drama and production. Clinics-politics of transmutation, of immanence, of events and differences. Desiring enjoyment that is always articulated to the propagation of a field, proliferation of forces, for the construction of the plane, even if it seems to be individual, is always political, involving collective assemblages, becomings-social (Deleuze & Parnet, 1977).

The actualization of these movements leads us to the path of producing differentiation from the variation of degrees of power, from the incitement of affects as passages. Producing and experiencing intensities and new existential territories incites a social transformation that is not only macropolitical. The mutation of the incorporeal, the desiring transformation, which is the passage of becomings: the guerrilla of active forces. That is why, especially in times of death, one must live and desire. Fight and experiment. We quote the commander of the Colombian guerrilla M-19, Jaime Bateman (1983), possibly another schizoanalyst who never read Deleuze and Guattari, but who knows so much about the relationship between affects, power, and becomings, and who inspires us to produce new knowledge, new clinics, and politics: "One must dance and sing. And not only to death, nor sing only to defeats. One must sing to life, because if someone lives in function of death, they are already dead. People who live only from memories are dead, memory without becoming only brings sadness, and sadness never generates struggle, never."

Living desiring is becoming-revolutionary. It is to operate micro-revolutions, molecular revolutions. It is the movement of agitation of the molecules in such a way that it can generate fissures, new lines, and transmutations in the diagrams of forces, even if they are momentary and ephemeral. So, the molecular revolution can be an affective fold, a twist of desire, which traces a new singularity, another way of seeing and feeling the world and the people who surround it: a new softness and sensitivity. It can be lived as another regime of affection, emergent, when coming into contact with a song, story, painting, or aesthetic production. To accept the deviation and the difference that occupies our bodies in relation to the established standards that force us to consume and try to be and appear. To let sexual flows overflow in the direction they try to run, in a fracture of heteronormativity toward other possible sexualities. To affirm the color of the skin, the physical traits, our disabilities, the beliefs, community and ancestral values, which may be considered retrograde by the capitalist discourse, but which empower us and create meanings for living.

As much as we cite examples of molecular revolutions apparently from the individual sphere, they are not restricted to the individual. It is a practice that is not limited to the scope of the "office" or the "concrete institution." The molecular revolution can also be a picket, a protest, a collective demonstration, that fights for better living conditions and expression of desire. It generates such agitations, that the various molecular foci, in high vibration, can be linked to others, producing a great transformation. Both becomings-revolutionary, as well as the revolution itself, which "is the social power of difference, the paradox of society, the particular wrath of the social Idea" (Deleuze, 1968, 208). May 68 began as a molecular revolution that reached a great multitudinous movement. Or even, the Cuban Revolution, which resulted from the production of molecular foci, in various spheres, that achieved the revolution in a country that was in the hands of a dictatorship, and of

American entertainment, for decades. Molecular foci were able to produce the greatest event of liberation of the peoples in the second half of the twentieth century.

Therefore, the challenges we face, the blocks and desiring modulations should not be lived only in the individual sphere but also on the political plane. The anti-racist, anti-sexist, anti-homophobic, anti-ableist struggle, should not be just a fight for inclusion, for social recognition but above all an anti-fascist, anti-capitalist and anti-State struggle, in the deconstruction of these established desiring circuits, for the production of others. It should not be lived only as individual suffering and affliction, as it directly refers to a process of collective social capture and subjection aimed at maintaining the neoliberal diagram and the established relations of domination. It is necessary to articulate intersectionality to transversality, producing a *transectionality*[7] of struggles and becomings, a reticular mesh of heterogeneities that express the power of differences and dissidences. So the "individual" desiring scraping experienced from the schizoanalytic and schizodramatic devices must always be articulated to a political struggle against domination and subjection, in its various diagrams of forces, in its *n* spaces. A struggle that should not be based on the logic of negativity but on the actualization of active forces and of an instituting, insurgent, and creative desire. A *trans* practice, of creation and transition between the various corporealities, consciential modes, and groupalities. Movements that trigger a becoming-revolutionary, the will to power, against the coercive strata that only aim to govern and impoverish life, always in a zigzag between molecularity and molarity, in this permanent challenge that is the production of a potent life. Insist, vibrate, and reinvent; "dare to fight, dare to live."[8]

References

Baremblitt, G. (2019). *Esquizodrama: 10 proposições descartáveis*. Instituto Gregorio Baremblitt.

Baremblitt, G., Amorim, M. A., & Hur, D. U. (2020). Esquizodrama: teoria, método e técnica—klínicas. Ed. IGB.

Bateman, J. (1983). Bateman habla de su muerte. *Semana*, 21/08/1983.

Bateson, G. (1972). *Steps to an ecology of mind*. University of Chicago Press.

Deleuze, G. (1966). *Bergsonism*. New York: Zone Books, 1988.

Deleuze, G. (1968). *Difference and repetition*. New York: Columbia University Press, 1994.

Deleuze, G. (1969). *The logic of sense*. New York: Columbia University Press, 1990.

Deleuze, G. (1981a). *Spinoza: Practical philosophy*. San Francisco: City Lights Books, 1988.

Deleuze, G. (1981b). *Cursos sobre Spinoza*. (3rd ed.) Fortaleza: EdUECE, 2019.

Deleuze, G. (1981c). *Francis Bacon: The logic of sensation*. New York: Continuum, 2003.

Deleuze, G. (1986). *El poder: curso sobre Foucault (Tomo 2)*. Buenos Aires: Cactus editorial, 2014.

Deleuze, G. (1990). *Negotiations 1972–1990*. New York: Columbia University Press, 1995.

[7] The term "transectionality" emerged from the collective discussion in the course "Schizoanalysis I: clues and drifts of the Anti-Oedipus" (2022) of the Gregorio Baremblitt Institute, being of anonymous authorship, or better, from the "Gregorio Baremblitt Collective."

[8] Adapted from the famous motto of Carlos Lamarca, commander of the Revolutionary Popular Vanguard (VPR), Brazilian guerrilla organization: "Dare to fight, dare to win."

Deleuze, G., & Guattari, F. (1972). *Anti-Oedipus: Capitalism and Schizophrenia*. Minneapolis: University of Minnesota Press, 1983.
Deleuze, G., & Guattari, F. (1980). *A thousand Plateaus: Capitalism and Schizophrenia*. Minneapolis: University of Minnesota Press, 1987.
Deleuze, G., & Parnet, C. (1977). *Dialogues*. New York: Columbia University Press, 1987.
Fernández, A. M. (2007). *Las lógicas colectivas: imaginarios, cuerpos y multiplicidades*. Biblos.
Foucault, M. (1975). *Vigiar e Punir*. Petrópolis: Vozes, 1984.
Foucault, M. (1976). *Society must be defended: Lectures at the Collège de France, 1975–1976*. New York: Picador, 2003.
Fumiato, F., & Santa Cruz, S. (2005). *Filosofía bal-Buceante: de la resistencia a la insistencia*. Laspuertas.
Guattari, F. (1989a). *Schizoanalytic cartographies*. New York: Bloomsbury, 2013.
Guattari, F. (1989b). *The three ecologies*. London; New Brunswick, NJ: Athlone Press, 2000.
Guattari, F. (2013). *¿Qué es la Ecosofía?: textos presentados y agenciados por Stéphane Nadaud*. Buenos Aires: Cactus editorial, 2015.
Hur, D. U. (2015). Corpocapital: códigos, axiomática e corpos dissidentes. *Lugar Comum, 45*, 232–245.
Hur, D. U. (2018). *Psicologia, política e Esquizoanálise*. Alínea.
Hur, D. U. (2021). Discursos sobre a retórica governamental de Bolsonaro: louco, genocida, necroliberal ou cortina de fumaça? *Lugar comum, 61*, 190–210.
Kesselman, H., & Pavlovsky, E. (1991). *A Multiplicação Dramática*. Hucitec.
Kopenawa, D. (2015). *A queda do céu: palavras de um xamã yanomami*. Cia das letras.
Krenak, A. (2019). *Ideias para adiar o fim do mundo*. Cia das Letras.
Massumi, B. (1992). *A user's guide to capitalism and Schizophrenia*. The MIT Press.
Mbembe, A. (2018). Necropolítica. São Paulo: n-1, 3rd ed.
Rolnik, S. (1997). *Psicologia: subjetividade, ética e cultura. Saúdeloucura, 6: Subjetividade*. Hucitec.

Index

D. U. Hur, *Schizoanalysis and Schizodrama*,
https://doi.org/10.1007/978-3-031-94657-8

The manufacturer's authorised representative in the EU is Springer Nature Customer Service Centre GmbH, Europaplatz 3, 69115 Heidelberg, Germany. If you have any concerns regarding our products, please contact ProductSafety@springernature.com

Printed and bound by CPI Group (UK) Ltd, Croydon, CR0 4YY
30/09/2026
02225607-0016